PRAISE FOR JIM ROSS AND UNDER THE BLACK HAT

"I realized very quickly at the beginning of my WWE career that if I was going to be successful, I needed a conduit between me and the global audience watching from home. That conduit was Jim Ross. Proud to say we reached that global audience in a very big way."

—Dwayne "The Rock" Johnson

"Jim Ross is not only the greatest wrestling play-by-play man ever, he's the architect behind the greatest roster in WWE history. He's also a master storyteller, and this book is the perfect forum for his forty years' worth of tales. So put on your black hat and get ready for an amazing read that's anything but 'bowling-shoe ugly'!"

—Chris Jericho, former WWE champion, inaugural AEW champion, and *New York Times* bestselling author

"JR is a legend on and off the screen. He has been a driving force behind a big generation of wrestling fans, and has helped grow one of the greatest media marketing forces in history—and that's just the tip of the iceberg. His ability to connect with some of the most powerful entertainers of our time is unparalleled. Any book from JR will be a must-read."

—Mark Cuban

"[*Under the Black Hat*] is a candid, colorful memoir about the inner workings of WWE and the personal crises he weathered."

—Jim Varsallone, MiamiHerald.com

"Jim Ross's latest autobiography is available now in print and digital formats, and it is a fantastic read about the latter half of his career and some of the personal adversities he overcame. A follow-up to his bestselling memoir *Slobberknocker*, he talks about his career in the wrestling business, getting older, leaving WWE, and the sudden death of his wife, Jan."

—Wrestle Zone, Mandatory.com

"An earnestly written and entertaining memoir tailor-made for fans already familiar with the ringside legend."

—*Kirkus Reviews*

"[A] must-read for wrestling fans . . . Ross is most compelling when he reveals his vulnerability and explores the caverns of his psyche and his heart, detailing how both were tested in his turbulent years working for McMahon and in the wake of his late wife Jan's death. . . . A master storyteller at the broadcast table, Ross takes the reader on an entertaining ride in this fun memoir."

—Joshua Needelman, *The Post and Courier*

"I literally read Jim Ross's *Under the Black Hat* over the course of one day, and just two sittings. I even kept putting off much-needed restroom breaks so I could keep turning the pages. I found myself thinking "Just one more chapter," chapter after chapter. . . . It's an excellent book, and well worth your time. I definitely put it up there among the best memoirs in the business."

—Mick Foley, *New York Times* bestselling author and legendary pro wrestler

"Paul O'Brien is one of the best wrestling minds out there, and a truly gifted writer. I knew he and the legendary JR would deliver a book full of humor, pain, and triumph. I was not wrong. Loved it."

—Becky "The Man" Lynch, former WWE world champion

"A cursory glance at the television broadcasting industry shows that Ross is an anomaly. On-air roles are for the young and glamorous, and the elder statesmen are typically ushered out and replaced with their younger counterparts. Ross has persisted and endured, a touch of the past that fits seamlessly into the present."

—Justin Barrasso, *Sports Illustrated*

ACKNOWLEDGMENTS

I'd like to thank everyone who made this book—and my crazy life—possible, including Tony Khan, Vince McMahon, my daughters Kasi and Amanda, Barry Bloom, Rafael Morffi, Cowboy Bill Watts, Leroy McGuirk, Busted Open Radio, and Paul O'Brien.

ABOUT THE AUTHOR

JIM ROSS has been involved in professional wrestling for more than forty years. Elected into the WWE, NWA, and National Wrestling Halls of Fame, Ross is also a *New York Times* bestselling author, a BBQ guru, and the cohost of his own podcast, *Grilling JR*. He is the weekly voice of *All Elite Wrestling: Dynamite*, shown on TNT in the United States, TSN in Canada, and ITV and FITE in the United Kingdom. In addition to *Under the Black Hat*, he is the author of *Slobberknocker: My Life in Wrestling* and two cookbooks: *J.R.'s Cookbook* and *Can You Take the Heat?*

UNDER THE BLACK HAT

MY LIFE IN THE WWE AND BEYOND

TILLER PRESS

NEW YORK LONDON TORONTO SYDNEY NEW DELHI

An Imprint of Simon & Schuster, Inc.
1230 Avenue of the Americas
New York, NY 10020

First Tiller Press paperback edition March 2021

TILLER PRESS and colophon are trademarks of Simon & Schuster, Inc.

For information about special discounts for bulk purchases, please contact Simon & Schuster Special Sales at 1-866-506-1949 or business@simonandschuster.com.

The Simon & Schuster Speakers Bureau can bring authors to your live event. For more information or to book an event, contact the Simon & Schuster Speakers Bureau at 1-866-248-3049 or visit our website at www.simonspeakers.com.

Interior design by Laura Levatino

Manufactured in the United States of America

3 5 7 9 10 8 6 4 2

Library of Congress Cataloging-in-Publication Data

Names: Ross, Jim, author.
Title: Under the black hat : my life in the WWE and beyond / By Jim Ross.
Description: First Tiller Press hardcover edition. | New York : Tiller Press, [2020]
Identifiers: LCCN 2019049597 (print) | LCCN 2019049598 (ebook) |
ISBN 9781982130527 (hardcover) | ISBN 9781982130534 (ebook)
Subjects: LCSH: Ross, Jim, 1952- | Wrestling promoters—United States—Biography. |
Sportscasters—United States—Biography. | Discrimination in sports—United States.
Classification: LCC GV1196.R67 A3 2020 (print) | LCC GV1196.R67 (ebook) |
DDC 796.812092 [B]—dc23
LC record available at https://lccn.loc.gov/2019049597
LC ebook record available at https://lccn.loc.gov/2019049598

ISBN 978-1-9821-3052-7
ISBN 978-1-9821-3054-1 (pbk)
ISBN 978-1-9821-3053-4 (ebook)

I dedicate *Under the Black Hat* to the memory of my late wife, Jan, who always believed in me and was my greatest partner in life and love. You made me a better man.

And to the many fans, who were always there for me when I needed you the most.

Our journey together continues!

—Jim Ross

TABLE OF CONTENTS

FOREWORD

IN MY FORTY-SEVEN-YEAR CAREER, I've had the privilege of working with all the great commentators and announcers. The list started in my hometown in Minnesota, with the American Wrestling Association's Marty O'Neill, and expanded as I traveled to include legends like Bob Caudle, David Crockett, and Gordon Solie.

People might not realize that a good commentator can "make" a wrestler with his words and that a bad commentator can "break" even the strongest characters. The right voice coming through the TV is vital in making sure the audience responds to the wrestlers, the feud of the day, the dynamic on-screen. When it works, the talent thrives, and everyone makes money.

But of all the voices that have come and gone, only a very few belong in the "great" category. Whenever I'm asked, "Who was the best commentator of all time?" I think: Who has used their abilities to anoint new stars? Who has narrated the most legendary moments? And who has most helped the people at home feel the same passion we feel in the ring? My answer is always: "The incomparable Jim Ross!" And lucky for us, he's still going strong today.

WOOOOO!!

—Ric Flair

PROLOGUE

WrestleMania XV: We'll Do This Together

"MY GOD, WHAT A NIGHT," I said to the people back home as Stone Cold Steve Austin chugged down a couple of cold beers for a packed and raucous crowd in First Union Center, in Philadelphia. I was ringside, on commentary, watching *WrestleMania XV* come to a close.

As I spoke, Steve's mortal enemy—the real-life owner, chairman, and CEO of World Wrestling Entertainment, Vince McMahon—staggered to his feet in front of me.

In most other sporting events, if you see the authority figure at the end, he's there to present a belt, medal, or trophy to the winner. But this was WWE. So naturally, the boss was there to take an ass-whooping.

"Mark it down," I said. "Mark down the 28th. The Rattlesnake is back on top of the mountain."

Austin rolled out of the ring, knowing the crowd didn't want him to leave. In our business that's called "psychology"—when a wrestler uses their body at the right time in the right way to elicit the best response from the audience.

Steve threw his WWE title back in the ring and slid under the bottom rope for one more salute to the audience. The roar of the crowd was deafening. I wanted the people at home to feel what we were feeling.

"There're 20,276 fans here, and by God, they love him," I said.

Steve called for more beer as the chairman limped slowly around ringside.

I said, "Mr. McMahon is barely able to stand, and The Rattlesnake is toasting the referee, he's toasting the fans. He's toasting everybody who works for a living."

My longtime broadcast partner, the legendary Jerry "The King" Lawler, always a master of timing, chimed in: "You can't drink on the job, you idiot."

"The job is done," I replied, referring to Austin winning the title. "Has Mr. McMahon ever had a sadder day—a worse day, King?"

"No, he hasn't," my exasperated partner said. "This is awful."

"Long live The Rattlesnake!" I shouted. "Long live Stone Cold Steve Austin!"

The production truck cut to Vince standing at the end of the ramp, looking both angry and heartbroken that a working-class redneck was "his" World Champion.

In reality, of course, the boss couldn't have been more elated. His pick to draw WWE forward on a global scale was absolutely on fire, with huge mainstream interest, PPV numbers, merchandise sales, and about any other metric that could be used to measure success in our business.

But back on TV, it was Lawler's job to cement Mr. McMahon's pain and anguish, while it was my job to drive home to the viewing public that Austin was a blue-collar badass disrupting the corporate world.

Austin vs. McMahon had all the ingredients for a once-in-a-lifetime feud: worker against boss; redneck against blue blood.

And they weren't done yet.

Steve rolled out of the ring, where Mr. McMahon was waiting to berate him. *Boom!* Austin shut him up with a stiff right hand. The crowd went crazy. Then Stone Cold threw his boss into the ring, where everyone could get a nice clear look at what was coming: a kick in the stomach. Vince doubled over, and The Rattlesnake ended it with his finishing move, the Stone Cold Stunner.

"Stunner," I said with all the passion I could muster. "Stone Cold just dropped the owner."

Steve looked down at ringside and called for another beer. Luckily, our timekeeper had perfected throwing long passes of "'Steveweisers"' from almost any angle.

The Rattlesnake caught the incoming refreshment, cracked it open, and poured it all over the "unconscious" chairman.

"Aw, God, ladies and gentlemen, I wish you could all be here," I said. "What emotion, what electricity."

And it was amazing.

And just like that, it was done.

Then came the adrenaline dump.

The noise was gone, the arena had mostly emptied, and the electricity coursing through my veins had dissipated. I'd stayed behind a little longer than everyone else. The crew was stripping down the set and ring like hungry ants on a prone body.

I looked up the ramp toward the curtain.

Any curtain in the entertainment business is, by definition, a portal between two worlds. When you're on the public side of it, nothing exists except the story you're telling your audience. On the other side is real life.

In my business, that *other side* is where larger-than-life WWE Superstars become everyday people with everyday problems. They hobble in pain, dance with joy, break down in tears, or celebrate—depending on how their night went.

As I walked from the commentary table back toward the curtain in Philadelphia's First Union Center, I had no idea if joy or pain was waiting for me back there either.

I didn't even know if I still had a job.

I had returned to commentate on just one match, after several months away recovering from a second bout of Bell's palsy. *Before* Bell's, I was the voice people heard when they tuned in to the wrestling juggernaut known as WWE. *After* Bell's, I was confined to a dark room, in pain, while one side of my face hung paralyzed.

In truth, I wasn't yet healed properly, but the honor of being asked to commentate on the biggest match in WWE history was too great to ignore.

Even though I was wracked with nerves, I didn't want to let Vince McMahon, the CEO, chairman, and owner of WWE, down. Nor did I want to disappoint "Stone Cold" Steve Austin and Dwayne "The Rock" Johnson, as they were the ones who specifically requested that I be there to call their match. I had signed both men to WWE, and narrated the stories of both their rises to the top of the company each week for the viewers at home, so I wanted more than anything to be there calling the action on the biggest night of their careers.

But it wasn't easy. I had to hold my cheek up with one hand during the match just to enunciate correctly. It felt good that two of the biggest stars in wrestling asked for me, but I was under no illusions about the prospects in the entertainment business for a chubby, middle-aged man with a southern accent and facial paralysis.

If my career hadn't already been an unlikely climb, it would be a small miracle to keep my spot now. I knew my inability to smile was devastating to a TV personality, but there was nothing I could do about it. Even on the street, when unknowing fans approached, they would say, "Give us a smile, J.R."

How I wished I could.

I had worked decades in much smaller companies, hauling rings from town to town, refereeing matches, driving the wrestlers around, learning how to commentate in gyms, TV studios, arenas, and stadiums; I had spent countless hours, countless matches, countless special occasions away from my kids—all to get to my dream job as the voice of WWE.

And now that job was in jeopardy because of how I looked.

"Get well soon, J.R.!" one fan shouted as I got closer to the curtain.

The show was over and First Union Center was emptying, but a large number of fans had gathered at the security railings to applaud my slow walk back.

Professionally, I was wearing two hats: one as an on-air talent and the other as executive vice president of talent relations within the company structure. Part of me thought that if this were my last match, at least it was a hell of a way to go out. And I could still carry on in my duties as EVP in the company.

But deeper down, I knew I would go goofier than a pet coon sitting in an office all day, without the weekly rush of live TV and the satisfying chaos that came with it.

At least my wife, Jan, was backstage. Whatever was waiting, I knew she would be there to support me—she was my rock, my North Star in a business where a person could get lost without someone to go home to.

I turned and took one last look back into the arena. I wanted to remember what it looked like but, more important, what it felt like. Nothing compared to commentating on a live show: the adrenaline, the noise, the electricity—and the quiet when it was all over.

I TOOK A BREATH and split the curtain, heading straight into the production area, where Vince oversaw the whole show.

I was afraid to look up because I wasn't ready to retire. I wasn't ready to leave the job I loved.

I flicked my eyes upward, and the chairman gave me a smile and a nod. That was as close as he came to praise.

I had worked with Vince so long that I knew all his tics and tells. This nod was a proud nod. I hadn't let the team—or him—down. I was loyal to a fault—people mocked me for it—but I didn't care. In my field there was only one lead announce position, and I had it. I had earned it. I had worked for it for decades. Most important, I was proud of it.

Now I just had to see if I still had it.

I thought about trying to get a word with the boss there and then. No point in putting off the inevitable. But with throngs of talent and crew gathered celebrating, I couldn't get close.

The Rock and Stone Cold were happy too. Both men hugged me tightly.

"Thank you, Jim," Steve said in his raspy Texan accent.

The Rock was buzzing on pure electricity. He smiled that million-dollar smile. "We got them, Jim," he said. "The people were with us for everything. Thank you for being here."

"See you back at the hotel," Austin said, disappearing into the crowd.

Everyone was heading for the annual post-*WrestleMania* party that the company threw.

It was always interesting to me that some stayed, gathered around Vince, just so the boss could see them while others were reliving their matches, talking about what went right and wrong "out there." In wrestling, wrestling people talk about wrestling, even after the wrestling is done. Wrestling, wrestling, wrestling.

As I wandered toward my dressing room, I was just happy to feel needed again. I knew I wasn't one hundred percent out there yet, but my passion for the sport—and the spectacle—got me through. I had left my house, held up my face, and called my heart out.

I was so relieved I almost cried.

I changed from my tuxedo into my everyday clothes and stood in silence for a while until my door gently opened. My wife popped her head in; Jan was smiling from ear to ear, like always. Her brown eyes were sparkling with pride, and she looked resplendent.

"I'm so proud of you," she said, walking toward me with her arms outstretched.

"I was scared out there," I said, low enough so no listening ear might hear except hers.

She hugged me closer. "Whatever happens from here, we'll figure it out."

And with that one sentence, I felt better. She always made me feel better.

"Whatever is coming, is coming," she said. "We'll do this together."

UNDER THE
BLACK HAT

ONE

BACK IN THE SADDLE

On the Front Lines

ABOUT A MILLION, BAZILLION MILES away from WWE on TV was WWE corporate. The seven-story Titan Towers was WWE's headquarters in Connecticut. The brand may have conjured mayhem and excitement, but the offices looked and felt like every other in America.

Now, if your passion was administration and corporate jousting, it was perfect. But if you were a cherubic Okie who loved calling professional wrestling matches for a living, it was kind of a come-down.

I took the elevator to the top floor—my office was just steps from Vince's—and wondered why the boss hadn't spoken to me in the two days since *WrestleMania*. In our couple of meetings, he still hadn't mentioned my on-air role one way or the other. My wife told me to be patient, as my Bell's palsy was getting better; but I clearly wasn't "healed" or anywhere near it, and I knew time was of the essence.

Ding. Door opened. My office was nice enough, but I felt like running headfirst through one of the huge glass windows. The fact that I was actually good at the administrative part of my job felt almost like a trap. Not that I didn't love talent management—I did—but not on its own. The office side of my work was a welcome balance to the madness of live TV, and live TV was a beautiful escape from corporate governance.

But I wasn't on TV anymore.

"MORNING, JIM," people said as they breezed past.

I mostly grumbled back. I had a bit of a rep for being "prickly" at the best of times, so why not lean into it now? *Raw*, WWE's flagship TV show, had aired live the night before, and I wasn't asked to be on the broadcast. I had hoped my calling of the Austin vs. The Rock match would put me back in the lead announce position; instead, I was dragging myself toward my office with egg salad sandwiches in my bag.

My office door creaked open, and I got the distinct whiff of career death. Okay, maybe that was a bit dramatic, but the room could certainly do with an air freshener. I put my bag in its usual spot and sat in my usual position, ready to do my usual things.

Administration things.

Yippee.

I had called the goddamn Flair vs. Steamboat trilogy, and now I was trying to get punch holes to line up in the stupid paper on my stupid desk.

I wanted to be on the front lines, not behind a desk. I wanted to call classics and to see the wonders of the wrestling business in action. I looked at my sandwiches. Jan had said they were for lunch, and it was only ten o'clock, but I ate one anyway to regulate my emotions.

I leaned back in my office chair, looked at my Mickey Mantle and John Wayne memorabilia, and wondered if either of those guys would be happy in an office.

I was listless, detached—floating, if you will, in a sea of uncertainty. I had left home to join the circus but now found myself an administrator.

The *Raw* broadcast immediately after *WrestleMania* was a hugely important show; it set the tone for the full year. It was like a season opener on your favorite drama, where everyone of importance was highlighted and featured.

But I hadn't been highlighted or featured.

PREVIOUS RIGHT-HAND MEN TO VINCE, including the legendary Pat Patterson, retired wrestler and manager J.J. Dillon, and my old friend and creative powerhouse Bruce Prichard, had worked out of the same office before me. It was the only space in the whole building with windows that opened, thanks to Pat's love of cigarettes.

I saluted Pat's legacy as I lit my own smoke and leaned out that one open window. True power in the wrestling business is convincing Vince McMahon to open a window so you could smoke. The chairman hates smoke (and smokers). He basically had no tolerance for any sign of loss of control or weakness. Perhaps most remarkably he hated sneezing, his own even more than other people's.

I, like my predecessors, was a seven-day-a-week guy. I answered calls late at night and got into the office early in the morning—when I wasn't on the road. My usual schedule was Sunday and Monday traveling for Pay Per View and TV broadcasts, back to the office on Tuesday morning, work there until Friday, over to Vince's house on Saturday for meetings, and managing WWE's touring live events on the weekends.

In between, I was responsible for the talent—the Superstars, as we like to call them. It was my job to oversee the scouting and hiring of new prospects, monitor the drugs program, and sometimes discipline grown adults who should know better.

I was their boss, their counselor, their coach, and their sounding board. But my most important task every week was payroll.

Discretionary payroll.

It was just like regular payroll but with a ton of extra hassle involved for me because a person's self-worth is always attached to their dollar-worth.

Hell, mine is too.

So, if a wrestler's pay wasn't what they thought it should be, then I would hear about it pretty quickly. The way it generally worked was: after taxes, I was given 30–35 percent of the live-event ticket sales to pay the talent. The main-event guys got 3 percent of the after-taxes net, and I would pay a little something extra to those who went above and beyond—if they took two flights to make a show, or if they got "busted open hard way" and bled by accident, or if they got "a little color" and bled intentionally by cutting themselves to elevate the match. I always tried to make sure that no one—referees included—got less than $500 per event, which came to $2,000 a week over our four shows.

Of course, not everyone was happy all the time. Sean Waltman, a trailblazing Superstar with a smaller, more cruiserweight body type, once asked, "Hey, J.R., are you paying me by the fucking pound?"

I bonused him a little extra the next week for the memorable line.

No matter what was happening in my life, the payroll always got done. Even when I suffered my bouts of Bell's palsy, Jan went into the office and got the payroll for me to finish, in the dark, at home.

Quite literally, if I didn't do it, then no one would get paid. It was a responsibility I found a bit weighty at times, to be honest.

In becoming the head of talent relations, I knew what I had signed up for. The phone never stopped, the problems never lessened, and the payroll never went undone. It was something I got good at, but I never *cherished* it the same way I did being the voice of WWE.

That's why being left out was excruciating.

I flicked my cigarette out the window and slumped down in my seat. I knew Vince was in his office. On non-TV days he was the first in every morning and the last out at night—if he went home at all. Of all the crazy workaholics I've known, no one held a candle to McMahon. If his day was too full, he would go to the gym at two in the morning and still be at the eight o'clock conference call ready to smash another eighteen-hour day.

Problem was, he expected everyone to be like that, especially those in his inner circle. The boss was pushing an open door with me in that regard because I was born and raised to work morning till night.

My office phone rang. I saw the name on the caller ID was Beth Zazza, Vince's executive assistant. "Vince is ready for you now, J.R.," she said when I answered.

Vince and I met daily on a variety of issues, but there was only one thing on my mind this time. I knocked on the chairman's office door and tried to straighten my face as best I could.

"Come in, J.R.," Vince bellowed.

His office was red and big and loud but exceedingly well organized. He was sitting behind his big square granite desk with his head buried in a stack of documents.

"How are you doing, J.R.?" he asked in his deep voice.

I sat across from him. "I'm getting better."

Vince continued to sign paperwork. "You doing good? You sleeping okay?"

The boss slept only a few hours a night, but he always asked others how they slept.

"Took a call late last night that I probably shouldn't have," I said. "But I'm sleeping fine otherwise."

He stopped signing and looked up at me for the first time. "What call?" he asked.

I was reluctant to tell him any more, but he left a pause too big for me not to fill. "Well," I began, "one of the talent bought his girlfriend fake . . ."

"Fake what?"

"Tits," I said.

That got the boss's attention; he paused. "Why are someone else's fake titties an issue for you?" he asked.

"'Cause the idiot paid for them with his Mastercard."

Vince was still puzzled. "And?"

"Well, the Mastercard bill is paid by the idiot's wife."

"Goddamn." Vince chuckled. "You don't put things of that nature on a card."

"No, sir. I might have told him the same thing last night myself."

"Well, titties notwithstanding, you ready to come back to work, pal?" the chairman asked, as he returned to his documents.

I squealed a little inside. No joke. Those were the famous words people in my business loved to hear Vince say. I'd personally heard the boss say them a thousand times to former talent he wanted to bring back to TV.

Now "You ready to come back to work, pal?" was running through my fat ears. "Yes," I replied coolly. My mouth still wasn't working properly, so I tried not to dribble. I also didn't want Vince to know I was too eager.

"Okay," he continued. "We need you back in the booth on Monday. You and Jerry."

I was excited.

And now a little worried.

"Yes, sir," I said.

I had walked into Vince's office wondering if I'd ever return—now I was walking out worried because I knew I would.

At least it was with my longtime partner, Jerry Lawler. I could slip right back into the great chemistry we had together.

BUT I WAS STILL WORRIED about how I looked.

I mean, I was always self-conscious about my appearance, even before the Bell's palsy attacks. All those years as a chubby kid had left a lot of baggage, even in the best of times. But there's something visceral about being "rejected" because of your face. But I could hear my old friend Dusty Rhodes in my ear: "Jim, when you hand in your jersey, you're off the team."

And I wasn't ready to hand in my jersey or be off the team.

I said to Vince from his doorway, "Whatever you need me to do."

Vince stopped writing again but never looked up. He said, "If I could clone you, Jim, I would."

I'd been so beaten down and so worried about my future that Vince's kind words almost broke me. If I didn't know just how much he would see it as weakness, I might have shed a tear. But I'd spent a career so far trying to always prove my toughness around alpha males, so I knew how to be around Vince.

I waited until I got back to my office, and on the phone with my wife, to show any true emotion. It's amazing what a little good news can do: The office was suddenly brighter, my egg salad even tastier, and my wife's voice was as joyous as ever.

"Honey," I said. "I'm back in the game."

You're Putting Him Out Here?

"THE JOE IS SOLD OUT HERE IN DETROIT," I announced to the millions watching *Raw* at home. I was back in the booth, back on live TV, back where I felt most alive.

"Hi, everyone," I continued, "I'm Jim Ross here, alongside Jerry 'The King' Lawler, and King, what a night for the fans to be here with us on *Raw*."

The smoke from the show-opening pyro was still in the air, and the sell-out crowd was raucous and ready. The King laughed and replied, "It's gonna be big!"

I'd missed this so much.

As the opening chords of The Corporation's music hit, I felt a sense of familiarity—the adrenaline, the noise, the excitement, the signs waving in the crowd.

This was home to me.

"What an assemblage of humanity The Corporation is," I said as the stacked "heel" faction walked down the ramp. Shane McMahon, The Rock, Triple H, Chyna, Big Boss Man, Test, Ken Shamrock, The Mean Street Posse, and The Stooges all poured into the ring.

As a company, we were red hot and getting hotter. Austin and The Rock were thrilling the fans with their bitter rivalry, and the rest of the roster was stockpiled with a colorful, over-the-top blend of wrestlers, performers, and athletes. Many had that magic combination of all three.

As Vince's real-life son, Shane McMahon, ramped up his rhetoric in the ring, the boss's alter ego, "Mr. McMahon," made his own bombastic entrance.

One big secret to WWE's success was that many of the folks at home—and in the company, for that matter—took Vince's on-air persona seriously. If

Steve Austin was our number-one draw—and he was—it was largely because he had such a fantastic bad guy to bristle up against every week.

As I looked at all the talent in the ring, I flashed back to the days I spent lying at home, unable to even open the shades because of the blinding headaches. I was not able to leave my house because I was genuinely afraid people were going to laugh at how I looked. I relived all over again the fear, frustration, and pain I'd gone through.

But here I was. In the exact place I wanted to be, doing the exact thing I wanted to do.

When I was most down, I imagined what it would be like to call wrestling again. It helped take my mind off what was happening to me. It helped me remember who I was and what I loved to do for a living.

And now I was back.

I knew that, as a company, we were going through a special time, and I wasn't going to let it pass me by. My face couldn't smile anymore, but just because I couldn't *show* the world how I was feeling didn't mean I damn sure couldn't *tell* them.

There was magic in the air: a transfer of exhilaration from the performers to the audience, the audience to me, and from me to the people at home.

And then, suddenly, I was the story.

"LOOK AT JIM ROSS DOWN HERE . . . returning to *Raw*." Shouting into the microphone, the younger McMahon was berating his father in front of the world. "Jim Ross," he continued. "The guy can barely speak, and you're putting him out here?"

The audience didn't like that one bit.

Shane then turned to me and said, "You know what, Jim? I'd fire you right here on the spot."

The crowd booed; they didn't want to see me get shit on after the bad run I'd had. Their defense of me made me feel even more welcomed back. They weren't heckling me, as I'd feared they would in my darkest hours. They were protective of me.

Man, if I didn't get emotional again. It's silly sometimes how the reaction of fifteen thousand strangers can make—or break—your day.

Wrestling is a unique business that way. All of us—the McMahon family included—were in the service of the story, the TV show, and WWE in general. Not much was off-limits, and a blurring of the line between our real lives and our characters was common.

WWE was pushing the TV envelope with edgy, raunchy, and provocative material, and that meant all of us were in play—even the usually off-limits announcers.

WHEN I GOT BACKSTAGE, Vince approached me with a smile on his face.

"Did you hear them, J.R.?" he said.

"They were a pretty hot crowd," I replied.

"No, did you hear them when Shane went after you?" he said.

Before I could answer, Vince had already slapped my shoulder and walked off.

"*I* heard them," the chairman shouted back over his shoulder.

Vince's excitement about the crowd reaction told me something else was coming, though. I'd seen that look before. It meant he had an idea—something different. If bringing up my name on the air helped the story or helped the team, then I was more than cool with it. I didn't know then that it would be far more than my name he used.

Good ol' J.R. was back on the air, and there were ass-whoopings, ass-kissings, humiliations, shockers, promos, scalpels, ambulances, bad skits, comedy, life changes, tragedies, and triumphs aplenty all coming my way.

The Steak and Sizzle

A BIG PART OF WHY no one else wanted my talent relations job is that it sometimes put you opposite the Boys. In our business, "the Boys" is a collective term for the men and women you see on TV every week—the wrestlers, the talent, the Superstars.

Most anyone outside of the Boys was seen as "the Office." That was me. Not only was I Office, I was the sharp end of the Office, the hiring and firing guy. I was the one who came knocking when bad news had to be handed down. Everyone getting into the wrestling business knows just what a fickle fuck it can be, but no one is ever truly ready to get the tap on the shoulder and told their time is up.

I sure as hell wasn't.

Now, I knew nothing in WWE stays the same—nor should it. I'd seen enough in life to understand that the moment you reach your comfort zone, you start dying. Everything in WWE is always in a constant state of flux—some of it necessary, in my opinion, but some not.

Naturally, this includes the talent roster. Going live fifty-two weeks a year means we burn through storylines, and stars, exceptionally fast.

In the world Vince has built, you need both your body and your story to stay healthy if you want to make a living. You have a certain amount of control over your body, but you have almost zero control over the storylines. It is the way of WWE. Sometimes you're cast to mean little in the global story sense—and then you're released because you mean little in the global story sense.

Now, you can take care of your body in terms of aesthetics and general fitness, but wrestling by nature means you give your body to your opponent in the hopes that they'll look after you as they drop you or jump on top of you.

Ours is a brutally tough business, both physically and psychologically. Every person on the roster knows that, in the end, either their body will fail them, or the storytelling will.

Either way, when it was time, I was the one the Boys saw coming. Even though the decision came from Vince, the words were delivered by me.

It was never pleasant news to give, but that was especially true when you had a longtime relationship with the person receiving that news. For instance, firing my good, personal, longtime dear friend Steve Williams, who had come up as a wrestler in the territory system with me when I was building my career as an announcer. In 1999, there was nothing on the WWE horizon for the man known as "Dr. Death," and Vince wanted his contract terminated.

"We're moving in a different direction," Vince told me.

I had to be professional, of course—Vince had made up his mind in a very dispassionate way. He hadn't hired "Doc" because he was my friend, and he wasn't firing him because he was my friend either. Like most everything in Vince's life, it was just business.

"There's nothing we can do?" I asked, already knowing the answer.

"It's time for a change," Vince said in reply. He handed me a larger list of guys who were no longer needed by the company.

"There's more on there, but I wanted you to hear about Doc from me," the chairman said.

Releasing anyone is tough, but to let go the man with whom you started in the wrestling business was extra tough. I tried to remind myself that all of us knew wrestling wasn't a guaranteed job for life. That it was like any other weekly TV show—you're hot, then you're not, then you're out.

TV shows in general feed on the new, and Doc was far closer to the end of his career than the start. But that's what made it even more tough: This was supposed to be his last big run—and money-making contract—before he hung up his boots.

To get him in, I had pitched him as a viable heel to come and work a program with Steve Austin (whose real name, I should note, is actually also

Steve Williams; yes, two of my closest friends in the wrestling business both happened to be named Steve Williams). In any case, Bruce Prichard was keen on Doc, too, and both our recommendations led to him getting a shot.

We wanted to do with Doc what we'd done with Mick Foley, which was to bring in an experienced locker-room leader to work a program with an established top guy who needed a new, credible threat. Mick had gone on to be one of our main stars, and we were hopeful Doc could draw money with a final run too.

And for a while, it seemed like it could work. Doc's size and believable work in the ring made for a considerable obstacle for the red-hot Austin to overcome.

But unfortunately, Doc's body was breaking down due to his aggressive style and hard-hitting matches in Japan.

Even before he'd gotten into the wrestling business, he was putting his body through the wringer as a four-time consecutive All-American wrestler who, as a nineteen-year-old freshman, was wrestling guys much older than he was.

He never gave himself a day off, going from the end of football season straight into wrestling season, and then straight into pro wrestling. He debuted in Mid-South Wrestling before his senior year, where our friendship started. Even then he was an intense bull of a man, and all of that wear and tear had caught up to him.

There was nothing I could do. Doc didn't measure up to Vince's two Cs: *cash* and *creative.*

The cash WWE put into Doc's contract wasn't drawing a return, and the creative dried up after he ripped his hamstring the year prior during one of the dumbest ideas we ever let loose on TV: Brawl for All.

We took a tournament full of professional wrestlers, put them in boxing gloves, and had them fight each other for real on live TV. It was an all-around disaster, creating zero stars and racking up thousands in medical bills.

Doc was one of those who ended up hurt. Suddenly the physicality he had relied on—the steak—was gone.

Some of the other guys could lean more heavily on their charisma as they got older to keep them in the game, but Doc didn't have the gift of gab or a sparkling personality to fall back on. He was a gruff shit-kicker who mauled his opponents. WWE was always way more sizzle than steak, and that made someone like Doc particularly vulnerable. His presentation in wrestling was that of an athlete, not a performer.

After Doc returned from his Brawl for All injury, it was clear that WWE didn't have a plan for him. For a few weeks in early 1999, before *WrestleMania XV* and after my second Bell's palsy attack, the WWE creative even brought me back as a heel manager for Doc. Creative was headed by Vince Russo and Ed Ferrera at the time, a duo who had helped set the tone for some aspects of what people called "The Attitude Era," and they liked pushing the envelope with shocking storylines. I guess they thought seeing a bitter J.R., still stricken by the effects of Bell's palsy and angered that a newer announcer, Michael Cole, had replaced him on commentary, would wildly entertain the fans. (It didn't.) Maybe they thought my feuding with Michael Cole would sell tickets. (It wouldn't.) Maybe they thought it would entertain Vince. Whatever the thinking, boy, was it a sign of things to come.

After that plan failed, they had run out of plans for the wrestling veteran.

"Creative doesn't have anything for him," Vince said. "It was worth the shot to bring him in; it just didn't work out. Make sure he's looked after financially."

I waited until I had left the chairman's office before taking a second to figure out how I was going to do it. I wanted to call Jan, to hear her voice.

I picked up the phone and dialed home.

"He'll know it wasn't your decision," Jan said. "Doc knows you. He knows how you operate, Jim."

"The one thing he needs is his health—and I can't give it to him," I replied.

"He knows you love him."

"I wish I had the power to make him healthy, but it's just been too many injuries, too many surgeries."

"Did you get him the best care?"

"Yes."

"The best doctors?"

"I did."

"And he'll be taken care of financially?"

"Vince insisted on it."

Jan paused a second. "Well, I don't see anything else you can do to make this awful situation any better. He knows you're only doing your job. I'm real sorry you have to do this."

Jan's voice, her reasonable, caring tone, suddenly made me desperate to get home to her. I just wanted to turn on the TV, forget about wrestling, and be with my wife, doing nothing special and loving every second of it.

When I first got into wrestling, setting up rings and refereeing in small venues, I never thought I'd have to fire a great friend.

I knew there were other companies out there who would want to work with him, but WWE was the major leagues, with the most money. If Doc was going anywhere else, it was probably our rival, WCW, or back to Japan for less money and a lot more travel.

Jan said, "When the owner of the team says you need to get rid of a player, you do it. It's how you do it—that is all you can control."

She was right. I put down the phone and put in the call to my friend.

It was the hardest call I'd ever had to make. But that was my job.

T W O

OWEN

As Real Can Be

I HAD BEEN BACK at the announce table only weeks before the worst happened.

"We've got big problems out here," I said into my headset. My heart was thumping in my chest; I was trying to figure out if I'd actually seen what I thought I saw. We were live on PPV, but my words were meant for the people in the back, not the fans at home.

A couple of moments earlier, my broadcast partner, Jerry, had nudged me and mouthed, *He's fallen.* I saw something too, something not right, the flash of something falling from the rafters.

Or *someone.*

We were in Kansas City, and the lights in the Kemper Arena were dimmed for a video package that was playing on the big screen for the audience in attendance. I realized the man playing on the video package was the same man now lying prone in the ring in front of me.

In the darkened arena, Owen Hart—a fantastic talent, brother, husband, and son—had just fallen from the ceiling and landed hard in the ring.

Jerry jumped up from his seat beside me and told the timekeeper, Mark Yeaton, that Owen had fallen. Mark got the message backstage as King entered the ring.

The production truck—unaware that anything was wrong—continued the pretaped video of Owen, while medical professionals rushed toward my fallen friend, trying to save his life.

As the lights came back, the crowd in the arena was confused as to why the ring was suddenly littered with EMTs. Some of the fans believed it was part of the show—our audience was used to seeing medical personnel showing up on TV as part of the storylines.

But this time there was nothing "showbiz" about it.

The medical professionals removed Owen's in-character mask to better help him. From my vantage point I couldn't see Owen's face, but Jerry, who could, immediately turned ashen. I knew then that this was as grim as a situation could get.

My heart sank for my friend, who looked to be in serious, serious trouble. There was nothing I could do, nothing I could offer, to make the situation any better.

I could only watch as the people who knew best worked feverishly to resuscitate him.

I waited for instruction from the back, as the medical staff tried mouth-to-mouth and oxygen to get Owen breathing again. There was dead air. Nothing. No updates, feedback, or instructions.

For our audience at home watching the PPV, they suddenly cut back to me live in the arena—but I had no idea what to say.

WWE, rightly, didn't want to show the scene in the ring, and they didn't want to show the fans in the arena, so a whip-quick decision was made to cut to me instead.

I didn't have time to think or polish any thoughts. We were on the air, and my friend was dying in front of me. All I could do was try to form some thoughts for the people back home.

"Ladies and gentlemen, when you're doing live television," I said, "a lot of things can happen . . . and sometimes they are not good. The Blue Blazer, whom we know is Owen Hart . . . was going to make a spectacular superhero-like entrance from the rafters."

I couldn't believe the words that were coming out of my mouth.

"And something went wrong here. Certainly, Owen Hart, the Blue Blazer . . . is in a very serious situation."

I glanced up into the ring, still praying he would be all right. I reluctantly continued: "At this point, he's being attended to by the EMTs. This is not a part of the entertainment here tonight. This is real as real can be here."

My mouth was talking, but my mind was racing everywhere—to Owen's wife, his kids, his big Canadian family who were all in the wrestling business. Were they watching this?

"The EMTs are attending to Owen in the ring now. And we are again now . . . we are at a little bit of a loss with this situation. I've been doing this for more years than I'd like to admit, and this is the . . . well, one of the most shocking things I've seen."

All I could do was explain to the crowd that this wasn't a "wrestling angle." There was a human being—one of the best I'd ever met—fighting for his life in front of thousands of fans.

"This is a real situation," I said. "Owen Hart was to descend in a superhero-like entrance from the ceiling of this arena and something went terribly, terribly wrong. I don't know if the harness broke or what the malfunction was. And we are going to keep the cameras on the crowd at this point in time . . ."

We cut backstage, for an interview hyping the next match.

As cruel fate would have it, the interviewee was Owen's former tag-team partner and real-life friend, Jeff Jarrett.

Both J.J. and his on-screen manager, Debra Marshall, tried hard to stay in character, but both struggled to keep their raw reactions at bay as the camera rolled.

The show was in chaos.

The production people were cutting to video packages and interviews they had lined up—anything to give the EMTs time to work and to make sure they didn't show a single shot of the ring.

WWE had become edgier, raunchier, more over the top in recent years, and in this storyline, Owen was playing a wholesome character who railed against the grittier parts of what WWE was doing. In real life, he turned down more adult storylines that might have pushed him farther up the card because he didn't want his kids to be teased in school, or his wife to be made uncomfortable by his on-screen persona. Even though Owen loved the wrestling business, he loved his family so much more, and to him, no amount of money or fame was worth risking embarrassment for them. He held his convictions even though it meant he might not be featured as prominently on the show.

"J.R., we're coming back to you," Kevin Dunn, the longtime executive producer for WWE, said in my ear.

I didn't want to do it, I didn't want to go back on the air, but when that red light went on in front of me, I went on autopilot. "Ladies and gentlemen, again . . . Owen Hart was scheduled to descend from the top here of the Kemper Arena," I informed the viewers.

Now I could feel the tingle of shock running up and down my spine. My mouth and my brain felt miles apart. I was trying to explain to the audience at home what was happening without fully understanding it myself.

"Again, a superhero-like entrance in his Blue Blazer character. Something has gone terribly wrong with the equipment [as] Owen Hart was being lowered down to the ring. And the paramedics are working on Owen Hart. Let me tell you, we're going to have, and already had, some entertaining things . . . this is not a part of the show. I don't know any better way to put it: This is not a wrestling angle. This is real life."

I was struggling to continue.

"Owen Hart, with the equipment malfunctioning," I said, "is being attended to right now by a host of EMTs. We are not going to put this on television. It is not a sensationalistic attempt to leave a mark here on this event. It was . . . Again, we don't know what malfunctioned. Obviously, something in the apparatus, we assume—and that's all we're doing is assuming—that went wrong. Unless Owen inadvertently released himself before he was near the ring. So again, we will have our mixed-team matchup . . . we will have the rest of this broadcast. But the bigger issue now is that a human being . . . Owen Hart has been terribly injured here on this live broadcast."

In the ring, Owen was still unresponsive.

"Again," I said, "so many things have happened here, but right now nothing is more important than the health and the welfare of not only a great athlete but a very unique and a good human being who is now being attended to in the ring. And again, I can only reiterate the best way I know how—and if I'm not being as articulate as I would like to be, I hope that you can understand—that this was not, I repeat, this was not a wrestling angle. This was not part of the storyline. This was a terribly, terribly tragic situation. And the EMTs now are giving Owen Hart external heart massage. They are . . . Several . . . several folks are there to attend to him."

The King rejoined me back at the announce table. He was clearly distressed himself, but the cameras kept rolling.

"And Jerry Lawler [is] back, joining me here," I said. "King, I was just reiterating to the fans this is not part of the show. We're here to entertain the fans and have fun. But this is neither."

Jerry muttered, "No . . . it's . . . it doesn't look good at all."

Owen was taken from the ring and wheeled to the back on a stretcher. King and I were both numb.

Everyone was.

The show kept going.

Matches happened.

The show was a runaway train.

King and I were on an island by ourselves.

No one was talking.

Neither of us knew what was happening.

It was all a slow-motion blur until about an hour after Owen's fall.

I heard the voice of the producer in my headset. "J.R.," said Kevin, "we're going to come back to you and have you give an update on Owen."

I pressed my callback button so that I could reply. "Kevin, I don't know what the update is," I said.

He replied in a calm voice, "Owen has died. And we're back in 10 . . . 9 . . . 8 . . ."

A cameraman knelt down in front of our announce table, ready to capture the live shot. I had no idea what to say or how to say it.

My countdown continued: "3 . . . 2 . . . 1 . . ."

"Here at . . . in Kansas City, tragedy befell all of us," I said. "Owen Hart was . . . set to make an entrance from the ceiling, and . . . he fell from the ceiling. And I have the . . . unfortunate responsibility to let everyone know that Owen Hart has died. Owen Hart has tragically died from that accident here tonight."

That was the last thing I remember saying, though the show went on and we called a few more matches.

After the show ended, I sat on my own for a couple of minutes. Backstage veered from quiet confusion to anger, from sadness to tears. I cried for my friend. I cried for his family. And then I felt like I had to wipe my eyes and offer counsel to anyone who needed it.

Just an ear, someone to listen.

I had to put my own feelings aside and be the coach that the talent could talk to, or shout at, or vent in front of. So I sat and listened, shared the wrestlers' anguish, their pain. I prayed with some and cussed with others.

I felt I had a responsibility to help in any small way I could. But I just wanted to cry some more myself.

Even in tragedy, I was programmed to hide my anguish. So I waited until everyone was gone. Then I left for my own hotel room, where I could weep unseen—and, more important, pick up the phone.

I just wanted to talk to Jan; to hear her voice again. I knew she would have been watching the broadcast, because she always did when I was commentating.

She was the only person on the planet that I could cry with, be honest with, be in love with, at that moment.

I wanted to go home. I wanted to hug her, tell her how much I loved her. I wanted to make sure she knew just how much she meant to me.

And in the same way that I listened to the talent as they angered up and fell apart, Jan listened to me.

But this was the wrestling business, and as much as I was hurting, I knew I couldn't go home just yet. There was another show to do.

So I had to make do with my wife's voice and kindness as I mentally prepared for another day of chaos, anger, bewilderment, and human frailty in the WWE.

My friend was gone. And there was more work to do.

THREE

CASH AND CREATIVE

Package Delivered

I WASN'T DOING WELL, but I couldn't really tell anyone. Owen's death had affected me badly; I couldn't sleep, couldn't focus. And every time I closed my eyes, I saw that horrifying scene replay over and over again.

I knew I wasn't the only one; we were all trying to handle what was in front of us without looking back too much. Some days were harder than others. Vince was quieter than usual—withdrawn. He went about his business but in a muted way.

My own workload didn't slow down either. I was heading into a blur of talent signings, re-signings, and negotiations.

WWE was all-consuming, and I knew I needed to be careful. After years on the road, watching marriage after marriage break up—including my own a time or two—having an understanding partner at home was invaluable.

Thankfully, Jan always understood when I had to work late, or rush across the country to meet new talent, or fly halfway around the world to call a PPV. Instead of resenting the business, she got involved—everyone was welcome in our home for a meal or a spare room in which to sleep.

She was like a coach's wife—she washed ring gear for weary travelers and made the wives and families of talent feel at home. Instead of being on the outside of my crazy business looking in, she became an ear for frustrated wrestlers and their partners; she was empathetic and caring in an industry that was short on both.

Any time I felt guilty about how hard I was working, she would say, "I'm your biggest fan. Let me know how to help." Her kind words made the seemingly impossible, possible. She knew that if we put our heads down together, and made our money, it would all be worth it when the business cooled off again. We were making hay while the sun shined.

And boy, was that sun shining.

WWE had gone from a company in financial peril only a few years before to a multimedia global entertainment powerhouse that was boasting record numbers.

Such rapid growth meant more talent was constantly needed, which just naturally meant more work for me. And when it came to talent, my priorities usually boiled down to Vince's two main headings: *cash* and *creative*.

Talent basically wanted to know: "How much will you pay me, and what will I be doing for that pay?"

We already had a locker room of which I was hugely proud, but I knew that my talent relations department couldn't rest on what we'd built. The wrestling business always needs something new to survive—new faces, new ideas, new talent, and new directions. We needed to find people with the right attitude, skill, and temperament to make it in WWE. Sometimes those people were former athletes, and sometimes they were already pro wrestlers being wasted in our rival company, World Championship Wrestling.

THERE WAS ONE GUY IN PARTICULAR whom I wanted to make sure got through the bullshit and onto Vince's radar, and that was Chris Jericho.

"Who?" Vince said.

I knew from his reaction that Chris's name hadn't made it to him yet. I had been pushing it in upper-management meetings for a long time, but I was being met by the usual nonsense argument against him—that he was short. As if he could help that.

"Chris Jericho," I replied. "He's really good. He can fly, brawl, and he wrestles big."

A tape was the key, so I had asked our production guys to make me a Chris Jericho highlight package no more than two minutes long, because that's all Vince needed to make his mind up.

I was also prepared for the criticism, but I knew that if the chairman could watch Chris work, his height would be less of a dealbreaker.

I pressed play. Right on cue, Vince said, "What height is this guy?"

Bingo. I paused the tape and actioned my plan to give Vince a range, so I could find his threshold. "Five-seven or -ten," I said, acting not sure.

"*Five foot seven?*" Vince said, almost in disgust.

It was in that moment that I saw how a creative bubble forms. The company in general thought short was bad, not because the people thought short was bad but because Vince did. Then, in meetings with the people he was paying to offer differing opinions, the chairman just heard his own philosophies regurgitated back to him.

I looked at my notes. "He's five-ten," I replied.

Vince was still looking at me like I had asked him to swallow a shit sandwich. "Five-ten," he muttered to himself.

"He's good," I answered instead. "Real good." I pressed play again, and Jericho's highlights began. "He's the next guy I want to bring in," I said. "He's a world traveler, experienced, comes from an athletic family, and has no locker room baggage that I know of."

I knew Vince trusted my judgment—he'd given me the autonomy to hire anyone I wanted to bring in—but I wasn't pitching Chris to come in as a midcard guy.

I was showing Vince because I believed Jericho could be a main-eventer, and for that to happen Vince himself had to see something in Chris—from the beginning.

"What do you see for him?" Vince asked, as he took in the highlight package on-screen.

"He can be a babyface or a heel," I said. "He's durable. I think he comes in for a top program."

I could see the chairman was beginning to think, beginning to imagine Chris on his TV—the height issue was diminishing. "On top, you think?" Vince asked.

"Absolutely," I said.

The chairman had seen enough before the two minutes were up. "See if you can get it done." McMahon stood, ready to move on to the next thing. "Actually," he said, correcting his own thought, "meet him first, and then bring him to the house."

"Bring him to the house" was always a great sign that Vince really liked someone's upside. Whenever the boss wanted to impress a new talent, he'd have them brought to the McMahon mansion in Connecticut, to sit by the pool. The fact that he wanted Jericho to get that treatment was a real "fuck you" to the rest of management, who kept passing Chris over whenever his name came up.

"I'll get right on it," I said.

I wanted to act quickly, before someone else got in Vince's ear and dropped Jericho's height by three inches. I could see that closing this deal would be a matter of catching the boss in the right place at the right time.

I called Chris and arranged to meet with him and the best talent scout WWE ever hired, WWE Hall of Fame wrestler and fellow Oklahoman Jerry Brisco, at the Bombay Bicycle Club in Tampa.

When we sat down, I immediately knew I was in the presence of a huge talent. Chris was well spoken, handsome, charismatic—and he also knew what he wanted to do with his career. It was easy to see that he was a creative guy who would flourish if given the right kind of guidance within the WWE system. Sometimes creative people thrived with us, and sometimes they burned out from the frustration of having to deal with writers and agents filtering, changing, and straight-up ignoring their ideas.

I got the vibe from Jerry that he felt the same about Chris. If there was one guy I trusted implicitly to spot talent, it was Jerry Brisco. My Native American "brother" was a world-class amateur and professional wrestler himself—but he also had the best eye for raw ingredients I'd ever seen. Jerry could tell from sheer instinct whether someone had the tools to cut it in the wrestling business or not.

That's not to say that everyone we signed was a hit, but everyone to whom we handed a contract certainly had a good shot; after pen hits paper, it's largely up to the talent if they make it upstream or not. Wrestling is an upstream business, with more factors pulling against you than for you.

Jericho already had one major advantage in that regard: He'd gotten over in every territory in which he'd competed. Swimming upstream was this guy's forte.

"The good news is that Vince wants to meet you at his house," I said to Chris. "The bad news is that I can't pay you up front what you're getting at WCW."

I didn't get the impression that money was a big factor one way or the other. He just wanted to be part of the biggest company in his field. "What can I expect?" he asked.

"Well, your base salary will be roughly half what WCW is offering you now," I replied. "But the way we work it, you could actually come out with a lot more every year based on bonuses, merchandise sales, appearances, and other revenue streams if you do well."

"The doing-well part doesn't faze me at all," Chris said.

I thought as much. "Vince wants you to go visit him at the house," I said.

"His house?" Chris repeated.

"Yep," I replied.

I didn't much visit Vince's house myself on booking days—the creatives and I didn't gel all that well—but I wanted to make sure Chris was introduced in the right way to the boss so I'd be joining him there.

At the airport, Jericho met Vince's limo driver, who drove him to the McMahon mansion in Stamford. Shane answered the door and brought Chris to the table, where the boss was waiting with his creative team of Vince Russo, Ed Ferrera, and Bruce Prichard.

I could tell Vince was warming to Chris when he asked him about a finish of a match that he was booking for that week's *Raw* TV show.

I smiled when I heard Chris chime in with his thoughts. I didn't give a shit if Jericho was five foot seven, ten, or two. He was a package delivered, as far as I was concerned. A prospect who could do major things in WWE no matter his size. Talent doesn't give a shit what height you are.

I left Vince's place a happy man. I knew Chris had so much to give to WWE, and he certainly ended up living up to that potential. But maybe I should have stayed with the creative team once I heard what they had in store for me.

While Jericho was on his way to WWE, good ol' J.R. was on his way to get his ass beat by a six-foot-four, 250-pound wrestler known as Triple H.

The Conduit

VINCE HAD MENTIONED a few weeks before that they were going to try something with me and Hunter Hearst Helmsley, or "Triple H," as he was now known. The boss's smile told me that it wasn't going to be a typical gig.

"I want to get Triple H in there with Austin," Vince said. "But I need you to be the conduit."

"Conduit?"

"Yeah."

I waited for an explanation, but Vince didn't offer one.

"What kind of conduit?" I asked. "Not that I'm . . ." I didn't want the chairman to think I wasn't masculine, that I was scared or anything.

"Well, the audience knows you and Austin are friends, J.R.," Vince explained. "So if Triple H beats the shit out of Austin's friend, it would . . ."

Vince wanted me to finish the sentence.

"Get him ready for Austin?" I said.

"Exactly," Vince replied, like he hadn't just told me the answer.

"Okay, I can be a conduit," I told him, still not really knowing what that meant.

Turns out it meant getting my ass beat by Triple H on live TV.

Now, I had been used in angles before, but this was new ground: I was stepping from the announce table straight into a multiweek storyline with the biggest heels in the business. I had been the *voice* of the show for years, but what Vince was laying out was the birth of J.R. the *character*—the man behind the voice.

And I wasn't all that sure how to feel about it.

Vince McMahon wanted to build "The Game," Triple H, into a mega heel for the hero, Austin, to battle, and one way to build a heel was to have him do dastardly things to someone the audience likes, roots for, and cares about. Vince hadn't forgotten the reaction I got on my first night back after Bell's palsy, when the audience defended me against his son's verbal insults. Now the chairman wanted to use that feeling to make his lead bad guy even more hated.

I wasn't sure that people would care to have me on their TV sets that way, but if that's what Triple H needed to get to that next level, then I was sure willing to try.

The story put The Game on guest commentary beside me at the start of the summer. By this stage, I knew what was coming—or, more important, *who* was delivering it—and honestly, it put me a little more at ease. If someone was going to take me behind the woodshed, I was happy it was a professional like Triple H—a man I had christened "The Game" and the "Cerebral Assassin" because of his chess-like approach to violence.

The Game and I once shook hands on a new deal in Evansville, Indiana, on one of the Anvil cases that we used to transport our gear. His rise up the ranks had placed him around the "magic number," as Vince liked to call it—one million dollars a year guaranteed salary. That was rarefied air in the company, and getting there meant you were in Vince's plans for a long time to come; the boss didn't like dropping that kind of guarantee on anyone unless he smelled money coming back his way.

This night, though, Triple H punched me in the mouth. I fell off my seat and did my best impression of a dead fish. As I lay on the ground, I smiled to myself as I heard the smashed-glass first note of Stone Cold's opener.

The arena went nuts.

It was so satisfying to lie there, face hidden, and listen to the passion in the building. Triple H had hit the wrong man, and now my friend, the Texas Rattlesnake, was going to serve The Game the receipt he'd earned.

Austin slid into the ring, pushed Chyna over, continued at full speed out the other side, and met Hunter with a barrage of stiff right hands. Both men beat each other around the ring until they ended up back inside the ropes—with the crowd at fever pitch—where Austin could hit his signature move: the Stone Cold Stunner.

I lay on the ground knowing that Austin and Triple H were set up perfectly. I could return to doing what I did best. I wouldn't have to take any more beatings.

WAIT A SECOND.

A short month later I was back in the storyline, on *Raw*, again.

"Ladies and gentlemen," I said on the microphone from the ring. "It is my honor to welcome the new WWE Champion."

My line was a setup to make the audience think they were getting fan-friendly Mick Foley, but instead Triple H marched down the ramp, flanked by his hulking female bodyguard—and real-life girlfriend, Chyna—instead. The next part of The Game's story was about to play out live—with me as his dance partner.

Both Triple H and the "Ninth Wonder of the World," Chyna, entered the ring.

"There's not going to be any celebration," Triple H said. As I tried to leave the ring, The Game stopped me. "You don't go anywhere. I want you to hear this. You stand there and you listen to me."

I turned to see Hunter's bully posture fully blown in front of me. I did as I was instructed and waited in the ring as he began to list his grievances from the PPV the night before.

Hunter and Stone Cold had had a match and Triple H felt he had Austin beat; he told the audience that he'd taken the air from Stone Cold's body, that he'd taken his very soul. The crowd booed as Triple H expertly turned the verbal screw on their hero.

The crowd began to chant in unison for Austin as the Cerebral Assassin played with their emotions like a conductor leading an orchestra.

I just stood there praying I wouldn't screw up the momentum that Hunter was clearly building.

"Steve Austin will never, ever, be the same again," Hunter exclaimed. "And now Steve Austin is watching this very interview flat on his back in some hospital in Minnesota, with his legs in the air like some cheap prostitute."

I'd had enough—or I'd heard my cue line—so I turned to leave, but The

Game wasn't having it. "Oh, what, you got something to say about this?" Hunter asked me. "Oh, wait, that's right, I forgot. Mick Foley, Austin, they're your boys, right?" he said.

I nodded emphatically. Both in storyline and in real life, Mick and Steve were "my boys." I had signed them; I had huge respect and admiration for both.

Hunter continued: "You're enjoying this . . . seeing Triple H out here in front of the world not getting what he wants. You're enjoying it, aren't you?" he shouted at me. "Just like I'm about to enjoy what I'm about to do."

This was it—the moment we'd all find out if the audience actually cared about an announcer being brought into the storyline. I wasn't afraid about any pain that might come, only silence—the empty sound of no one giving a shit.

Triple H locked me in a standing armbar that took me to my knees. "Now, Mick, I know you're back there and you have what's mine," Hunter said, referring to the WWE title. "I want your ass out here, or I'm going to break his arm."

Well, I'll be damned: I could hear people caring.

As Triple H handled business on the mic, I was on my knees. My anxiety quickly migrated from the reception of the audience to the quality of my performance. I wasn't trained to be in the ring, but I felt an obligation to try what Vince wanted. I could hear my hard-working, no-nonsense, tough-as-nails father saying in my head, "Son, if you're going to take the man's money, at least try to do what he asks."

So, I grimaced in agony and I tapped on the mat, on Hunter's leg, and on Chyna's leg when I could reach it. But it didn't matter—Triple H wasn't letting me go. The dastardly heel locked my arm even tighter to convince Mick to give him a title shot.

Even when Foley appeared and granted Hunter what he wanted, The Game simply leveraged my arm further and "broke" it anyway. That no-good dastardly bastard. WWE, the masters of subtlety, played a snapping sound over the sound system, which I guess was supposed to be my arm breaking? Problem was, the *Snap!* came *after* Hunter had broken my arm.

I hit the mat and left my newly broken arm twisted beside me.

As the crowd went crazy, I lay on the mat, happy it was over with. (Well, except for being taken out on a stretcher and put into an ambulance—you know, standard medical practice for a broken arm.)

Judging by the audience reaction, it landed just like we'd hoped it would. I wondered as I drove out of the building that night if that was a good or a bad thing for me personally. I knew the old temptation to keep going with something that was working. When I got to the hotel, I found out Vince was thinking the same thing. "There might be more for you and Triple H to do," he said.

Sure enough, two weeks later, I was looking at Triple H live on TV again.

"C'mon, let's hear it for good ol' J.R.," Triple H shouted from the ring.

I was dressed in black again because I was scared shitless, again.

There was a steel chair set up in the ring for me, as The Game was about to bully and beat good ol' J.R. once again. I reluctantly left the announce table, got between the ropes, and sat down, just like The Game told me to.

"What do you think a guy like Austin thinks of me?" Triple H asked me through the microphone.

I didn't miss a beat before replying, "He thinks you're an asshole."

The crowd went crazy.

Triple H was so good. He'd left it wide open for me to come along and deliver a line that would get me cheered. The crowd reaction was like a warm blanket wrapping around me.

Triple H continued: "What do *you* think of me, J.R.?"

I channeled my idol, John Wayne, and paused for a second before replying: "You really want to know?"

"Yeah," he said.

I got good and close to the mic and replied, "I think you're a sorry, low-down SOB."

Hunter turned away, seething, but he was really just giving room for the audience to react—and boy, did they react. For a second, I thought I was a badass.

Triple H replied, "That's a . . . that's a pretty good piece of business." Then he charged me and clotheslined me backward off my chair. The cheers turned to boos, music to my Okie ears. They went with me on the cheers, and when the time was right, they booed Triple H too. Hunter seized the moment to kick me in the ribs and rain down some smack talk. *Stomp. Stomp. Stomp.*

The Game's music played triumphantly, and I lay on the mat once again, happy that it was over.

As I was helped to the backstage area, I hoped we'd done enough to get me back to my real job at the announce table.

"Goddamn, we got something here," Vince said excitedly as I walked through the curtain. "I'm thinking we do a match with you and Steve vs. Triple H and Chyna, J.R.," he said "What do you think?"

"A match?" I said.

"It'll be good, J.R.," Vince replied.

"I think I need to go and buy some more black clothes," I said.

"What?" Vince asked, not knowing what the hell I was talking about.

The next week on *Raw*, Stone Cold called Triple H out. The Game made his entrance around the ring, but instead of getting between the ropes to fight Steve, he was prowling around the *Raw* ring as Stone Cold waited inside.

Hunter suddenly turned away from Austin and approached me at the announce table instead. He slapped the hat off my head and pushed me over when I stood up.

I'd had enough.

Triple H turned again to face The Rattlesnake in the ring, and I picked up my desk fan and hit him as hard as I could. Hunter turned and looked at me like he'd just gotten hit by a child.

Didn't matter. Stone Cold had seen enough.

Austin slid out of the ring and started laying in hard right hands, to the delight of the massive crowd in the Georgia Dome.

I sat down, but Austin sent Hunter flying over the desk and into my lap. It was glorious chaos as my announce partner shouted, "J.R., look what you caused!"

I wasn't finished yet.

I entered the ring as Stone Cold stomped a mudhole in The Game and walked it dry.

The Georgia Dome was going crazy.

Austin held my tormentor wide open and I asked the audience if they wanted to see good ol' J.R. punch that dastardly bastard with all I had. They replied in kind, and I proceeded to drive a right hand into Hunter's stomach. He sold it like he got shot; down he went, and Austin continued to beat the snot out of the WWE Champion.

But still my night wasn't over.

Chyna ran down the ramp, slid into the ring, and speared me into the corner. She drilled me in the temple over and over until Stone Cold grabbed her, stood her up, and disposed of her with a single strike.

Triple H grabbed the mic. "J.R., you want to get yourself involved? Well now, goddamnit, you're involved. The two of you, tonight, against me and Chyna. If you got the balls."

"We're going to have a match! Look at J.R.'s face, he can't believe it," The King said. He was right. Damn right.

AS I WALKED DOWN THE RAMP later that night, my hands were shaking. I knew the focus would rightly be on Triple H and Austin, but I had to hold up my end with the "Ninth Wonder of the World." Backstage, Chyna—or Joanie, to her friends and family—was a soft-spoken, kind, and considerate human being. In front of the camera, however, she was an ass-kicker. And I was about to get my ass kicked.

Triple H and Chyna were already in the ring. I waited at the end of the ramp for my tag partner to appear. As I turned around to see where Austin was, Triple H rolled out of the ring and attacked me from behind. A couple of seconds later, Stone Cold's music blared over the speakers, and the Georgia Dome crowd roared its approval.

Austin stopped Triple H from beating my ass any further, and champion and challenger brawled around the arena, through the crowd, and into the concession area.

I still had my Chyna problem to deal with. She choked me, punched me, and tossed me back into the ring. She hooked into Triple H's finishing move, the Pedigree, where my head would be driven into the mat. The choking, punching, and general beating that came before wasn't too bad and I knew that Joanie would never intentionally hurt me, but her Pedigree knocked me loopy.

She was wearing heels, and the extra lift knocked her calculations off. Good ol' J.R.'s head, by way of my face, bounced off the mat.

I lay there half functioning, but happy.

Happy the crowd remained engaged, happy my jeans didn't rip, happy my belly didn't pop out, and, once again, happy it was over.

Except it wasn't over.

Far from it.

FOUR

THE NEW AND THE OLD

Goddamnit, J.R.

"ARE WE GETTING ANY EXTRA MONEY FOR THIS, J.R.?" The King asked me.

"What do you think?" I replied.

We were heading into the spring of 1999, and The King already knew the answer. He'd asked it a thousand times in the days leading up to our new assignment.

Monday Night Raw had been WWE's flagship show for many years, and tonight was the debut of its sister show, *SmackDown*, on UPN.

Most people in the company hadn't even known we were in talks for a new show, but out of nowhere we were live on the air.

"We're coming back from break," Kevin Dunn said in the headset.

First nights of anything were fraught, but this particular night there was real anxiety in the air. Actually, the anxiety was in my ear, courtesy of a Mr. Vincent K. McMahon.

"Goddamn, J.R., make sure you explain to the people who's in the ring and why they're fighting," Vince said through my headset. Actually, he more shouted than said.

The boss was pissed at me for something, but I wasn't sure what. I'm not sure he knew what either. Vince was always opinionated, animated, and sometimes sharp in my headset, but rarely was he so aggressive in his producing of my work. He wanted *SmackDown* to be perfect from day one, and he was putting that pressure squarely on me.

King gave me his favorite-son smile. Jerry never got notes from Vince—not one fucking time.

Kevin Dunn chimed back in: "5 . . . 4 . . . 3 . . ."

"This is a whole new audience, J.R., goddamnit," Vince shouted. "Talk to them, tell them who we are."

King's smile turned to a chuckle as he heard what a shitty night I was having. Jerry didn't like drama, and Vince knew that The King didn't have the mindset to deal with long-term tension. If Vince wanted the best performance from Jerry, he knew not to confront him. So I got it instead.

"You got it?" Vince asked.

"Yep," I replied to the boss. "I got it."

And we were back live. New set, new colors, new opening, new channel, same announce team. I think that's what was bothering Vince so much.

I was finding out live on the air that we weren't ready. The deal with UPN had been put together quickly, and Vince wanted to plow ahead and get the show on the air "yesterday." The speed with which we found ourselves with a whole new show to write, staff, and produce put everyone on the back foot.

The business overall was hotter than hell, but keeping the machine running was tough enough without adding a whole new show to the mix.

"The audience has no product knowledge, J.R.," Vince yelled at me for what felt like the hundredth time.

I had more patience than most when it came to taking shit from the owner, but his tone was starting to get to me. I was commentating live on a match, adhering to the run-sheet, while at the same time listening to my announce partner, and the owner of the company was shouting in my ear. Anyone else would easily get confused or flustered with so much going on. But not me. I had a skill only a few had mastered.

"For God's sake, J.R., explain things to them," Vince said. "Don't take for granted that this audience knows who we fucking are."

I was not only doing my best—I was doing exactly what I had done successfully for Vince on his flagship show for years. But tonight, midshow, he suddenly wanted me to be a different commentator altogether. I had no idea what he wanted, to be honest.

We went to another break.

"Are you sure we're not getting paid extra for this?" The King said, his chuckle now a raucous laugh.

Didn't matter to me that we weren't getting paid extra, because I could tell I was going to be relieved of my *SmackDown* duties the second the show ended. And I was more than happy with that, because my professional plate was already overflowing. Adding another show every week was something that I knew I couldn't handle.

"J.R.," Vince began, and I could sense there was another load of heat coming my way.

I pressed my call button and interrupted him. "You never told me you wanted me to change up what I'm doing out here," I said.

"You're not making things clear enough," he snapped back.

I was backed into a corner. If I'd known going into the show that the chairman wanted something different, I would have given him just that. But he and his new network had specifically asked for J.R. and The King to be the announce team.

Jerry whispered, "So you don't think we'll get any extra—"

"King!" I shouted. I was getting flustered, and Jerry loved that.

"If you're going to get yourself thrown off the show, can you see if you'd get me canned too?" Lawler was a capitalist: He just wanted the cash, an easy work environment, and as much time at home as possible.

Me? I had long forgotten what an easy workweek was like.

"Vince," I said, "we never talked about any of this. We never talked about me changing up how I announce. I'm doing my work as I've always done my work. I didn't know you wanted something different."

"Goddamnit. Tell Jerry his work is off tonight too," Vince shouted back.

I could tell by Jerry's lack of reaction that Vince had piped his message only into my headset, not his.

"Why don't you tell him?" I said to Vince.

There was silence. The only thing worse than Vince shouting in your ear was Vince not shouting at all. I pressed the button to mute the boss as I leaned over and said to Jerry, "I hope you enjoy this next week without me."

We finished the show, and I knew my fate.

Afterward, on the WWE private jet, Vince and I sat together in silence for most of the trip. He did his work and I did mine.

"I'm going to put Cole with Jerry on *SmackDown*," he said just before we landed, referring to Michael Cole, who had replaced me previously during my bout with Bell's palsy.

"He'll do a great job," I replied. I was happy to see him get his break.

"I want you to produce him," Vince said. "Help him get up to speed."

I was happy to do that too. Michael was a good talent, a great family man, and a wonderful guy. I could already hear The King in my head saying, "Cole is green, J.R. I'm not making any more money, and now I have to work with someone who's green too?"

But man, I was relieved. Vince would get no pushback from me. I already needed more time than I had to focus on the talent relations department.

The only time I was with the whole roster was on TV days, preparing for my own part on the shows. It wasn't fair to the Boys that I was often busy when they wanted to see me. I always carved out time, but sometimes it was just five minutes walking the halls or one minute before we went live.

Losing my *SmackDown* slot one night in was a blessing in that regard. Now I'd be on the road on a TV day, when everyone was there, and I'd be freer to talk to whomever needed it. It gnawed at me that I was doing a lot of jobs reasonably well but none at the level I wanted to; halfway through one task, something else would always claim my attention.

That's one thing I came to know and accept about the wrestling business: Everything hinges—and changes—on a whim. You're hot, then cold. You're the main event, then unemployed. You're vital to everything, then needed by nobody. One day you'll never have enough time, then the next you'll have all the time in the world.

Losing and Gaining

THE PET-COON CRAZY YEAR showed no signs of normalizing, as word came from WCW that the executive vice president, Eric Bischoff, had been fired. Bad creative and falling ratings meant that WCW were looking for a new leader—and a new creative direction—to try to correct the promotion's downward course. And it looked like WCW's new vision was going to be coming from within the WWE ranks.

"It's just another day at the office, J.R.," Vince said as we walked to his office.

Our head writer, Vince Russo, and his number two, Ed Ferrera, were all of a sudden heading to WCW. Russo was already burned out trying to keep up with the nonstop grind that was WWE; adding *SmackDown* to his to-do list seemed to have been his breaking point.

"What's the plan?" I asked.

"This isn't fucking rocket science, we just move on," Vince said.

I could feel a tension within the locker room with the head writer leaving. Personally, I couldn't care less; I had enough of my own shit to worry about. Russo was definitely a huge part of what the company had achieved, but I saw enough to conclude that McMahon was often curbing Russo's worst impulses.

Routinely, Vince would ask me, "What do you think of this idea, J.R.?" or "How do we make this angle better?" And routinely I'd disagree with the way some of our creative guys was going. I couldn't argue with the eyeballs it was pulling in, but the edgier, low-road stuff wasn't my personal cup of tea. Some of it, frankly, was more Howard Stern than pro wrestling. But it was a formula that had helped us pull ahead of our main competitor, WCW, in the ratings.

Even though I was booking the nontelevised, weekend house shows with Vince, I wouldn't go to a TV booking meeting unless drugged and dragged. Russo had such high regard for himself that it was impossible to get any booking idea off the ground without him leading the charge. Those meetings often felt like an audience with the writers rather than an exchange of ideas. And I was too busy to spend hours listening to anyone else doing their job, when I should have been over in the other side of the building doing mine.

I also understood that, my personal tastes aside, Vince McMahon and Vince Russo together made a winning team, with Russo cooking up all kinds of ideas and McMahon filtering them down into something we could use.

If Russo was going to leave, WCW was the obvious move. There was nowhere else in our field to turn for equivalent—or better—money, for fewer hours of work.

And I certainly understood his burning out. We had only a small staff to "feed the monster" in WWE, so working all hours, all days, wasn't anything unusual. It's hard to keep that up forever.

When word of Russo's leaving got out, I had to calm the minority panic with some of the Boys. Like most creatives, Russo had people he liked more than others, and he would therefore pitch for his pals and some were worried they would no longer be looked after. On the other hand, those who felt like they hadn't gotten a proper shake were suddenly hopeful they would now be given another look.

With any change of booking philosophy in wrestling, there are those who are going to be worried and those who are going to be happy. I saw a lot more happy faces in the locker room that day than worried ones. Most everyone was making great money, and the WWE brand was stronger than it ever had been. It was so strong that Vince was making moves to bring his company from a privately owned, family-run business into the public square.

I knew all about it because of my morning meetings with Vince. He would run by me details that linked to the bigger corporate picture. Those meetings were like a crash course in how to service the duality of a leadership position in an entertainment company.

"We're heading into more exciting, uncharted waters that will change the company for good," Vince said.

The chairman had a big ace up his sleeve that he wasn't yet ready to share with the world: WWE was going public, and having Russo leave wasn't going to even mildly disrupt that.

"We're going to float the company on the New York Stock Exchange," the boss said. "You're going to be made whole financially."

"Me?" I said.

"Yeah, J.R. When the stock hits certain markers, you'll see a significant difference."

I had grown up on a farm. I talked to animals a lot. I wasn't a Wall Street guy. Although Vince had grown up in trailer park, he nevertheless seemed to have a great grasp of what we were discussing.

"Of course, I'll make a significant difference," I said, not knowing a single thing I was talking about.

Vince continued: "The top guys and those that have been with us a long time will see some stocks too," he said. "I want you to tell the Boys when the time is right."

"Of course I will," I replied.

I could see why Vince McMahon wasn't perturbed by Russo leaving. The chairman was frying much, much bigger fish.

Now, I knew that me trying to tell the likes of Stone Cold, The Rock, and Undertaker about stocks would be like a turnip trying to teach a spoon the theory of relativity. I had no idea what Vince was talking about, but I pretended that I did.

I sought out Ed Kaufman, who was WWE's chief legal counsel. "This will be the best thing to ever happen to you financially," he told me.

"Ever?" I said.

"Every year we hit our marks, you get more stock," he said. "And that will be worth millions of dollars to you."

"Millions?" I asked.

"Millions," he said with a smile.

All of sudden I felt the strong urge to kiss Ed. Or Vince. Or Jan. Yeah, my wife would probably be more welcoming than Ed or Vince.

When I got the green light, I caught up with the Top Guys and told them what had been told to me. They didn't understand the finer points either.

"Vince isn't putting any extra money in your hand today, but he is putting it there. You might have to wait a little while," I explained.

All the Top Guys wanted to know was what the other Top Guys got. I felt a little like The Rock as I explained, "It doesn't matter what anyone else got, you're getting it too."

On the day of the IPO, we were invited to ring the opening bell on Wall Street. I could feel how big an occasion it was to the McMahon family, and Vince in particular. Apart from the optics of professional wrestling showing up on the stock market, the move also gave us more than $160 million in capital injection. That money would be our shield against any oncoming threats. WWE and pro wrestling in general were now legit, and growing. The panic about Russo being gone was suddenly a thing of the past.

Or so I thought.

The Old-School Handshake

AS ALWAYS, THE CALM DIDN'T LAST LONG. Trouble came by way of a contract negotiation with Russo's friend Jeff Jarrett.

Something told me it was going to be a long day in Cleveland when I arrived for *No Mercy* in 1999—well, actually, *someone* told me first.

"You really screwed up this time, J.R.," Brian "Road Dogg" Armstrong said as I entered the arena.

"Did you wait here to tell me that?" I asked him.

His face lit up with delight. "You messed up big time, man."

I kept walking. I'd never had a talent wait by the door of a building to gleefully declare I was "in trouble" before, so I no-sold him. In wrestling, if you let anyone know what gets to you, they'll keep poking—just like in prison.

Plus, I knew that if I really was "in trouble," I would know why soon enough. After all, as we say in the business, if you want bad news to travel fast, "Telephone, telegram, or tell-a-wrestler."

This time, the bad news was that Double J., Jeff Jarrett, was leaving WWE and joining WCW.

A talent leaving wasn't usually that earth-shattering. We were knee-deep in a wrestling ratings war with World Championship Wrestling, and talent from both sides crossed over frequently.

The thing that made the Jeff situation unique is that he was our Intercontinental Champion, and he was threatening to leave that night, *before* the show, unless he was paid cash money before the bell rang. Jarrett was scheduled to lose to Joanie "Chyna" Laurer, who you'll remember was Triple H's partner in kicking my ass.

As timing would have it, Jeff's WWE contract had lapsed the day before, so he was legally free to walk if he wanted to, without "putting over" Chyna and losing the Intercontinental title on his way out.

And I should have seen it all coming.

In the weeks leading up to PPV, Jeff asked his father, Jerry Jarrett, to negotiate a new contract with me on his behalf. Jerry had grown up in the business as a wrestler himself, then as a longtime promoter, and he was even a consultant for WWE at one point.

If anyone had excellent product knowledge, it was Jerry.

Jeff knew his old man knew our business inside and out and could possibly get a better deal in the long run. The only problem for both men was that Jerry, as a father, was blind to his son's real worth to WWE.

Both men felt that Jeff should be working a program with Steve Austin on the top of the card. Austin felt differently: He had no interest in working with Jeff until Double J. got over enough to make their match something people wanted to see.

Austin's thinking seemed pretty reasonable to me, but Jerry was adamant his son was main-event level despite what audiences thought, what the merchandise sales said, or our ratings displayed every week.

But numbers aside, it was ultimately Vince McMahon who disagreed with Jerry's lofty assessment of his son, and he backed Austin's take.

I did too.

"Jeff was told that he was in line for Austin," Jerry said.

"He was told?" I asked. "By whom?"

"He was told," Jerry replied, obviously not wanting to get into it.

I knew who was feeding Jeff that fantasy: Vince Russo. The same Vince Russo who gave Jeff an opening on *Raw* to claim that the "Austin 3:16" slogan, from which Steve and WWE were making millions, was "blasphemy" because it mirrored a biblical passage.

The same Vince Russo who was pushing so hard for Jarrett to face Austin that it made Steve dig in his heels at a quick meeting with Vince and me. "Goddamnit," The Rattlesnake said, "I told you I don't want to work with him, and now I keep hearing his name come up and you're making me the bad guy for squashing it."

Jeff wasn't getting to Austin, no matter how hard Russo pushed for it.

In fact, the more Russo pushed, the less likely it became, because Steve felt like he was getting railroaded, and that wasn't going to happen under any circumstances.

The evidence that Jarrett wasn't a top-tier talent was there in black and white, week after week, year after year. And that wasn't a knock on Jeff: He was a great talent, but he had a ceiling, like 99.99 percent of the roster.

Not everyone can be main-event level, which is why so few have reached the top in professional wrestling. But we wanted Jeff on our roster, and we wanted him to re-sign for a number that made everyone happy.

So the negotiation, as they always do, turned to money.

Turns out Jerry had exceptionally high expectations for his son in this category too. The number he sought was way beyond what Vince had instructed me to pay.

Jerry, more than anyone, knew how the system worked. WWE's model with all talent was to agree on a downside guarantee—a gross dollar number that you got, divided by fifty-two if you preferred to be paid weekly.

Your salary could not fall below that guarantee. So you knew that, no matter what, that amount was coming in every week, just as if you were working in a factory.

On top of that base number would be your discretionary slice of merchandise sales, PPV buys, live-event ticket sales, and other monies. This number depended on where you were on the card, how much of your branded merchandise you sold, et cetera. Those extra monies were pooled together and paid out in one lump sum at the end of every year.

Jeff had always made considerably more than his downside guarantee because business was red hot and everyone was making great money. But Jerry felt his son should be making even more.

Vince held firm on his number.

"Is this coming from Vince?" Jerry asked me.

"You know it is, Jerry. All these numbers come from Vince," I said.

"And he ain't going to move?"

I shook my head. "Vince gave me the number. He's not going to move."

Jerry thought about it for a second and put out his hand.

I shook it.

"We got a deal?" I asked.

"We got a deal," he said.

"Tell Jeff I'll see him at the Pay-Per-View and we'll sign there," I said to Jerry.

"Will do," Jerry said, still shaking my hand.

There and then as far as I was concerned Jerry Jarrett and I struck a deal on his son's behalf; we shook hands on it and exchanged our good word.

Based on that agreement, we built up Jeff's match with Chyna on our TV shows; we shot angles, we agreed on creative and the finish. We were full steam ahead. All that was left was for Jeff to sign his new contract in Cleveland.

Exactly where I was now standing backstage.

"I was under the impression we had a deal," I said to Jeff in the locker room.

"I'm leaving for WCW," he told me. "They're going to pay me what I'm worth, so I want my PPV payoffs, merchandise money, and anything you guys owe me, Jim."

I didn't answer immediately because I wanted a pause to calm the situation. I also needed what was happening here to settle in. Twenty-five years I'd been in the wrestling business, and I'd never been involved in anything like this before.

"You sure this is what you want, Jeff?" I asked.

"Yep," he replied.

"Okay, if you're sure."

"I want it now. In cash," he said.

"How much?" I asked.

"Three hundred grand," he said. "That's what I figure I'm owed."

"I'm going to have to talk to Vince on a number like that."

"Do what you gotta do," he said. "I've already been in there with him."

This was something I had never seen before, and it was way above any decision-making power that I had in the company.

I left the room. I was surprised—and not—because Double J. had been raised in this business. Unfortunately, professional wrestling has a split personality when it comes to its unwritten rules and traditions.

On the one hand, there is a custom of "doing business" before you leave any one company for another. Champions, especially, drop their titles in the ring before they move on to any new company or territory. This is to ensure the ongoing integrity of the belt they're holding, to "bless" the new champion, and to help make whole the company they are leaving behind.

The flip side of wrestling, though, houses a dirty, carnival-like, smoky backroom mentality of cutting throats and stabbing backs. This is a mentality where wrestlers can screw over owners when they have leverage, and owners sure as hell screw over wrestlers.

I found myself caught somewhere between those traditions: operating on the old-school handshake, even as we were rapidly entering a screw-or-be-screwed era.

I had trusted Jerry's word that his son would operate without a contract for a few hours—that was on me.

When I got to Vince, he was calm. "We need to protect Chyna," he said. "We want this to be her night. She's going to be the first female Intercontinental Champion."

"What happened?" I asked. "He said he was in here already."

"He came into the building without his bags or the title," Vince said. "Said he was going to leave and get on a flight if he didn't get what he was owed."

I was beginning to wonder just what was happening behind Jeff's decision.

"We've been building Chyna," Vince said, snapping back to the business of the night. "So we negotiate Jeff's number down and get this match on."

"I should have handled it differently," I said.

"What happened with the contract?" Vince asked.

"Well, it ran out at midnight, and I brought the new one with me here today for him to sign. I apologize," I said.

All along the way I had kept Vince fully informed of the tricky negotiations, but the boss wanted to keep the program of Jeff and Chyna on the air no matter the dicey predicament of the legal work.

Vince stood. "He wants you personally to give him the money," he said.

"He what?" I asked.

It was then I knew the root of this whole thing. Jeff had signed a couple of years before on a bigger, $350,000-a-year contract. We tried everything to make his money worth the outlay, but Jeff just wasn't clicking with the fans. It was at that point that Vince wanted to drop Double J.'s downside guarantee to $250,000—which I did, and Jeff agreed to it. Turned out, with bonuses and PPV money, Double J. made more than the $350,000 he'd dropped down from anyway.

But he'd clearly held Vince's pay cut against me personally—and this was just a way for the Jarretts to humble me.

As Vince and I talked, his office door was being pounded on like crazy. I knew the sycophants in the company couldn't wait to get in the chairman's ear to try and use this situation to discredit my work in toto. The only thing I had in my favor was my record. I was good at my job, and I had learned a valuable lesson about wrestling, contracts, handshakes, and integrity.

"I can bring him his money," I said.

"No," Vince replied. "You're the head of talent relations, J.R. We won't have you degraded like this. You go, negotiate him down. Send him out there to put Chyna over. Let him move on."

Vince picked up the phone and told someone to find out what the box-office take was that night, just in case we needed the cash.

"I didn't know Jeff had it in him to do this," I said before I left.

"Make sure it never happens again," Vince replied. "Ever."

As I walked the hallway back to Jeff, the last piece of the puzzle clicked for me as to what was going on.

Vince Russo and Jeff Jarrett were friends. Russo was now in power at WCW, and he needed someone he trusted around his new locker room.

Jeff was right to take the better offer at WCW, and he was also right to look for the money that was owed. But he was way wrong in how he was doing it.

He got his money—far less than he'd looked for—and he put Chyna over in the ring. Vince never mentioned him again. (Until twenty years later, when he hired Jeff to come back to WWE in a producer's role.)

I, on the other hand, immediately instituted new policies in my department to make sure that a handshake could never be trusted going forward. It was necessary. But it made me sad.

The whole situation with Jeff could have been averted with a little communication. Instead, we'd regressed to the smoky backroom dealings of wrestling's seedier past.

WWE moved on with its business, and Jeff followed Russo to WCW—which no doubt was his plan all along.

FIVE

TALENT AND TELEVISION

Issues Stacked High

WWE WAS SERVICING A LOT of TV hours across different networks, and our number of weekly original hours was growing. For me, that meant we needed a lot of new talent to facilitate the endless cycle of content being consumed, not only in the United States, but in many countries around the world.

If I wasn't meeting with talent, I was scouting them. If I wasn't scouting talent, I was listening to them put forth the case as to why they'd want to come to WWE—or why they wanted to leave.

I became obsessed with striking the right balance in our locker room. I knew I'd have to navigate some tricky waters if I just filled our roster with bodies, without considering character and leadership, not to mention chemistry.

My days off the air had turned into nonstop meetings; my desk was stacked high with issues month after month, year after year.

And to keep it interesting, as we left 1999 and headed into 2000, no two talent "issues" were the same.

Sable, a wildly popular but athletically limited Superstar, left the company because she felt it was a hostile work environment. I was made aware by WWE counsel that she had filed a lawsuit against the company. I'd never known the real-life Rena Mero to be anything other than professional, and she rarely hit my radar unless it was because of others becoming jealous of her success.

Rena first came to WWE for a meeting with her husband, Marc Mero. Marc was playing a Johnny B. Badd character in WCW and, to his credit, very well. So we knew Mero had the sizzle that Vince liked. He was also a well-spoken guy, very well conditioned, and he had a good look. But the second Vince saw Rena, a switch flipped.

After the meeting, I showed Marc and Rena out and thanked them for being there. When I got back to my office, Vince had already left a message for me to call him right away.

I called, and he jumped right in. "Did you see what I saw?"

Knowing Vince, I replied, "Yes, I think I did."

He said, "I'm glad we're signing Marc, because she's money."

I said, "I think you're right."

I wasn't just ass-kissing the boss. A blind man could see Rena had "it."

Vince didn't wait long to put her on TV. She didn't even know how to be what she was supposed to be character-wise, as nobody was giving her any real instruction. Usually I liked all new talent to go to one of our feeder territories in smaller, less-risky environments to learn the business, but Vince wanted Rena's striking beauty front and center right away.

All I could do to help bring her along was to make sure that Sable, as she was now known, was surrounded by talent who knew the ropes, like Ivory, Jackie Moore, and Jazz. All these women had the experience and knowledge that Sable couldn't possibly have. I was relying on them to help Sable raise her game.

And to Rena's credit, she was in great shape—a cardiovascular machine. She just didn't know the wrestling business.

And all of those things made her a target of jealousy.

The wrestling business really dislikes a person cutting the line and getting fame and fortune, while others who have been toiling away for years don't.

It's understandable, but it's also bullshit when you think about it.

A star is a star is a star, and the wrestling business is as star-driven as any form of entertainment.

Sable came in, blazed through the business, and left as one of the hottest acts on the roster. I hadn't been aware of the specific issues she was facing, but I was certainly sorry she was gone.

On the tougher end of the spectrum, Ken Shamrock, an MMA legend and solid wrestling star, wanted to leave WWE to take some big-money fights back in the mixed martial arts world.

It took us a while to understand what Kenny's plan was, because at first he told us he was injured, but that didn't add up. Then he started to miss some shows. Eventually, it seemed that the problem was a combination of some substance issues and the schedule grinding him down.

Talking to him was one of the scariest conversations I've ever had.

"Kenny," I said.

"What?"

"You're missing towns." I was trying not to comedy-gulp as the former UFC Superfight Champion (the precursor to their heavyweight title) and King of Pancrase walked toward me. "We can't book you if we don't know you're going to be there," I said.

Kenny had partied a little heavily in El Paso and had missed his flight. "The World's Most Dangerous Man" was the world's most stranded man.

So he missed his booking.

Now it was my job to bring him to the "principal's office" the following Monday at *Raw*.

"You can't do this," I said.

"I know," he replied. "I apologize."

"I gotta fine you. A thousand bucks." As the words left my mouth I looked up and down Kenny's whole body for signs that a kick, punch, or headbutt was coming my way. Thankfully not. "Kenny, you've got nothing in this business if you're not reliable, buddy." I secretly hoped calling him "buddy" would dissuade him from killing me.

I was still alive and now feeling a little bit more sure of myself. "If we can't rely on you to make the damn towns, how are you gonna get a push? You want a push, you wanna make a lot of money, right?"

"Yeah! That's what I came here for," Kenny said, his sudden enthusiasm scaring me a little.

"Okay, then," I replied, nice and softly. "Go back to work and make that money."

Kenny opened the door to my office to leave. I wondered if he noticed that I always had Jerry Brisco around outside when Kenny was in my office—to pull Kenny off if he started to kill me.

I took a deep breath, glad it was over. Until Shamrock missed another show several weeks later.

"Aw, fuck," I said when I heard. I was mad Kenny was missing shows but angrier that I had to go face-to-face with him again.

I sent somebody for him at *Raw* again, but not before I had cornered Jerry Brisco again.

"Jerry," I said.

Jerry smiled before I had finished my sentence. "Kenny?" he asked.

"How did you know?"

He laughed. "'Cause I can smell fear, J.R."

"Look, I gotta talk to him again, and he's not going to be happy with what I have to say."

"I know, I know," Jerry said. "If you're not back in ten minutes—"

"Call the cops, an ambulance, and a priest," I said.

I was joking, but not really. Shamrock had a short fuse, and he was more than a little unpredictable.

This time I didn't want to be in an enclosed space, so I waited by the loading dock of the building. Kenny walked toward me with that signature wide strut of all truly tough bastards.

My nerves were jangling. "Kenny," I said. "We had this conversation already."

"Jim—"

"Now, apparently you didn't give a shit," I said, surprised at myself. Adrenaline is a helluva thing. "And apparently I don't mean nothing in your life, where you're gonna do what you're gonna do anyway."

I waited a beat for Kenny to jump in, but he didn't. He just stared. I looked over his shoulder for Brisco before continuing. "But that's not how it's gonna work here. So here's where we are. I'm gonna fine you a week's pay for missing this town. And no, you would not have made nearly this much money on the payoff from the town. But I don't know any other way to reach you."

Kenny was silent. Hard to read.

"So I'm gonna fine you your week, or we can part ways. We can't do business this way," I said. "I talked to Vince about it. We're very disappointed; we see great things in you."

"I'm sorry," he said.

You are? my inner voice said. "You should be," my outer voice actually said.

"Tell Vince it won't happen again," Kenny said, before walking away.

I looked to my left and Jerry Brisco was behind some crates, laughing with his double thumbs-up.

Kenny got more responsibility; he was booked a lot. I had him booked on every show, but I guess he got a little bit burned out on the road. And he had opportunities and offers—significant offers—to go back into MMA.

In the world of mixed martial arts, instead of wrestling four nights a week, he could fight two, three times a year and still make good money.

He could also be home training, except for fight week or something. And so that's what we discussed.

When he left, I said, "The door's open, you can come back any time you want. We don't wanna lose you."

I felt like Kenny was leaving money on the table, but he clearly felt he had unfinished business in the octagon.

Ken Shamrock was very, very close to becoming a megastar in WWE. Vince and I liked him for the top of the card at a *WrestleMania* or something similar. We believed in him because he was damn real.

Kenny wasn't playing a character; he knew what he could do, and every move in the ring was so damn smooth and realistic. So losing him to MMA hurt us. We put a lot of money into him, a lot of time.

Week after week—some talent in, some talent out. Some of the wrestlers I dearly wanted to bring in, some I didn't want to lose—and some I could take or leave. But when I heard rumors in the locker room that Eddie Guerrero wanted to come to WWE, I was immediately interested.

The arrival of Vince Russo in WCW had only further heightened the tensions backstage there as various personalities jockeyed for control of the company. As unrest grew, word going around was that WCW had offered snap releases to any of the talent who were unhappy and wanted to leave, so a band of top talent got together and asked to go. Our first piece of business in my department was to make sure that anyone coming from, or still involved with, WCW had the green light to talk to us, because we didn't want to get caught up in a tampering issue with WCW's parent company, Time Warner.

The paperwork came through showing that not only Guerrero but also Chris Benoit, Perry Saturn, and Dean Malenko were free and interested in coming to WWE. The four of them were unhappy with their treatment in WCW, and they saw how Chris Jericho was being booked as a top star, no matter his size, since making the move to WWE a few months prior, after similarly hitting the ceiling of what WCW would allow him to achieve. We began to realize we might have lucked into a possible amazing "faction" that could electrify our expanded TV hours.

I was particularly interested in Eddie and Chris as potential main-event talent because of their next-level work in the ring. Meanwhile, Dean had grown up in the business, had wrestled around the world, and was considered one of the best mat wrestlers around. And Perry was strong and charismatic. They would be stellar additions to the roster too.

Eddie called me and told me he wanted to meet. Bruce Prichard and I met with all four for dinner and immediately knew we had to get these guys in front of Vince. They spoke with passion and solidarity, and their issue with WCW seemed to be more creative than financial.

"What are the hurdles?" I asked Bruce back at my office.

"Vince needs to meet them," Prichard replied.

"Couldn't agree more."

As with Jericho, we didn't want Vince hearing about any of these guys from the wrong people in the company. Inevitably, the conversations would turn to a guy's height and weight instead of his passion and skill.

I met with Vince first thing the next morning and quickly filled him in. I knew the best route was to highlight one rather than try to sell the chairman on all four right there and then.

"Eddie Guerrero," I said. "You should really meet him at the house."

I remembered what had worked well for Chris, and I wanted to stick to the same game plan.

"Bring him over," Vince said.

Those three words from the boss let me know we were off to a great start.

I wasted no time in getting Eddie to the McMahon family home in Stamford. When we arrived, I could see Eddie was a little in awe, just as I had been the first time. The McMahon house was certainly large, but it did have a homey feel—meals were eaten there, arguments had, holidays celebrated, and music played.

The first thing that Eddie noticed was the giant painting of Vince in a polo shirt hanging in the hallway.

"When you think of Vince McMahon, you think of polo, right?" I said to Eddie.

Eddie smiled, and it broke the ice a little. He was nervous, but I knew he could be charming and professional when he needed to.

Bruce was already there, waiting for us to arrive.

"I just want to be used right," Eddie said to Vince. "We all do—me, Chris, Perry, and Dean."

Vince was impressed with Eddie's candor and straightforwardness. The boss's favorite saying was "Don't tell me how to make the damn watch, just tell me the time."

"Well, if you want to come work for us here in WWE," Vince said, "we'll make sure you have every chance to get to the heights you want to get to."

At the end of the meeting Eddie left first, giving me a second with Vince to gauge his interest.

"What do you think?" I asked.

"Man, he's tiny," Vince replied.

"He's not a giant," I said. "But he's a helluva talent."

The boss always had his mind set on a certain look, but I knew that Eddie's talent would overcome any initial reservations. I always fought to bring in those who weren't the "ideal" size because I never believed there was an ideal size to begin with. I had seen too many guys under six-foot become legends in the wrestling business. I knew looks and size could be a key component, but they weren't everything—especially when the talent was this obvious.

Broadly speaking, I wanted to bring in great workers, good human beings, and especially diverse personalities who could make our overall locker room stronger. It was my job to help the WWE goose that laid the golden egg stay healthy, and I knew that Chris Benoit and Eddie Guerrero in particular could help our overall WWE goose thrive.

"And they left because they weren't happy with their creative?" Vince asked.

"Yep," Bruce replied. "We put these guys on TV as a faction. Bring them all in together. That way we can introduce them with some steam behind them."

"All right, J.R.," Vince said. "Let's do it."

The chairman liked to take calculated risks, but I didn't see much risk at all. The Radicals, as we would call them, were established talents. Malenko was a great technician, Saturn had the skills and the look and personality to be a star, and Eddie and Chris were two once-in-a-lifetime talents coming along at the same time. They were also technically brilliant, Chris with a more mat-based approach, and Eddie coming from the high-flying lucha style. But it was their ability to engage the audience that set them apart. Everything Chris did looked crisp, solid, and flawless in its execution; Eddie had a unique charisma that made him a man of the people and easy to root for.

"I'm telling you," Bruce said to Vince as we left. "Eddie Guerrero is like the goddamn Mexican Shawn Michaels."

Meanwhile, I had a date with the real Heartbreak Kid on the books.

Shawn Michaels, "The Heartbreak Kid," was a WWE veteran who had retired a year prior. A back injury ultimately took him down, but ongoing issues with drugs and alcohol had made his departure fraught and messy, to say the least. But word had it Shawn had cleaned up his act and gotten straight in his personal life, and had found a more spiritual side of himself since he left.

Just as I wanted to bring Eddie Guerrero in, I also wanted Shawn back in the locker room someday. I didn't know whether he was truly happy to be outside of the wrestling world. After all, he'd left WWE as one of the best ever, and to my eyes he had unfinished business in the ring.

I met Michaels and his agent, Skip McCormick, in a restaurant in Alamo City. Skip was a nice guy and really seemed to have Shawn's best interests at heart. I was happy to see The Heartbreak Kid looking so fresh and rested.

"Would you ever think of coming back?" I asked as we tucked into our meals. "Not even in the ring, but in the locker room, where people could really need your guidance."

"I'm not sure, J.R.," Shawn replied.

I could see that part of him really wanted to come back. A lot of guys, when they come off the road, find that they like being in their own bed every night for a while. It's a break from the craziness. But eventually the itch comes back. Shawn was clearly happy with the new avenue he was on, but there was a serious competitor still knocking around in his person somewhere.

I said, "You're going to be known as one of the greatest of all time, but you need to write a different ending for yourself."

"My faith is very important to me," he said.

Shawn knew, like I did, that most guys who got spiritual in the wrestling business did so because they got caught cheating on their wives or crossing the boss in some monumental way. Usually, spirituality in wrestling was temporary. But not with Shawn.

"I would like people to see and experience your new attitude. You can help a lot of guys in our locker room," I said. "I don't care whether you wrestle. You're an amazing resource we can't replicate."

I actually did care if he wrestled. In truth, as long as he was healthy, I knew that Shawn could come back and be one of the best in the world again.

I continued: "I don't know how bad your back is, but to me that doesn't even matter. I just want you back around the company in any way you're comfortable."

I could see that what I was saying struck a chord. Shawn clearly still loved the business.

"Maybe we can do something," he said.

I told him, "Take your time and let me know."

I don't know which part of the job I loved most: finding new beginnings for wrestlers from elsewhere, or helping longtime WWE talent find new paths for themselves. But I do know that the seeds that were planted with those conversations in 1999 helped drive the direction of the business in the years ahead. By 2002, Shawn was back in the ring. And by 2004, *WrestleMania XX* was main-evented by two championship matches—one seeing Eddie Guerrero, now the WWE Champion, successfully defend his title against former Olympian Kurt Angle, and the other pitting World Heavyweight Champion Triple H against two contenders—Chris Benoit and "The Heartbreak Kid" Shawn Michaels.

While Shawn's story ended happily—with The Heartbreak Kid staring in many more unforgettable *WrestleMania* moments until his retirement in 2010—both Chris and Eddie's did not.

Eddie died suddenly at only thirty-eight years old due to heart failure, and, a couple years after that, the horrifying circumstances around Benoit's tragic suicide rattled us all to the core.

Three men, three signees, three amazing talents, three completely different paths and legacies.

A Bottom-Line Move

EVERY THURSDAY MORNING when I wasn't on the road, I met with Vince's executive assistant, Beth Zazza, and his wife, Linda's, executive assistant, Liz DiFabio, along with the general counsel of the company, Ed Kaufman. It was my job to give them an overview of talent issues so the assistants could fill in the owners, and Ed could see if there was anything coming down the pike that might need his attention.

Early 2000 was no different.

I was happy being left to captain my own ship inside WWE. I was responsible for the most important cog in the wheel—the talent—and Vince more or less left me alone.

We were hiring a lot of new wrestlers, and the sheer number of new deals, renewals, terminations, and developmental deals to process was getting mountainous. WWE was always growing, moving, reinventing itself—which meant plenty of logistics.

One Thursday after the meeting, my phone lit up with the name V MCMAHON.

It wasn't unusual for Vince to call after I filled in Beth—he often wanted the report straight from the horse's mouth. When I popped my head into his office, Vince was eating a sandwich with a knife and fork.

The chairman is a bit of a germaphobe. Even on longer days, when pizza was delivered, Vince would fold a slice and eat it up to where he touched it, then bin the rest. It was my daily challenge at WWE to ignore this while sitting across from him.

"We're moving networks, J.R.," he said as I sat down.

"We are?"

"It's a bottom-line move. USA isn't willing to give us what we're worth, so we're going to TNN."

"Viacom?" I asked.

"Yep."

TNN had Extreme Championship Wrestling—the gritty, hardcore, upstart promotion run by my old mentee Paul Heyman—on its airwaves but hadn't done much to promote it.

I had a feeling that if Vince was moving his programming at such a vital stage in WWE's overall expansion, he must have gotten some concrete guarantees. At the executive meetings, I had heard that negotiations with our long-term home network, USA, had been slowing down.

"USA isn't going to let us go easily, but I've got Jerry dealing with that," Vince said, between dainty bites.

The "Jerry" Vince mentioned wasn't my partner, The King, but Jerry McDevitt, the most badass lawyer I had ever seen in action. If I ever found myself in trouble, it's Jerry I would call first; he's the best I've ever seen, a rare mix of book smart and street smart, with an amazingly high IQ. Over the years, I'd witnessed him doing great work for WWE and making a fortune in the process. I was sure that whatever we needed to move on from USA, Jerry McDevitt could get it done.

"The talent doesn't need to know just yet, but you do," Vince said. "Viacom is very happy to have us come aboard."

On the immediate surface it kind of made sense. TNN was looking to actively target young males, and that was our exact demo.

However, leaving our long-term partner, USA, was a risky thing.

I was even more surprised that Vince was leaving Dick Ebersol's neck of the woods. Ebersol was a rock-star exec at USA's parent company, NBCUniversal, which many years before had given Vince the network rub at a time when professional wrestling wasn't exactly mainstream. The two went on to foster a great working relationship and a personal friendship that lasted decades.

Dick had said more than once that Vince McMahon was "the greatest partner I ever had."

Both men were TV trailblazers in their own fields, who then joined together to bring *Saturday Night's Main Event* to NBC prime-time, in the heyday of Hulkamania, brother!

But their relationship went beyond just business. Dick's wife said her husband's wish—if anything were to happen to him—was for Vince to become the legal guardian over their kids, so he could watch over them and protect them if Dick wasn't around.

McMahon and Ebersol's bond was tight, but this was a business move, not a personal one for Vince. "They preempted us for the fucking dog show," Vince muttered as he finished eating.

Vince was right, they had. *Raw*—WWE's flagship show and USA's top-rated program—was preempted every year for the Westminster Dog Show.

"We've given USA notice, and we won't be re-signing our contract when it comes up in September this year. We need to get ready."

"Ready?" I asked.

"TNN is going to rebrand and refocus attention on us," Vince said. "We'll be going somewhere we'll be appreciated and promoted, J.R."

"I look forward to it," I said.

Most other people I knew nearly always threw in a token "It's not about the money," but to Vince McMahon it was always about the money. "It'll be business as usual," he said. "We'll reestablish our own brand on Viacom's networks."

He was acting casual, but the move was the first in a run of decisions that would change how the business was seen and how it operated. TNN knew we were big fish, and it would put the full weight of the network behind our show. Yet we could hardly have known, at the turn of the century, how much more the future held.

The Hereford Bull

WE WON THE LAWSUIT AGAINST USA. Not that I had ever doubted: Jerry McDevitt didn't lose often. So we were full steam ahead to our new network.

The boss never looked back, always forward: *what* was new and, more important, *who* was new.

And he saw it with his own eyes, as we walked backstage at *Raw* in Minneapolis.

In the packed hallways, filled with changing TV segments, nervous adrenaline, and packs of the most unique-looking people in the world, Vince McMahon saw a prospect that literally made him turn his head.

"Who is that?" he asked.

I turned and looked, knowing exactly who had stopped the boss in his tracks.

The "that" Vince was inquiring about was Brock Lesnar.

"Jerry Brisco and I thought you should see this kid," I said. "His name is Brock Lesnar, and he's—"

Before I could finish my sentence, Vince made a U-turn and walked over to Brock.

I stood back and watched the chairman shake the hand of the big, reserved farmboy. In the past I'd always had to get tapes made or arrange for certain wrestlers to meet Vince at the McMansion, but I could already see this time would be different.

If Vincent Kennedy McMahon could Frankenstein up the wrestler of his dreams, it would be Brock Lesnar. He looked like a Viking but moved like a cat. He gave off an unpredictable vibe—like someone who could snap at any second and go on a rampage. He had a nervous energy, a quick trigger, and the natural ability to draw people in. He wasn't a loudmouth, didn't have the classic traits of cocky charisma.

Lesnar drew you in with something more primal.

In truth, he came from humble beginnings, the son of a South Dakota dairy farmer accustomed to hard work and tough times. Brock made it clear to us up front that he was done relying on Mother Nature to feed his family, and he wanted to make some real money in WWE. He wasn't some lifelong fan who was happy to be there, or someone like me who had grown up with pro wrestling in his blood. He was just someone who possessed the tools and attributes to make serious money in our world.

That's what he wanted to do—nothing more, nothing less.

He was almost clinical in that way.

His meeting with Vince was the culmination of more than a year of anxiety, scouting, dealmaking, and plain old waiting.

I had seen tape of Lesnar compete in the National Junior College Athletic Association in his sophomore year and was struck by him immediately. I called Jerry Brisco, again. I knew if anyone had info on the person I had just seen, it would be Jerry. "You see this kid in Minnesota?" I said over the phone.

"Yeah, Brock Lesnar," Jerry replied. "I've been tracking him for a year already."

I knew Jerry would be on the job.

"We need this kid, Jerry," I said.

"I've already got the wheels in motion," he replied.

Jerry was the best pair of ears and eyes WWE had out there. When he told me he was already tracking Lesnar, I knew we were in safe hands.

"What's his deal?" I asked.

"Well," Jerry said, "he wants to leave school now and make some money."

"What year is he in?"

"Moving into senior year," Jerry replied. "Brock's coach, J. Robinson, was a former amateur wrestling teammate of mine at Oklahoma State. He doesn't want Brock to know that we're interested yet. He's afraid Brock will walk out of school right now if he hears we want to sign him."

I got the feeling that if Lesnar wanted to walk out of anywhere, there wasn't much anyone could do about it.

"Is it true that he can deadlift 720 pounds, squat 695, and bench-press 475?" I asked.

Jerry laughed—he knew those numbers were for Vince more than me. "That's true. Now, he's bullheaded," Jerry continued, "so we're going to wait a while to offer him a deal."

I was anxious about waiting. Not that I wanted Brock to leave school early, but with someone so gifted I at least wanted something on paper saying that Lesnar would talk to us first after graduation.

"We won't need anything written down," Jerry said. "Coach says he'll call us once Brock is finished school."

Coach Robinson needed Lesnar to compete at the NCAA tournament his senior year, certain he would win. Sure enough, Lesnar ripped through the competition, becoming the top heavyweight in the country. And Jerry got the call, just as promised, to come sign Brock.

"Coach wants us to sign Lesnar's training partner too," Jerry said a few days before we put pen to paper.

Anyone who could hang with Brock in the gym and on the mat was someone in whom I was immediately interested. It became clear very quickly that Lesnar's training partner, Shelton Benjamin, was an amazing find too. He was quick, strong, well mannered, coachable, and as athletic a person as I'd ever witnessed.

We signed both men and slotted them in as the foundation of our training promotion, Ohio Valley Wrestling.

Lesnar and Benjamin joined fellow rookies Dave Batista, Randy Orton, and John Cena to make up what would become our most successful class of all time.

But during those first weeks I knew our challenge would be to keep Brock happy while training, before the big lights and bigger paydays that I knew he wanted so badly. Lesnar and patience weren't all that friendly with each other, so I'd bring him up to *Raw* every now and again to keep him in the mix and get him used to what life in WWE proper would be like.

VINCE AND BROCK exchanged a couple of words before the boss walked back over to me. Or perhaps "glided" would be a better word.

"J.R." He beamed. "That guy is something I haven't seen in a long time."

"He's money, ain't he?" I replied.

Vince nodded with a giant grin on his face. Like most of the other bookers and owners for whom I had worked, he loved big guys on his TV.

"Jerry is taking him under his wing," I said.

"Goddamn," Vince replied. "He looks like a Viking."

"Yeah, or Hereford bull," I replied.

"What's a Hereford bull?" Vince asked.

"A bull from . . . Hereford," I said, not really sure.

"I like 'Viking' better."

"Yeah, me too."

"How is he doing in developmental?" Vince asked.

Developmental back then was Ohio Valley Wrestling, a small local promotion in Louisville, Kentucky, which was staffed by the all-star training team of Danny Davis, Rip Rogers, Jim Cornette, Al Snow, and others who helped shape, guide, and promote the prospects of tomorrow.

Even though Brock had unlimited potential, he was still very much a rookie, assigned to do rookie things in developmental. Didn't matter what contract you were on—and Brock was on the highest-dollar deal by far—you still cleaned the small building down there and built the rings for shows. We were big on making the trainees learn the business from the ground up, as it helped keep egos in line and gave them an understanding of how much of a team effort went into keeping the business a success.

Some guys never liked to sit down, and Brock was one of those guys, so the more work and leadership responsibility we could give him, the more we'd keep his head busy and make him feel more at home.

"He's the foreman of the ring crew," I said.

"Is he?" Vince smiled.

"He likes driving the trucks and dragging the rings around," I said. "Helps the big bastard burn off some energy down there, I suppose."

Vince laughed. He loved the image of Brock caveman-ing his way around the training facility.

"Hey, did you know he can deadlift 720 pounds, squat 695, and bench-press 475?" I said.

That was it: Vince was totally smitten.

"Do you see any downside?" Vince asked.

"The only thing we'll need to manage is his enthusiasm," I said. "The big son of a gun has no idea just how strong and quick he is, and we want to make sure he doesn't really hurt someone."

Even though there was early talk of bringing Brock up by the writers, Vince knew what I was saying.

"We don't want him here until he's ready," the boss said.

"We'll have to put a bit in his mouth to hold him back a little," I replied. "He's more complex than he might look."

"How so?" Vince wondered.

"He's not just a big country boy. He knows exactly what he wants to do here."

"Make fucking money," Vince said, finishing my thought. "Well, let's make sure he does just that."

Vince McMahon, owner, chairman, and CEO of World Wrestling Entertainment, strutted off down the hallway, his day made from meeting the Hereford bull.

Or the Viking.

Either way, the boss was happy, and so was I.

SIX

THE WRESTLING GUY

Tryouts

VINCE MCMAHON WASN'T A "FOOTBALL GUY," but he wasn't necessarily a "wrestling guy" either when he started working in the wrestling business. When WWE was born, Vince reimagined your grandfather's wrestling as sports entertainment—a mix of steak and sizzle. He took the old tropes of smoky, back-hall wrestling and made it a glamorous TV spectacle, a live-event business that you just had to see.

So when Vince told me that he was starting his own football league, I wasn't a bit surprised.

"The Genetic Jackhammer," as he liked to call himself on TV, wanted to take another American staple, football, and reimagine it as the "Xtra Fun League" where "Past Meets Future." His plan was to take the attitude that made his wrestling empire so successful and bring it to the football field.

It was early in 2000, and Vince wanted to start off the new millennium with a bang.

I was excited by the announcement, excited we were growing, but most of all, I was excited because football was my other great love. My true beginning as a commentator came from watching all those football games with my dad and breaking down the pertinent information for his attention. I'd prep and get all the info ready before the game, and then when the action started, I'd give my father the stats and previous scores; I'd tell him what to look out for, including rivalries between players.

I knew the XFL needed a few commentary teams to handle the main NBC games, the UPN games, the TNN games, and the NBC regional telecasts. I honestly couldn't help but wonder if I had a shot when Vince's assistant said the boss wanted to talk to me about the XFL commentary teams.

"NBC wants you . . ." Vince began.

I was immediately overjoyed.

". . . to be the other guy in the auditions for announcers."

I was immediately devastated.

"They want me to be . . . ?" I left a gap to see if Vince might fill it with something positive for me.

"They want you to help them find their guy, J.R.," he said.

And that was the end of our meeting on the XFL commentary teams. My tiny little pigskin-covered Oklahoman heart broke like a fragile egg. If NBC was auditioning commentators, I didn't want to be the "other guy," I wanted to be "the guy."

As I left Vince's office, I couldn't help but wonder why I wasn't being considered—but as soon as I met the people from NBC, I got my answer.

"Jim's the wrestling guy," one of them introduced me.

It seemed that the company that carried our wrestling show, was in business with our wrestling boss, and promoted our wrestling stars, didn't want a "wrestling guy" on commentary.

I had thought that if there was ever a time when being the "wrestling guy" wasn't going to be a disadvantage, this was it. Same network, same executives—they would have some imagination.

Nope. The stigma of calling "fake" sports followed me everywhere, even to the network that aired it.

Vince had a long-standing relationship with Dick Ebersol—the president of sports at NBC—on which he was counting to help bring his vision of "football after the Super Bowl" to the U.S. market. NBC had just lost the NFL to CBS and FOX, and Dick wanted to get back into the football business. The XFL had been pitched to NBC as faster, grittier, and sexier than the alternative, with the hottest promoter on the planet, Vince McMahon, behind it.

Of course, because no one wanted anything wrestling-adjacent involved with it, they promptly hired former wrestler and wrestling commentator Jesse Ventura to be on their main commentary team. (In fairness, Jesse was sitting governor of Minnesota, so he brought with him added intrigue and eyeballs.)

I got called in to help find Jesse's partner.

Person after person came and went, but I could tell by Dick's face that he wasn't happy with any of them.

"Hey, J.R.," he said. "We'd like for you and The King to audition. I'm not saying anything, but just to see."

There was hope for a wrestling guy after all. Maybe even two, if The King and I got on the air together.

"You think we have a shot?" Jerry asked when I told him.

"Well, put it this way," I said. "I know the caliber of the other guys because I sat beside them in their auditions."

"And?"

"Let's go show them what two wrestling guys can bring to football," I replied.

I never thought for a second that The King and I had any real shot. I was just focused on having fun. Sometimes people think the job is about *what* you're announcing rather than *how* you're announcing it. And of course, it helps to love what's in front of you, but all the true greats I'd grown up listening to could make anything better—not just their sport of choice. I loved professional wrestling, and I loved football, and I was sure I could make any sport more engaging if given the time to prepare.

"You think we'll get paid extra for this, J.R.?" Jerry asked as we sat down for our audition. "I hear Ventura is getting a million a season."

"Yeah, we ain't Ventura," I replied. "We'd get fifteen hundred bucks a game."

He laughed. I didn't.

He saw I was serious. "Are you ribbing me?"

I was not. I knew that while Jesse wasn't making a million a season, he was making a whole lot more than we would. But I'd already made the mistake of letting Jesse's ability to negotiate more money than me cause bad feelings back when I worked for WCW. He was working as a part-time announcer then and taking home a truckload more than I was, even though I was full-time. I let my resentment of Jesse's good business sense cloud my judgment of him, and I acted like an asshole by no-selling his setup lines and purposefully trying to cool any chemistry he tried to make between us both on the air.

This time I wasn't annoyed about Ventura's money at all—best of luck to him. All I cared about was my own dream coming true. If that meant settling for fifteen hundred a game, so be it.

As the red light came on, I imagined I was back home on the farm with my dad, channeling my broadcast heroes Curt Gowdy, Ray Scott (who also suffered from Bell's palsy), and Keith Jackson. I felt instantly at home.

I had never focused too much on calling the nuts and bolts of wrestling. I cared more about verbalizing the emotion of it: the stakes, the struggle, the information the viewer simply had to have to enhance the experience of watching it.

But at NBC, with Dick and Vince watching, I called my heart out. All auditionees were shown the same tape: the fourth quarter of Super Bowl XXXIV, St. Louis Rams vs. Tennessee Titans, with St. Louis taking the game, 23–16.

The longer the audition went, the more I wanted the gig. I wanted to show everyone that I might be just a "wrestling guy," but I was a wrestling guy who could kick all your guys' asses when it came time to calling a damn football game.

And my chemistry with Jerry translated instantly. Our timing was good, our homework was done, and our years of teamwork were evident.

After it was over, we waited.

"Gentlemen," Dick said as he approached us, "we're going to go with you two for the XFL."

Fuck yeah!! Eat that, everyone who said I couldn't—

"You guys are going to call the regional broadcast games," Dick said. "Congratulations."

The B games.

Before I could open my mouth, Dick continued: "We don't have much time before the season starts, so we'll be in touch soon about how to do this."

"So, when are we starting?" I asked.

"In a few weeks," Dick replied.

A few weeks? I knew Vince liked to get stuff on the air as quickly as possible, but that felt rushed, even by McMahon standards.

"How long have the teams been together?" I asked.

"Couple of weeks," came the reply.

That sounded risky to me, but who was I to say anything? If WWE and NBC said they knew what they were doing, I was happy to be solely talent, go where I was sent, do what was asked.

"Okay," I said. "Thanks for the opportunity."

Of course, I wanted to call the feature games, but for now I was happy just to be on the team. Now all I had to figure out was how to squeeze this new gig into my already packed week.

When I got home, Jan was waiting for me, grinning from ear to ear. She wasn't mad that I had once again overloaded my wagon. Like I always said, "Don't worry about the mule, just load the wagon."

"We'll just make some adjustments," she said. "If this is your dream, sweetheart, we'll make this work."

So, adjustments it was. Or at least adaptations. I was still flying to *Raw* every Monday to call the show, flying to *SmackDown* to produce and manage talent on Tuesday, flying back to the office on Wednesday and Thursday to my EVP job, flying out on Friday to wherever the XFL game was and calling the game on Saturday, before flying home briefly on Sunday, to again fly out to wherever *Raw* was on Monday.

Rinse and repeat. (Paul Heyman will ask for royalties on that line.)

On XFL days, I got a suite with a VCR to watch tape of the players and games I was about to call. I worked late into Friday night pulling stats, plays, and player information that the viewer might want to know. Saturday was production preparation and, of course, game day.

I was tired, cranky, and stressed, but happy to do the XFL. Happy my wife was supporting me. Happy my father would have been proud of me.

Also, it had been a long time in my career since I was purely talent. It reminded me just how much I loved announcing.

Until it came time to use the bathroom.

"I hear Jesse has the Minnesota highway patrol to move people out of his way if he needs to take a leak," The King said. "He arrived like he was a Kennedy, I heard."

It was halftime, and we were standing in the bathroom line with the fans. The XFL was so "edgy" it didn't have any cover over the announce table or bathrooms for the B team.

I didn't mind standing in line, but the game was not going to wait for us if the line was taking a little longer than it should. To make matters worse, fans who had finished their business would see us in the queue. "It's J.R. and The King," they'd say and try to hug us or shake our hands.

"I'm not shaking pee-hands, J.R.," Jerry said.

After a couple of close calls, The King bailed first.

I followed.

We instead decided to apply our years of practice of peeing-into-a-bottle-while-not-looking-like-you're-peeing-into-a-bottle-under-the-desk. Trust me, we were both pros.

"Jim," came a voice in my headset.

"Yeah?"

"We're cutting into the Orlando game."

I wasn't sure whose voice it was because I had five of them in my ear at any one time, and none of those could hear when another was talking.

"The game in Vegas is flatlining. We're coming to you," the voice said.

I smiled at The King.

"What?" he asked.

"We're going live," I said. "The B team is cutting in on the A team."

Luckily, our game had excitement, and The King and I gave it our all, just like we tried to do every single week on *Raw*.

When I got back to my room in the Marriott, Dick Ebersol and Vince were already on the line for me.

"We're going to move you to the main game next week with Jesse," Dick said.

"What?"

"Next week, you and Jesse."

"What about The King?" I asked.

Luckily, Jerry didn't care; he barely wanted to be there at all. The King didn't have the love for football that I did; he was there only because he felt he owed it to Vince to at least try.

"We want you to go to the A team, J.R.," Dick said.

I was so excited: My performance was good enough to be elevated to work with the honorable Jesse "The Mind" Ventura. We had never called a game before, and there would be no practice or safety net—but I was living the dream.

Until the ratings began to fall, and then the "wrestling guy" was back down to the B team, baby. By that point I didn't mind; I didn't make much money calling the games, and they added more work to my week, but I really felt like I had accomplished something.

The football itself might not have been great, but I didn't hire the talent or call the plays. I was just there telling the story of the contests as they unfolded. But the writing was on the wall for the XFL.

"I took a calculated risk," Vince told me as the XFL ship went down.

WWE had taken on $50 million in debt, but the chairman wasn't brooding or self-pitying. He was defiant, taking it on the chin. I could tell he was putting on a brave face for me so I would wear that same look when I went to the talent. No matter what was happening, Vince always kept his poker face.

"I would do it all again," he said, and then he moved on. I never heard him talk about the league again, but I knew he carried it around. For me, it had been a chance to be back with my dad again, and that made every second of it a joy.

SEVEN

FRICTION AND FRIENDSHIP

Difficult

CHANGE IS PART OF LIFE, but it's an even bigger part of the wrestling business. When you burn through two live TV shows a week and a live PPV every month, talent turnover is inevitable.

The only place that was consistently "staffed" was the announce table, with The King and I. We had been successfully paired for so long that we become known as the "Madden and Summerall" of the WWE.

But nothing lasts forever, and times were turbulent. Our competitor, and my old employer, WCW, was failing. Even though they now had our former head writer, the dysfunction remained—or grew, depending on whom you talked to. Their weekly ratings were dropping at a shocking rate, and they were shedding fans by the truckload.

Every now and then I would stick my head up from the trenches to see what they were doing, but my overall philosophy was that the more time I spent looking, the less time I spent helping us. I had a lot of friends in WCW, but I had all I could say grace over in Stamford without worrying about what was happening in Atlanta.

With a locker room full of fragile egos, daily demands, relationship issues, long hours, long roads, booze, supreme talent, friendships, payoffs, positioning, and turnover—I knew my own next trying situation was never too far away. I just didn't expect from whence it came.

I don't think The King did either.

I went looking for Bruce Prichard, who was still involved with talent relations. We were in Arizona getting ready for a *SmackDown* taping when I heard what I had to do.

"Bruce," I said, when I caught up to Prichard, "I need you to come with me."

Bruce knew by my tone that something was wrong. "Everything okay?" he asked.

"I just got word that Vince wants Stacy gone," I replied.

Stacy Carter—or The Kat, as she was known on WWE television—was Jerry's wife. She was set to be a focal point of that night's TV taping, but after the production meeting, at which writers, agents, and producers met Vince to discuss the show, it was decided she was to be fired instead.

And as head of talent relations, I was the one to fire her.

Apart from my longtime partnership with The King, they were both dear friends. Jan and I had been guests at Stacy and Jerry's wedding.

"OH, SHIT," BRUCE REPLIED. "I'd heard her name coming up as being difficult."

"Difficult?" I said. "First I've heard of it."

"What can I do?" he asked.

"I want to say it to The King's face out of respect. But I don't know how he's going to react, so I'd like you there so it doesn't become a 'he said, she said' after the fact."

Bringing a witness to a potentially heated situation was best practice when sensitive subjects like terminations were on the agenda.

"I just hope he doesn't quit in protest," I said.

Bruce, The King, and I gathered in my makeshift office at the arena—we were alone, away from everyone. I stuttered some, genuinely trying to find the right words.

"I just spoke to Vince, and I don't know what to do," I said.

The King was immediately concerned by my demeanor. "What is it?" he asked. "J.R.," he said, "what's wrong?"

"I've got some bad news and I'm sorry. It's Stacy," I replied. "She's too hard to work with, Jerry. That's what they're telling me. Vince doesn't want to go ahead with the angle, and he's asked me to let her go."

The King smiled; he wasn't sure if I was joking him or not. I think he knew somewhere in his mind that I would never joke about something like that, but it was so serious that he hoped I was.

"I wanted you to hear it from me," I said. "We're friends, and I don't want to be doing this at all. Not one bit, King, you know that."

"Stacy?" Jerry said. I could tell he was struggling to see where the description of his wife being "difficult" came from.

I nodded in agreement. I had never seen or heard of his wife being difficult in any way either, but that was the reason I was told to fire her.

"I do not, under any circumstances, want to fire her," I said. "This is one of the hardest things I've ever had to do."

"Well, what did you say to Vince?" Jerry asked.

"I said I'm sure there's a way here to fix this."

"And what did Vince say?" Jerry asked.

"He said she needs to go," I replied.

"He did?"

"I'm sorry," I mumbled.

"Well then, I need to go too," he said.

The genesis of the friction with Stacy seemed to be creative. Some of the writing staff and producers had told Vince she was too difficult to work with—and earning a rep like that can be a death knell professionally in WWE.

Jerry had pitched a story for his wife that we were going to run with, but the assembly of that story led some writers to complain to Vince. Stacy was to have her character revitalized, and the last thing she needed to be in that situation was "difficult."

The King wondered, "What if you asked her to go home for a couple of weeks, until we figure out . . ."

I said, "I promise you, I tried, King. But Vince told me to give her notice anyway."

"Is Vince here?" Jerry asked.

"He's here," I said. "Do you want me to tell Stacy?"

Jerry said, "I'll tell her, on our way home."

He left to go talk to the boss. I waited, hoping they could work something out, but, knowing Vince, I didn't have high hopes.

"He thinks it's me now," Bruce said when Jerry was gone.

"Why?"

"Because I'm on the creative side, and now I'm in this meeting too."

After a while Jerry returned. "What happened?" I asked.

"I told Vince that I'd have to leave too," The King said. "And he put out his hand and told me he appreciated everything I'd done for him."

"You're gone too?" I asked.

The King nodded; he was clearly in shock. "This is horseshit, J.R. You know she's not like that," he replied.

Jerry moved to leave my office.

"Will you think about this for a second?" I said.

"If it was Jan they were firing, would you stay?" he asked.

I had to be honest. "I don't think so."

There was no hint of drama from The King. He was simply going home to support his wife, which I fully understood.

"I'm really sorry," I said. "What are you going to do from here?"

He replied, "I have a contract on my desk at home from WCW, J.R. You must have known I was going to leave with her. Vince must want me gone too," he said as he left.

I was mad as hell for my friends. Some of the writers squealed like a pig trapped under a gate any time they had to deal with something as simple as creative differences. Vince didn't want to listen to any drama—he just wanted the problem to go away.

So it had gone from no significant issue at all to firing her in the course of one meeting.

A number of the writers would look me in the eye the rest of the day. It confirmed which ones were easily affected, spoiled assholes whose collective testicles would fit effortlessly in a thimble—not that I needed confirmation.

I had to jump in to take King's spot with Michael Cole that night to commentate on *Smackdown*. It was one of the most challenging nights of my career. And, come the following Monday, I would be back on air for *Raw* without my longtime partner. I wished Jerry would just take some time off, cool down, and we'd figure this all out, but the second he told Vince he wanted out, that was that. Vince McMahon would never take him back after that.

To make matters worse, The King went public with his grievances, releasing WWE e-mail addresses for fans to petition the writers. Naturally, this only made the chairman more resolute.

A few weeks later, when things had calmed down a bit, I got a fax at my office from The King, saying he and Stacy would like to come back. Unfortunately, not only had Vince moved on from Stacy, but he had Jerry's replacement picked out too.

No Celebrations

"HELLO, EVERYBODY, AND WELCOME. We're live here in D.C., and I'm Jim Ross," I said directly into the *Monday Night Raw* camera.

Out of shot, a familiar voice interrupted me: "They already know who you are, now tell them who I am."

"I'm joined by Paul Heyman," I replied.

The shot pulled out a little to frame my old broadcasting protégé, Paul Heyman, sitting beside me at the announce table. The fact that his first act on WWE television was to interrupt me really set the stage for what our new partnership would be.

"You're joined by Paul Heyman because last Tuesday night The Kat was released, and her husband, Jerry 'The King' Lawler—to his credit—walked out right alongside her," Paul told the viewers at home. He continued: "But where there is chaos, there's opportunity. The King is gone, and in his chair is Paul E. And the 'E' is for 'Extreme.'"

I shook my head for the camera, but inside I knew my new partner would extract another side of my game. Paul Heyman was extremely skilled at being unlikable—and he reveled in using his antagonistic persona to create friction on the air.

The King and I gelled; Paul and I bristled.

Proud of himself, Heyman turned to me and said, "How's that? Not bad, huh?"

I could only reply, "I don't know what I did to deserve this."

I half meant it.

Paul and I had become close years before in our old company, WCW, when I took the brash young loudmouth under my wing and saved him a few times from being fired. Eventually we both left WCW, with me coming to WWE and Paul taking over the creative direction of, and eventually buying, the smaller, more hardcore company called Extreme Championship Wrestling.

ECW had been on life support since the global juggernaut known as WWE moved to their network, and TNN decided it no longer needed ECW and canceled it. Paul tried to find another national broadcaster, but no luck. They had the talent—just not the television.

Of course, many saw WWE as the bad guy in the story, but the truth was we had been doing deals with the ECW that could help keep the company afloat. Vince knew that the wrestling business was better off with some kind of competitor. But without distribution, and debt piling up, ECW was unsustainable.

Paul's subsequent jump to WWE was surprising to some fans but almost inevitable to those who followed the business closely. A talent like Paul Heyman was never going to be on the open market for long—even as his own company was going through bankruptcy.

In a time of massive changes in the wrestling landscape as a whole, having Paul on our team was a great advantage.

And he slipped in beside me on commentary like we'd never been apart.

THE WRESTLING RATINGS WAR, which launched careers, also killed careers, went over the top, got personal, made stars, recast legends, caused pain, gave joy, and nearly financially ruined the McMahon family; it ended, as most businesses do, with a deal.

Turner Broadcasting, which housed WCW, had already merged with Time Warner in the mid-1990s, and now Time Warner was merging with America Online in one of the biggest corporate deals of all time.

The new CEO of Turner Broadcasting, Jamie Kellner, quickly decided that WCW was no longer a good fit for the network and decided to cancel it immediately.

WCW was to be sold, but who would have the money or the desire to buy such a niche product without any TV time in the deal? After some talks with other interested parties, Turner execs realized that there was only one person on the planet who ultimately made sense—so they placed a call to Vince McMahon.

Vince only seemed interested at first if he could keep WCW's time slot on TBS. McMahon wanted to run World Championship Wrestling as a "separate" company, with its own stars, network, and feel.

When it became clear that Turner Broadcasting didn't want wrestling, period, Vince became less interested—especially when he found out that the contracts for the top WCW wrestlers were locked. That meant that even if Vince wanted to bring in WCW's top stars—names like Hulk Hogan, Kevin Nash, and Scott Hall, who had become major stars while previously in WWE, and homegrown WCW stars like Bill Goldberg and Sting—he couldn't. Those guys already had ironclad deals that promised them every cent they signed for, even if they only sat at home and collected the mail.

But in the end, the Turner people made the price so shockingly low that the WWE chairman couldn't refuse—even without having their TV slot or control of their top stars' contracts.

WCW, a company that generated hundreds of millions in revenue, went out with a whimper—valued and bought for less than $5 million.

One perk of the deal was that we now owned WCW's tape library. A lot of current and former WWE wrestlers had passed through the doors of World Championship Wrestling, and owning the rights to the company's previous content would be something we could monetize. And WWE was already very active in acquiring old tape libraries for other, smaller regional and defunct wrestling companies. WCW's content alone was worth considerably more than the price of the company.

But it wasn't just the tape library on the boss's mind—he wanted to use all facets of his new purchase.

"We can own both brands," Vince explained to me the day before he acquired WCW. "Put them on our different networks and pit them against each other."

It sounded like a great idea. We had two TV slots on two different networks, and any business is always healthier with competition to keep it fresh. I just wasn't sure how that was going to work.

World Championship Wrestling's last episode was a simulcast of both its flagship show, *Nitro*, filmed in Panama City, and our flagship show, *Raw*, which was being broadcast from Cleveland. It was just another day in the wrestling business. I was sad—for my friends who worked there and my wrestling brothers and sisters who now had only one place to work. But backstage Vince was all business; even though WCW—and the people in charge of it—tried to put him out of business, Vince wasn't celebrating—he was just focusing on what was coming next.

"I want you to go to Atlanta," he said. "Get a suite and interview whomever you'd like to sign from WCW."

WrestleMania X-Seven was right around the corner, but Vince wasn't pumping the brakes at all.

"When are you thinking?" I asked.

"Now," he replied. "I want to start this right away."

So I went down to my old stomping grounds in Atlanta and to the final night of my old employer, WCW. That final night had a surreal feeling to it. I was used to change in the wrestling business—quick change. But I couldn't shake the feeling that this was going to be harder than it appeared.

Heyman and I called the program the night of WCW's last show.

"You a little sad, J.R.?" Paul asked me as we sat at the announce table.

"Not sure," I said.

And then the red light hit, and we were live.

Vince explained to the audience that he was now the owner of both companies, and he fired Jeff Jarrett live on the air—in case anyone was wondering whether the chairman remembered J.J. jumping to WCW with a briefcase full of cash.

"We are back live on *Raw* from the Gund Arena here in Cleveland," I told the people watching at home. "Tonight Mr. McMahon's attention is on his acquisition of WCW."

As the chairman was walking down the ramp toward the ring, Heyman said, "They say that Alexander the Great sat down on a rock and cried, for he had no worlds left to conquer." As we watched a shot of Vince swagger-walking to the ring, Paul continued: "Tonight the Monday Night Wars are over. And the victor of the Monday Night Wars is clear: It's that man."

It was hard to argue—impossible, in fact. Vince McMahon now held the keys to both his own global brand and the company that nearly put him out of business only a few short years before.

I wasn't sure whether this was a good thing or a bad thing.

We were about to find out.

EIGHT

THE CHANGING OF STEVE

He Earned the Right to Be Wrong

HANDING OUT CHECKS BACKSTAGE was always a risky proposition. In the same locker room, those envelopes could make one person rich and another person angry. But around this time most people seemed happy: Numbers were big, crowds were big, pay was good.

It was the order on payday, though, for some of the Boys to lie to others about how much they made. You know, just to cause trouble.

"Oh, you only made that much?" they'd say to someone gullible or the new guy. "I made four times that for half the matches you worked."

My office door always got busier around payday. Almost every week, someone who'd been worked by the Boys would knock on my door and give some versions of this exchange:

"Such-and-such got paid more than me," they would say.

"Did you see such-and-such's check?" I would ask.

"No," they would answer.

"How do you know how much they got, then?" I would ask.

"Because that's what they told me," they would say.

And then I would wait for a few seconds to see if the person in my office actually heard themselves. Lot of times they didn't, so I'd continue: "Well, I know what you got, and what such-and-such got."

I would haul in both guys—the liar and the rube—to hash it out with them. Even though I secretly found it funny, I couldn't have talent not trusting me. So my door was always open.

But one week a visitor I didn't expect—nor would I ever expect on payday—showed up.

"I'm losing steam." I knew the raspy voice before I even looked up from my work. Stone Cold Steve Austin.

I gestured him inside and closed the door. There was a pause. I had just given Austin a merchandise check for seven figures; I assumed he was joking.

Turned out he wasn't.

"I'm growing old with the audience, J.R., so I'm turning," he said. Steve was WWE's version of John Wayne—the lone gunslinger who didn't back down from anyone. Now he was talking about making himself a bad guy. "I want to do it this coming *WrestleMania*," he said.

I got up and walked over to Austin. "It's too soon," I replied.

Steve shook his head. As was typical with Austin, I wasn't sure whether he was telling me what was happening or asking for my advice. I looked him in the eye and said, "The people are still behind you."

I knew it wasn't a money thing; he had more money than he knew what to do with. It was the creative reasoning he was mulling over.

"You caught lightning in a bottle. Why would you give that up?" I asked.

Steve quickly replied, "I want to stay ahead of the curve. I want to change before I lose the audience altogether."

I understood Steve's rationale completely: He was always taking the temperature of the crowd; he prided himself on knowing what they wanted before they did. But it wasn't the plan of Steve turning heel that I was opposed to—it was the timing.

"You've got big money still on the table as a hero, Steve," I said, trying to appeal to the businessman inside of him.

"We're doing it, Jim," The Rattlesnake replied with a slight smile. "I just wanted you to hear it from me."

"You turning heel is like John Wayne turning into a Nazi," I said.

Austin patted me on the shoulder and left.

I'd clearly failed, but I hoped the big boss could talk some sense into him.

THE NEXT MORNING in Vince's office, as we went over other business, I waited for the chairman to bring up Austin's proposed character shift. I figured if Vince didn't know about it, then Steve was just ribbing me.

"What are your thoughts on making Steve a heel, Jim?" Vince asked.

Nope, it was real.

"It's horseshit," I replied. It was hard to tell by Vince's poker face if he agreed with me or Austin. "I know Steve likes to be ahead of his audience," I said. "But the time isn't right."

Vince nodded; I could see he was torn. But why? Surely this was an easy decision. Austin was still making WWE a ton of money as a babyface. What was there to be torn about?

"I'm torn," Vince said.

"I can see that," I replied.

Historically speaking, Vince hadn't allowed most talent to have creative say in their characters. Some wrestlers just don't know, or want to know, how best to present themselves, but Austin was different. Steve knew from day one. It was when Vince, and the company in general, started listening to Austin's ideas that the biggest spark in wrestling truly ignited.

Austin's feel for his character had proven right time and time again—in everything from his T-shirt designs to his on-air promos. Steve became WWE's top draw, generating more revenue across merchandise, ticket sales, and PPV buys than anyone else in the history of wrestling. It certainly wasn't a one-man show, but the Texas Rattlesnake was a massive part of the creative success of his character—and now he was proposing a radical new departure.

The dilemma for Vince was whether to bet on Austin's gut one more time.

"Have you tried talking him out of it?" I asked.

"It means a lot to Steve, so we're going to try it," Vince replied. If Steve was adamant—and he was—the chairman wanted to back him. "Steve deserves the opportunity to see if we can make this work," Vince said.

Sitting across from the boss, I suddenly understood his true conflict. Vince wanted a happy, motivated Austin so he could get a few more years out of Steve's huge earning power—but Vince also appreciated and respected what Stone Cold had achieved. "I owe it to Steve to try," McMahon said.

Even though Vince had created more main-event stars than anyone in the history of our business, he never thought he knew everything. When talking about his ability to make stars, he'd simply say, "I encourage you to look at my track record." But now Stone Cold was the engine that was powering record numbers and previously unheard-of profits, and any change in that formula was risky.

Very risky.

"We'll just make it work," the boss said.

And that was it: Steve had raised the idea of turning heel; Vince backed it.

I'd made my position clear to both Vince and Steve, but now it was my job to help the chairman and his top star get this new version of Stone Cold over with the fans.

My personal opinion didn't matter. My job now was to help.

On commentary, I could paint a picture for the PPV audience that would help them dislike Steve—help them accept the journey as their biggest babyface hero turned dastardly heel. I'd have to summon passion, disgust, and anger about it—not too much of a stretch.

Stone Cold Steve Austin was going to become a bad guy, and he was going to do it in his own home state of Texas, at *WrestleMania X-Seven*.

The Turn

THE MAIN EVENT was Austin vs. The Rock, the second meeting of the two hottest stars in the business. It was also Austin's coming-out party as a heel.

WrestleMania X-Seven was top-to-bottom electric—the kind of event where everything clicked and every performer dared their colleagues to "follow that." Paul Heyman and I, in our commentary positions, knew we were a part of something great as we sat in the Astrodome in Houston, Texas. I could feel the talents in the ring overdelivering, and it drove me and Paul into high gear.

The table was set for the last match and the huge change in direction that was coming with it.

The buildup to Austin vs. Rock II was pure gold; both men were at the top of their game, and it produced some of the most entertaining, intense, believable TV in our business. What the feud boiled down to was two alphas, two worldwide Superstars, two of the all-time best, battling it out in front of seventy thousand fans in attendance and over a million watching at home on PPV. It was personal, it was believable, and it felt momentous.

Heyman and I reset, teed up the package, and set the scene for the viewers at home. This was the main event, the reason we were all here.

Over the speakers in the building, the glass broke to signal Steve's arrival to the ring. The arena came unglued. Austin was coming in as the challenger for the world title, in his home state of Texas. He prowled down the ramp with a scowl on his face and a swagger in his step; he was the baddest son of a bitch on the planet, and he knew it.

"The journey has culminated here tonight," I said to the people at home as Austin took in his rapturous applause. "The spinal surgery, the knee injuries—

the Texas Rattlesnake could be called the Bionic Redneck. 'Cause we're deep in the heart of Texas, and Stone Cold is going to challenge to become the top man in the industry."

Austin took in the scene around him as he waited for The Rock's music to hit. "What must be going through his mind at this very moment?" I said. "Knowing the journey that he has been on."

"IF YA SMELL WHAT THE ROCK IS COOKING!" boomed out in the Astrodome: The champ, The Rock, was ready to enter the fray. While Austin had stomped down to the ring, The Great One glided with intent. His face was a picture of focus; his movements were deliberate; his confidence radiated to the very back row.

"This is a very partisan Texas crowd," I said, setting the table for the heel turn to come. "Austin is revered, he is a folk hero. Austin has reached legendary status in his home state of Texas."

The Rock marched up the steps and into the ring.

"No doubt," Heyman said from his announce position beside me. "And for good reason. Stone Cold Steve Austin is a man of integrity. Stone Cold Steve Austin has backed up everything he's ever said in his career. But tonight, Stone Cold Steve Austin must take the championship from The Rock."

Heyman and I were building up Austin's credentials, struggle, and moral code so The Rattlesnake could pull everything down to maximum effect when the time was right. With the prefight pageantry still in full flow, Austin stalked the champion before the bell. Steve waited for The Rock to turn around, then delivered multiple right hands to his jaw.

"Here we go! Here we go," Heyman shouted.

The Houston crowd exploded.

And so it went, brick by brick, subtlety by subtlety—the most popular babyface in wrestling was constructing his heel turn. Inside the ring, outside the ring, into the crowd, the two Superstars told their story in front of a red-hot crowd. While The Rock was relying on throws and suplexes, Austin was looking for little shortcuts, like attacking The Rock before the bell, trying to hit him with the title belt, and removing the turnbuckle cover to expose the steel brace underneath. Ironically, it was the reverse of the formula that had subtly helped turn Austin from heel to face in his *WrestleMania* match four years earlier at *WrestleMania 13*, against Bret "The Hitman" Hart, when Austin's refusal to quit cemented his antihero status and began his ascension to the top of the WWE.

Because Steve's character was so full of piss and vinegar in general, the audience didn't immediately register his looking for a cheap advantage as something dastardly. Part of his appeal was that he didn't play by the rules—the more he attacked, the more the crowd loved him.

And that was Steve's new problem.

How does a guy who is beloved because he doesn't adhere to the rules become a bad guy whose job it is to break the rules?

You add the chairman of WWE, of course.

Austin vs. McMahon was the greatest rivalry in wrestling. For years these two alpha personalities had clashed, bristled, fought, bled, and drawn truckloads of money together all around the world. Now they would join up on TV to help Austin complete his transition.

Inside the ring, both The Rock and Austin gave it everything they had. They were both busted open, with blood streaming down their faces. They beat each other, pinned each other, and broke each other. They hit each other with their own finishing moves and then the other guy's finishing moves. It was too close to call, with neither man willing to quit or be pinned.

And then out came Mr. McMahon.

The boss walked down the ramp, stone-faced, toward the ring. A hail of boos and heckles rained down.

In the ring, The Rock hit the People's Elbow, and Austin was in trouble. One . . . two . . .

And the chairman of WWE slid into the ring to break up The Rock's count. The owner had saved Austin. The Rock stood, turned, and stared down McMahon with fury in his eyes. The Brahma Bull gave chase, and Vince took off at speed around the ring. The boss rolled out of the ring and The Rock followed him—only to run into Austin, who was waiting. Stone Cold hit The Rock with The Rock's own move, then a nut shot, and then The Rattlesnake called on Vince to hand him a chair.

The audience was confused: Why were Austin and McMahon working together? Paul and I sold the same confusion on commentary.

Steve dropped The Rock with a chairshot and got a close two count. More Stunners, chairshots, close counts, and Vince interference followed.

"Oh my God," I shouted into the headset as the intensity in the building left the charts. The mission in the storytelling wasn't just to get Austin over as a bad guy but to solidify The Rock as the top good guy. "He won't stop!" I said as The Rock kicked out of everything the newly formed duo of Austin and Vince could throw at him.

And then The Rattlesnake snapped and just laid waste to The Great One with chairshot after chairshot after chairshot until Austin finally got the three count.

"Why, Steve, why this way?" I shouted with all the passion and hurt I could muster. "I thought I knew Austin. I thought I knew The Rattlesnake. For the love of God, Steve, stop."

As Austin and Vince celebrated in the ring, I had a feeling that it might take a little more to get Steve where he wanted to go. I just had no idea that journey would include kicking my ass.

A Bit of Color

GROWING UP A FAT KID makes you do strange things as an adult. I've always just wanted to fit in and be accepted; that's where a lot of my prickly nature comes from, I think. I will call myself fat before you can; I'm reflexively defensive in anticipation of a hurtful comment. I grew up idolizing cool, strong, silent types like John Wayne and my dad, always knowing that I was never going to be like them.

Yep, growing up fat makes you do weird things—like letting Stone Cold Steve Austin cut your forehead with a scalpel and beat the living shit out of you on national TV.

Let me explain.

On the *Raw* immediately after *WrestleMania*, the newly crowned heel version of Steve Austin wasn't getting booed as much as we wanted; the audience just wasn't ready to turn on their ringleader. They liked that Stone Cold used any means necessary to "open a can of whoop-ass" on his opponents, so the traditional methods of getting wrestlers booed wasn't going to apply to Steve. We all knew we needed to try something else the next night on *SmackDown* to get the Bionic Redneck that heel heat he needed to be a success.

"Hey, J.R.," Steve said backstage. "You know what we're doing?"

I replied, "I sure do. You're going to kick my ass."

Steve laughed; he didn't deny it.

I had heard rumblings during the day that Stone Cold was going to take old J.R. behind the woodshed. The feeling was that if Austin turned on his best friend, surely the audience would begin to boo him in earnest. The only thing left to do was to get me to sign off on it.

Vince walked over to us, having clearly overheard. "We need Steve to attack someone who is sympathetic with the audience," he said.

I was proud that the boss thought of me that way. Traditionally, commentators were kept out of storylines, but, more and more, Vince was using my good standing with our fans to help get the in-ring talent over. It was heartwarming to me that the people cared that much about me. At least I could bask in all that love after catching a beating.

"You okay with this?" Vince asked.

The fat kid in me replied: "Of course."

I just wanted to prove every day that I belonged on the team, that I was willing to do whatever was needed.

"We probably need a bit of color," Vince added.

"Color" in wrestling means blood. The chairman of WWE was talking to me about slicing my forehead open so it looked more violent when Austin was beating the ever-loving snot out of me.

"Okay," I said. "I'm fine with it."

Even if I wasn't fine with it, I would have been fine with it. I was willing to do anything to get my friend, Stone Cold, over.

"I'm going to use a scalpel blade. That cool?" Steve asked.

"That normal?" I asked, knowing full well it wasn't. We usually used the corner of a razor blade, which guarded against the cut going too deep.

"It'll be fine," Steve said.

"Scalpel sounds good," Vince said.

Oh yeah? Easy for you two assholes to say, I thought. But what I actually said was: "Yeah, it does sounds good."

Steve had gotten the surgical knife from a doctor in the building; it was far more deadly than a razor blade—not that I'd ever say that to them. I was trying to fool the two manliest men I had ever been around into thinking I wasn't scared out of my mind. If taking a scalpel to my head in front of millions on live TV was the way to impress the alpha crowd, then cut me.

"See you out there," Austin said as he left the dressing room.

Vince slapped me on the shoulder and left too.

I can't say I wasn't a little ashamed of myself for feeling good about being macho in front of Vince and Steve. I basked in the glow of being a tough son of a bitch for one more minute before giving in to the terror of what was about to happen.

Getting beat up and cut was, of course, pretty standard for the Boys, but for me it was laced with anxiety. It had nothing to do with Steve or the angle—more with me as a performer. I liked on one hand that Vince saw me as someone who could help get the very top talent to where they needed to be; but on the other, I was always worried about messing it up.

Not that I'd ever admit that to anyone in the company.

"*SmackDown* is live, coming to you from the sold-out Myriad Convention Center from Oklahoma City. It's the home state of good ol' J.R., who goes one on one with Austin, coming up," Michael Cole said on commentary only a few short hours later.

They cut to me walking the hallway toward the ring, and boy was I nervous.

The Sooners music played, and, thankfully, my home crowd gave me a great reaction as I entered and walked down the ramp.

I took the microphone. "It's always great to be around WWE fans wherever we are around the world. But I got to tell you, it's especially great to be back home."

In wrestling, a line like that is usually a "cheap pop," as my good friend Mick Foley used to call it. But I really did love being in Oklahoma.

"Folks," I continued, "tonight, I have the opportunity to talk to the new WWE Champion, Stone Cold Steve Austin. I think there are a lot of questions that need answers. I think you deserve an answer; I think our fans at home deserve an answer. So, without further ado, I'd like to introduce to you the new WWE Champion, Stone Cold Steve Austin."

CRASH.

The glass shattered to start Austin's entrance music, and I knew a monumental ass-whooping was coming my way.

"Can you imagine what's going through the mind of Jim Ross as he stares into the eyes of The Rattlesnake?" Cole said on commentary.

Here's what was going through my mind:

. . .

. . .

I was so damn scared. Steve was a big, intimidating son of a bitch on his best days. But when I knew what was coming, it made him spine-chilling.

Austin's music stopped and he waited expertly in the ring to let the heat in the building rise. I took his cue and didn't say anything either. The longer we didn't talk, the louder the noise got.

I remember saying, "There's a lot of things I'd like to say to you in private."

The next thing I knew, he was slapping my hat off my head. The man who had once rescued me from a beating by Triple H was now ready to give me the same treatment.

My heart was racing so damn fast and my adrenaline was pumping so damn hard. I could feel Stone Cold's intensity ramping up; his eyes were narrowing; he was getting in my face, poking my chest.

"I think this interview was a mistake," I said. "This interview is over."

I turned my back to walk out of the ring, and *BOOM*, he clocked me from behind. I fell into my preordained corner, and boy did that son of a bitch stomp a mudhole in me.

In all my years calling that move at ringside I never knew those boots Austin was laying in were so goddamn stiff.

"Damn it, damn it, stop it right now," Mr. McMahon shouted over the microphone. The truck cut to Vince on top of the ramp admonishing Austin. "That's your best friend out there, and you're taking it easy on your very best friend." Vince's face contorted into pure hatred. "Damn it, Steve, open him up," he shouted.

This performance from the chairman was a sleight of hand to draw the audience's attention away from the ring so Steve could cut my forehead with a scalpel.

Yep. That's a real thing.

Austin tried to control the blade job on my forehead but the scalpel cut fast, and it cut deep. I didn't really have time to worry about the blood streaming down my face because Steve had moved on from that to punching me in the head.

Like, he really laid those blows in there.

It was the old-school way.

If the camera is close and you're trying to convince the audience at home that the new version of Austin was a low-down dirty SOB, then the punches he was landing on defenseless old J.R. needed to look real.

And they did. Because they were.

I wiped some blood out of my eyes and caught a glimpse of Austin's face. He was so "in the moment" that I genuinely thought he'd tipped over into insanity. My Stone Cold friend had sliced me open, punched me repeatedly, and, in his eyes, I could see the devil looking back at me.

But I wanted to show Steve, Vince, and the whole damn company that I was willing to do whatever it took to help the team. I saw wrestlers do the same thing every night of the week, so even though I wasn't trained and I was scared and it hurt like hell, I was proud of the beating I took.

Vince was shouting, the crowd was booing, Austin was beating the shit out of me, the refs were scrambling around ringside, and all I was worried about was: *I hope there's enough blood.*

I wanted the picture to match the occasion. Now that I was in it and the fear was gone, I wanted to make sure that Steve had what he needed, visually, to become the most hated man in the company.

He choked me with his belt, kicked me in the nuts, ground the title into my face, and left me a bloody mess in the ring.

All while my family watched at ringside.

When he finally left, I began to breathe a little more. He carted me out of the ring during a commercial break, and I've never been so happy to see that curtain again.

That curtain meant it was done, over. I could stop worrying.

"What was up with you out here?" I asked Steve from across the dressing room.

Austin was chuckling. "I had to make it look good, kid."

My head was busted open from the blade and knotted up from Steve's notoriously hard punches.

"You heavy-handed son of a bitch," I said. "I thought I owed you money or something."

Steve's chuckle turned into a laugh. "Gotta make it look good, kid. We're on live TV out there."

Usually, Austin's philosophy would have been one hundred percent correct. Except for one thing.

"Steve," I replied. "It's *SmackDown*, you asshole. It's a taped show."

"Oh yeah." Steve left the room cackling.

I sat alone and smiled. My inner fat kid was proud.

NINE
WINNING AND LOSING

To See Who Could Work

IT WAS APRIL 2001, and Jan and I were checked into the Buckhead Ritz-Carlton down in Atlanta. I was there to interview talents from WCW who I felt would be good for WWE.

My wife and I hadn't been spending much time together, so I was hoping we'd get a chance to go out for dinner or something if my schedule opened up. I wasn't proud of living a life in which my marriage was on standby, but Jan was her usual understanding self—as it was such a crazy time in WWE with several major companywide events happening, one after the other after the other.

I had just three days and a lot of people to meet. My brief from the boss was to hire on-air talent, agents, writers, referees, producers, and anyone else needed to run a wrestling company. The goal now was to run WCW on TNN under a tight budget and a short leash; we hoped to prove the market for World Championship Wrestling was still there—and to grow accordingly. The working assumption was that WCW would air late on Saturday nights, but nothing was concrete.

It seemed to me that TNN was a little apprehensive, but we made a start anyway. Vince wanted to maximize his new investment.

We had a couple of months to build a whole new company that would service both TV and live events.

I was more than a little anxious about so many good WCW people throwing their hats into the ring for WWE. I knew a lot of them personally, and others were friends of friends. Even though the Monday Night Wars between our companies had been quite vicious at times, the relationship—for the most part—between the talent and production staffs was always one of brotherhood. We all knew that, in wrestling, everyone is one call away from looking for a new job.

I wasn't in Atlanta to see *who* could work; I was pretty familiar with all of them. I mostly wanted to hear *where* their heads were at. There was added pressure, internally and externally, to get a potential WCW relaunch right, since the XFL had just been canceled after its first season, and Vince didn't want two misfires so close together on his résumé.

I tried to be up front with everyone about the financial realities of a "new" WCW. Some of the salaries in Turner's WCW were massively inflated and no longer feasible for our smaller-budget project. I also told people that nothing was finalized on the TV front, but WWE had brought in executives to try and secure a TV deal.

I hired a guy named John Laurinaitis—or Johnny Ace, as he was known in the wrestling business—to help me out. John was working backstage in WCW—I also knew him from his time working in Japan for their top promoter, Giant Baba—and he seemed most interested in talent relations, so I hired him as my assistant.

If Vince wanted to have two companies, and two rosters, and two TVs, it would be two times the work—so I sold Vince on Johnny, as the chairman didn't know who he was.

I also met with ECW's Rob Van Dam, as that company's demise meant its former talent roster was also looking for work. At its peak in the late 1990s, wrestling fans had three distinct choices on their TVs: WWE, WCW, and ECW. Now WWE was the only one left, with WCW being purchased and ECW filing for bankruptcy.

WE WERE SHORT ON HEADLINERS, and Rob was a naturally athletic, handsome, charismatic guy who could do things between those ropes that no one else could. His sticking point was that he didn't want to work the number of dates WWE wanted from a potential top talent. Both Van Dam and his longtime rival, Sabu, were keen to come aboard, but I held them off until I talked to Vince.

It was tough to be out negotiating with no absolute times and dates to tell people.

It was a whirlwind of many names and faces, but I quickly drew up a list of who I wanted and who I thought could be added to WWE overall. I wanted to find the best talent that I could, within the budget I had, who were willing to work without many guarantees about the future.

I had a deadline of about a couple of weeks to get together a whole new company of wrestlers who would gel, bond, and complement each other's style both in the ring and the locker room. Most of the people I was talking to or about had worked together already in WCW, but that locker room didn't have the greatest reputation. We also wanted to sprinkle in new blood, new hires, and potential players for future.

Most of all, I wanted to be clear and concise with the talent. I'm not a sugarcoat kind of guy; I was honest to all, and I'm sure it was sobering for some. WCW wasn't going to be a surefire hit; there was risk involved and more than a little ambiguity.

We'd given up on going after WCW's biggest names because they were on guaranteed contracts from before we bought the property. Time Warner had to pay most of World Championship Wrestling's top stars their full amount to sit at home and do nothing. With everything so up in the air, we certainly weren't going to match or better those offers, so I had some work to do to fatten up the main-event picks.

I signed about twenty names first, then added more as the deadline approached. WWE reached out to the fans through its official website to ask what the name of the new WCW show should be.

It was full steam ahead.

Until it wasn't.

Turned out I had hired a company full of people, but no TV station worth talking about wanted to have the tainted name of World Championship Wrestling on its network—especially without its top stars.

As I was building the roster for WCW, word came through that the XFL had lost tens of millions and was officially disbanded. I knew this news would make everyone a lot less likely to jump in on the WCW project. Vince wouldn't want another failure on a new show, and his reputation would no longer inspire blind faith from the prospective networks.

So, suddenly, it was all over before it had even begun.

I had signed and amassed talent, agents, referees, and production people for a new company that had just evaporated. Vince had bought his competition, but he had nowhere to try to maximize its name, history, or identity.

There was only one way to turn, and that was inward.

"I'm going to have an affair on Linda," Vince said, talking about his wife. "She's going to catch me, and then as part of the divorce settlement *Raw* and *SmackDown* will be divided." The boss was grinning ear to ear. He continued: "Linda will get one show where WCW will be, and I'll get the other where WWE will be. You see, J.R., we'll be separate companies under the same umbrella."

"Okay, Boss," I replied. "Let's go."

Vince was one hundred percent onboard, and touring schedules and new names for the WCW show were drawn up. We began to experiment with what Vince called a "soft launch" of WCW on our own programming when Lance Storm became the first WCW wrestler to hit our rings. We wanted to get people talking; to create an atmosphere of WWE being under attack. The next few weeks we mixed in more WCW personalities to get people to tune in to see who else might show up. We even had Booker T make his presence felt at the *King of the Ring* main event and almost cost Stone Cold the title. Unfortunately, the WCW's bad luck continued as Steve broke his hand when he took a routine sideslam from Booker to end the night.

The following night on *Raw*, Vince squared off with his son, Shane, who was written to be the owner of WCW on WWE television. While Mr. McMahon and his son were verbally sparring, Booker T ran in and hit the boss with a kick to the head. This one move spurred the WWE locker room to empty in defense of its boss, both on TV and in real life.

The chairman felt that the WCW wrestlers needed a few wins in their column to establish themselves as a threat.

We programmed WCW's first main event on *Raw* when Buff Bagwell and Booker T fought for the WCW Championship in a bowling-shoe-ugly encounter. Both guys were talented—Booker particularly so—but this was a match that needed to be great but never got off the ground.

"That was the shits," Vince shouted to no one in particular backstage.

Even when Kurt Angle and Stone Cold interfered in the match it was too late to salvage the audience—they had experienced the "new" WCW and they hated it. Their displeasure was clear and vocal; the Tacoma Dome let the boss know that this wasn't going to work.

I had a feeling Vince was getting frustrated by the whole experiment. He liked to get his new ventures on their feet as quickly as possible so he could control every facet of said project. With this project, Vince began to listen to "advisors" who were telling him there was no way WCW guys should be beating WWE guys. Personally, that logic melted my brain because "WCW guys" were WWE guys now. But I could tell that Vince was growing more impatient. All signs were pointing to Vince turning on the very premise that WCW should be a threat at all.

When the boss left *Raw* that night, there was no doubt in my mind that the clock was already ticking on World Championship Wrestling.

There's No Money in Fragile Egos

"WE'RE CHANGING DIRECTION," Vince said over the phone. It was the morning after the WCW main event had bombed on *Raw*. "We're moving forward without a separate TV idea for WCW."

Our plans of doing distinct TV shows, leading to separate Pay-Per-Views leading to dual touring live events, was gone. WCW was dead as an independent entity.

"What's the plan?" I asked.

"We're going to have them invade our programming instead. Mix our stars into their talent pools."

Vince could sense my reluctance.

"It will be good for everyone," he said. "The fans won't get burned out on seeing the same stars on both of our shows and they'll never know what's going to happen next."

I knew what was going to happen next: Vince was going to choke WCW to death. Something told me that the chairman wouldn't let the "enemy" win, even if he owned the enemy. And letting the other side win, every now and again, was the foundation of compelling TV.

But with Vince's new edict we, as a company, went full throttle into WCW "invading" WWE television slots, PPVs, and live events. The idea was called, eh . . . Invasion. Sorry, marketing decided "InVasion" was better than "Invasion." So InVasion was upon us!

WWE had WCW in its possession, but we'd also recently acquired the assets of the smaller, grittier, and financial insolvent Extreme Championship Wrestling in bankruptcy court too. Vince genuinely wanted ECW to survive because he wanted a farm system to cultivate guys in a smaller environment.

But when ECW couldn't get a TV deal to stay alive, Vince stepped in and bought its assets.

This meant Vince now owned and controlled all three wrestling companies that had any national penetration, but he had TV for only one: WWE.

"We're going to have them invade," Vince said.

"When?" I asked.

"At InVasion."

"Is the name giving it away?"

"No. We're going to promote it ahead of time, J.R."

"I was kidding."

Vince laughed like a guy who didn't know what I was talking about. He took my sarcasm as a sign I wasn't sold on the idea, so he got wide-eyed and put on his best promoter's voice. "WCW and ECW join forces to try to take down WWE, all under one roof," he shouted in his most gravelly voice. "That's good shit."

He was right: This would be the biggest angle in wrestling—if the pieces were placed correctly. McMahon had the fullest hand ever dealt in the history of professional wrestling, but he was also building a bubble around himself.

Not only had the amount of talent doubled in the company, the amount of corporate positions had grown too.

It was inevitable, I suppose, that more layers went between the boss and his core business—but all those layers weren't serving the interests of the business. They were mostly serving themselves.

New fiefdoms and allegiances began to spring up, one trying to outmaneuver the other. The smart ones knew how to talk to Vince, but the *really* smart ones knew *when* to talk to Vince.

If you got in his ear last, you had the best chance of getting your way.

For the first time since I joined WWE, I could see the chairman's mind and tastes changing over and over in the course of a day. He went from an owner who took only a couple of opinions on board to a man who took everyone's opinion. On the surface that sounds like a great thing—but not when decisions were made, changed, made differently, tweaked, then scrapped altogether, only to be remade again. The company was suffering serious whiplash from moving in so many different directions.

And it wasn't even like the new whisperers in the chairman's ear were offering an opposing view—they were just offering variations on what Vince already liked. They told him what he wanted to hear instead of doing their job by giving him what he needed to hear.

Vince had created an echo chamber.

So from that echo chamber came the idea that we ended up beating the shit out of WCW and ECW on our TV programs every week. We even put them both together in an ill-fated Alliance faction, "gave them" Steve Austin, and still beat the shit out of them every week.

No one from outside WWE would be allowed to win anything in any meaningful way on WWE television. This was Vince's instinct, fortified and cosigned by the gallery of yes-men around him.

One of the biggest possible money-making angles in wrestling history was being dismantled week by week, decision by decision, all because we couldn't let "them" look good.

Wrestling ego was about to kill the angle that was meant to fortify ratings, PPV, and the live-event business.

"If we let those guys win, it means they were the real stars all along" is the argument I heard. In the mix was Kevin Dunn and WWE's president and chief operating officer, Stuart Snyder, who had worked for Turner and wanted under no circumstances for WCW to "win" over WWE.

Stu didn't understand the basics of wrestling: that you want your opponent to look like a world-beater before you beat them because it only makes you look better in the end.

Vince didn't have all the answers, and as I saw it he listened to guys who had been successful in other areas in the past. They knew that stoking Vince's need to have WWE win would appeal to him, so that's what they did.

It hurt him, and it hurt the company. Stu didn't last very long, but the effect of throttling the InVasion did.

The original PPV of WWE vs. WCW did make the top three of all-time PPV buys for WWE. But the weeks that followed were one bad decision after the other. The one huge change, for me, came when my new broadcast partner, Paul Heyman, left his announce duties to become an on-screen character in the war against WWE—and was replaced with Jerry "The King" Lawler. It was J.R. and The King again on WWE's flagship show, trying to make sense of what was happening to one of the biggest letdowns in wrestling history.

After only a few short months of "warfare" with the "enemy," Vince made the decision to end the whole mushy saga at *Survivor Series* in a "Winner-Take-All" match.

"I've had it with this invasion crap," Vince said on TV. "What I'm proposing is a match to determine which entity will finally survive. It's winner take all."

I followed up on commentary with, "It's one match, winner take all. Either WWE stays in business or the Alliance stays in business."

"WWE will wipe the Alliance off the face of the earth," Vince proclaimed from the ring.

He wasn't joking, either.

The setup was simple: Two teams of five men battle it out, to see something about something. Actually, at that point no one could really figure out what was at stake, because out of the ten guys fighting, only two had come into the company under the invasion angle. So we had eight WWE guys fighting over which was the dominant brand. Shockingly, the final four were WWE guys, and the final two were our top two guys.

The Rock and Austin fought it out, with The Rock as the WWE representative but WCW Champion, and Steve as WWE's biggest draw but the Alliance's representative.

Yeah.

Exactly.

At the end of the night I shouted a line straight from Vince McMahon's brain: "The WWE wins and the Alliance dies at *Survivor Series*."

But with ratings going down across the board and live-event numbers dropping, I knew we were leaving the bungled invasion angle so we could move on to better TV and more engaging angles for our audience.

ChapStick and Hometowns

VINCE AND KEVIN DUNN had long wondered why our programming wasn't talked about in the same breath as all other entertainment shows on TV. The changes in the WWE vocabulary—from "wrestling" to "sports entertainment" and "wrestler" to "Superstar"—were all intended to make us more acceptable as a pure entertainment company—a mix of *Saturday Night Live* and *Days of Our Lives*, with a little action-comedy thrown in.

Soon our agents who put the matches together were called "producers," and the edict from Vince was to call us the "longest-running weekly episodic TV show in history."

We even hired writers from Hollywood to bridge the gap between what we did on TV and what everyone else did.

One day, as I stood in Oklahoma waiting to literally kiss my boss's ass on live TV, I too wondered why we weren't taken seriously in the TV business. After all, surely J.R. smooching Vince McMahon's bare buttery-smooth buns was award-show fodder?

Now, this wasn't just *any* ass storyline. No, no. This was a long-term ass arc, in which about half a dozen employees of the company would kiss Vince's ass because reasons.

I know people mightn't see that as comparable to the plotting of *The Sopranos* or the social commentary of *The Wire*—but I should mention that Vince had tan lines and he made his ass "do tricks" each time.

"Watch my ass do tricks," he would literally say.

I bet Walter White couldn't do ass tricks. You ever see Ray Donovan twerk, bitches? No? Exactly.

Now, just in case I'm being too subtle here, Vince literally pulled down his pants, cupped his junk, bent over a little, and had both cheeks hanging out clear as day.

Think about that. Grown men spent hours and weeks talking about their boss's ass in "creative" meetings.

"And the award for Best TV Show goes to . . ."

ANYWAY, BACK TO the Shakespearean tropes that we were about to honor on live TV. In my hometown, of course.

My wife, daughters, family, and friends gathered ringside to see their husband, father, and friend get on his knees and canoodle the shaved, tanned, tensed buns of his boss for "entertainment."

My only comfort was that the chairman was a clean freak, so I knew the runway would be clear of debris.

"These people are going to kiss my ass through you," Vince said as he unbuckled and unzipped his trousers.

I would tell you *why* this was happening, but who gives a shit, right? I mean, is there anything I could say to justify a middle-aged man getting people to pucker up to his badonkadonk on his own TV show?

Didn't think so.

The Olympic gold medal winner Kurt Angle was there too, as Vince's muscle. Angle grabbed me, and I struggled to get away while Vince pulled down his trousers.

Yeah, now that I think about it, this was all wrong from many different angles.

"I'd like to thank the Academy . . ."

Just as I was getting overpowered, Undertaker's music blared over the speakers: The Dead Man was coming to my rescue.

As the giant, ginger, beanie-wearing, leather-coat-clad Dead Man stood in front of me, I was feeling mighty tough.

In a nice moment, 'Taker picked up my cowboy hat from the mat, dusted it down, and handed it straight back to me.

The crowd loved it. J.R. had finally avoided some humiliation on TV. Yeah, right.

"Now, I've been here a long damn time," 'Taker said to Vince. "And just when I thought I'd seen everything, you got to take the cake."

I was thinking the same thing myself, Undertaker.

He continued, with a straight face. "Let me see if I got this right: You want J.R. to kiss your ass?" The Dead Man then turned to Angle. "And you want to force J.R. to kiss Vince's ass?"

Both Vince and Angle nodded.

The Hollywood writer thing was clearly paying off.

'Taker wasn't impressed. "You know, in eleven years I've seen a lot of people come and a lot of people go. Hogan, Warrior, Savage, Piper, Bret, Shawn Michaels," he said as he pointed to Vince. "I've seen the games they played and I've seen the games *you* played. But when it was all said and done, one way or the other, they all kissed your ass. You know what the saddest thing about that is? The one who kissed your ass the most . . . was me."

I had no idea where 'Taker was going with this. (Well, I did, but I acted like I didn't. I say "acted," but it was more like standing there.)

The Dead Man wasn't done yet. "Eleven years I've been here. Eleven years I've kissed your ass. I've stayed and I'm still putting up with your crap."

"Wow, he's baring his soul," The King said on commentary.

Shakespeare FTW.

'Taker walked back toward me. "So, J.R., just before I take care of this situation, I just want to know: Were you going to kiss his ass?"

"Hell no, I wasn't going to kiss his ass," I shouted into the mic.

The crowd rose up behind me.

"Do you want to kiss his ass?" 'Taker said, with more venom to keep the audience on their feet.

"Hell no!" I shouted, even louder.

The crowd made more noise.

"So, J.R., tell me this: Is that because you're better than me?" 'Taker asked.

The audience piped down quick; 'Taker wasn't so much with me anymore. As a matter of fact, the old Dead Man punched me right in my rotund face and down I went like a sack of shit.

"Are you better than me?" Undertaker shouted.

The crowd booed, and Mr. McMahon stood across the ring, shocked at

'Taker's new take on the situation—but happy he'd get to show the world his butt cheeks one more time.

'Taker said to me, "In front of your family, you are going to kiss his ass. Vince, drop your pants."

Even though my eyes were closed because I was "unconscious," I still rolled them.

'Taker seemed to change his mind. "He *can't* kiss your ass," The Dead Man said to Vince. "He *can't* kiss your ass . . . until you're wearing the man's hat."

Undertaker picked up my beautiful black hat and plonked it down on Vince's head. The chairman's ass was hanging out this whole time, by the way, like an excited dog waiting to be walked.

"Get over here and kiss his ass," 'Taker said as he slammed my face toward Mr. McMahon's can.

"I'd like to thank my agents for always believing that I could pull off a performance like this . . ."

I'm not sure what was going through my mind as I puckered up, except that this sure was a funny old business run by a strange dude. I also tried to count the number of times that "ass" was said in this one segment, but I stopped when my will to live began to dwindle.

All that talent in the ring. All that money and time spent on writers and production—and this is what we served our audience.

However, when I opened my eyes, I did see one boy who was nearly doing backflips with excitement.

It was Vince.

He was dancing around the ring while Limp Bizkit played over the speakers. The chairman was like a kid in Disneyland, hopped up on sugar after meeting his favorite character.

I swear he wasn't this happy the day his company went public. The man was literally doing laps around the ring while holding his junk, slapping his own ass with my hat.

And we went off the air to end the show.

Ugh.

TEN

DIFFERENT STARS, DIFFERENT PATHS

Start from the Top

IT WAS EARLY 2002, and that WCW-guaranteed money—or "mailbox money," as the talent called it—was coming to an end, so Vince wanted to bring his major star from the '80s and '90s, Hulk Hogan, back in the fold.

Signing "The Immortal One" back was the strategic first step in getting all the big names to leave their houses and come to work for WWE. We knew that if Hogan could be convinced to leave the bench and come back, WCW's other top stars, like Sting and Goldberg, might come on board too. Hulk was the lead—the top guy—and if he was happy with his deal, then word would soon spread.

However, before dollars and dates could be discussed, there was a hurdle to jump first. The last time Hulk was with WWE, he and Vince didn't end on great terms—a fact that didn't seem to bother the chairman much as we sat in his office to discuss the best way forward. Vince never let his personal feelings get in the way of business decisions.

"What's the best way to get Hulk's deal done?" I asked.

"How well do you know him?" Vince replied.

I did a little quick math in my head before answering: "I was around him some when I got here in '93, but he was soon out the door."

"I'm probably the man for the job, then," Vince said.

I agreed. Even if I negotiated on Vince's behalf, Hogan was going to want to speak to the boss anyway. Hulk liked to feel special—and he was right to expect that.

Vince knew that Hulk was the biggest star ever in wrestling, and having him back on our roster would be big news. But nobody was more aware of

Hulk Hogan's worth than Hulk Hogan. The real-life Terry Bollea was as cagey outside the ring as his persona was in it.

Vince and Hulk were once joined at the hip as promoter and top star, and they knew each other back to front and inside out.

"Terry and I might have to clear the air somewhat first," Vince said.

The chairman had wanted to move Hulk aside in 1993, not convinced that the audience wanted Hogan on top any longer. Hulk didn't like that assessment, and he eventually joined WWE's rival, WCW, and went on to nearly put Vince out of business.

So Vince and Hulk had spent the last several years, directly and indirectly, in competition.

I had grown to learn that every contract has its own personality, and Hogan and Vince needed to iron out their personal differences before the path was clear to talk business. Vince knew what was needed to land his guy. Even though Hulk was a special case, the chairman had been down this road thousands of times before.

The only thing that made this meeting different was that Hulk didn't need WWE.

"What's his incentive to come back here?" Vince asked, already knowing the answer.

"Well," I said, "Hulk knows better than anyone that being out of the public view for too long hurts his marketability and drops his asking price."

Vince nodded.

I continued: "So I think if you two can patch up old wounds and get together on a cash number, we'll see Hulk Hogan back here in WWE where he belongs."

"I do too," Vince said, sounding pretty confident.

We knew that when we were buying WCW, we were getting a glass only half full. Now Vince wanted to top up that glass with the talent that had evaded us in the beginning: the star names.

"Why start at the bottom and work your way up, huh, J.R.?" Vince wondered.

"That would be my approach too," I said. "But Hogan isn't going to come alone."

Vince nodded: He knew what I meant. "I'll meet with Terry and see where his thoughts are," the chairman said. "You put the feelers out around here and elsewhere about the others coming in."

The "others" were two men Hulk had spent the most successful part of his WCW run flanked by: Scott Hall and Kevin Nash.

Together, the three were known as the New World Order.

Vince went his way, and I went mine.

I soon discovered the mere mention of the nWo letters seemed to stir up something unpleasant backstage at WWE. In fact, I couldn't find anyone who actually wanted them in the company.

At senior level and at talent level, the reluctance to let Nash in particular back through our doors was jarring.

Vince had gotten good vibes off his meeting with Hogan, so he decided to float Kevin and Scott coming back at one of our management meetings. The response was almost unanimously negative.

The nWo in general had a rep for being hard to work with, for having their own agenda. It seemed that during their time in WCW all three men had made life tough for many people who worked there, people who had left WCW in part to flee the political forces like these veterans.

Despite the opposition, I saw the situation a little differently. Vince did too.

"Let's get them in here," Vince said to me after the meeting. "We can eyeball them and see how we feel."

"You want to bring them here?" I asked. "Or will we meet them off-campus?"

"Here," the chairman replied. Vince wanted word of the nWo's arrival to spread across the company.

So, at Vince's request, I asked Hogan, Nash, and Hall to come to a meeting in Stamford to have a talk. By that stage, Vince knew Hogan was in. And on paper, at least, Kevin seemed like a good fit too. But Scott was a little bit more of a risk, having earned a reputation for substance-abuse issues. By the end of WCW's run, Scott had been off a lot, missing work due to wellness violations.

Truth was, a lot of time had passed since I last saw Scott in person. I didn't know what to believe, because the rumor mill in the wrestling business could be unforgiving.

That's why Vince wanted to see them face-to-face.

We were surprised by how much older they all looked. Hogan, Nash, and Hall had all been resting at home for an extended period by the time they came to Stamford—but it didn't look like it.

Vince asked about their drive, and if they felt they could still do the job. I asked about their wear and tear, their injuries and fitness.

"Will you lose as readily as you're asked to win?" Vince said.

All three men were determined and said they were ready to go. We shook hands and they left.

Vince was sure about Kevin and Hulk, but Scott was still worrying.

"How do we take a risk on this guy?" Vince wondered.

"Well," I said, "we have checks and balances here. He'll be tested regularly, same as everyone else. One way or the other, everything will come out in the wash."

Vince had a vision, and he knew it might not work without all three guys coming in.

I think what made Hogan, Nash, and Hall hard to work with was that they knew the business. They were the type of guys who weren't going to be told what their character was by a young writer or just accept any old creative. They were opinionated and forthright, and they could muster a large dollop of asshole when they wanted to.

A lot of other talents didn't know how the sausage was made—nor did they care. They wanted to be pointed in the right direction, told what to say, and make their money. The nWo guys weren't like that at all.

The business of pro wrestling was complex, so it housed complex characters—Hogan, Hall, and Nash chief among them. They might be high maintenance, but I had to look at it from a manager's point of view—nothing personal.

Could I live with these men in the locker room? Absolutely. Their mix of experience, name value, and charisma on-screen more than made up for anything else. They were major names who knew how to get over in a major way. And that's what wrestling is all about—getting the people to care. In my role, if I dwelled on all the reasons something might not work, I would have gone insane.

I also wasn't going to be a martyr. The chairman wanted what the chairman wanted, and it was my job to figure out how to deliver on that desire.

We agreed to terms with all three, and we were happy with what we got them for. We didn't tilt the pay scale—in fact, I believe our guarantee to Hogan was less than he had at the WCW. But it was a good deal all around, as the guaranteed amount was more than earned-out.

After the ink was dry, Vince was all business again. We got our guys, but we also had over a hundred other talents to manage.

We'd heard all the right things from Kevin, Hulk, and Scott. Now we were going to find out if they could walk the walk.

Wrestling Shakespeare

THE WRESTLING NEWSLETTERS were making everyone in WWE management a little nervous about the nWo. Rumors abounded that Hall, Nash, and Hogan had creative control, and their mere presence was going to sink the mighty WWE.

Vince had other ideas. Not only was he not that worried about the nWo, he wasn't even that interested in the nWo. Not in the long term, anyway.

"We're going to do The Rock vs. Hogan," the chairman told me in his office.

I was a little surprised, as the nWo was only just settling into our programming—but *WrestleMania X8* was approaching, and it was being held at the seventy-thousand-seat SkyDome in Toronto.

"Goddamn it," Vince said. "What do you think?"

"That's one helluva match, that's what I think."

Because I did. And it was.

Vince could already see the billboard in front of him. "Icon vs. Icon," he said with a grin on his face.

As good as Hogan was in the nWo trio, Vince saw major dollar signs in Hulk breaking out into a singles match at the same venue where he had wrestled Ultimate Warrior twelve years before.

Even before Hogan came back to WWE, Austin had made it clear that he didn't want to wrestle Hulk. Steve felt their styles didn't mesh well and that the match wouldn't live up to expectations. Both Hogan and Stone Cold were battling pretty bad injuries: Austin's neck was worsening by the month, and Hulk's back was in bad, bad shape.

"I know people will say I don't want to do the job to Hogan," Austin told me, "but that ain't it."

I believed Steve, because if Austin and Hogan ever did match up, it wouldn't be Austin who was losing the match anyway. The truth was, my friend The Texas Rattlesnake was sitting on the front burner, and things were getting hot. Steve was weighed down by external issues, and he was constantly looking at his own mortality in the business.

Stone Cold was on the greatest run of all time, but he could sense it beginning to slow down. It was no disrespect to Hogan, just a dose of reality from the perfectionist streak in Steve.

The Rock, on the other hand, had a completely different style. Where Austin liked a hard-hitting brawl, The Rock excelled at a smoother approach.

The Rock was the icon of the present, and Hogan was the icon from the past. All we wanted to do was spark the flame that connected them. And that would come down to pure chemistry.

After Vince told me the plan, I wanted to find both Hulk and The Rock and get their take on the prospective match. Were both talents on board? Within ten seconds of talking to both, it was clear that they saw the same potential. The biggest hurdle for the match was Hogan's back issues.

Until Hogan's music hit.

"Ladies and gentlemen," WWE's greatest-ever ring announcer, Howard Finkel, began, "representing the nWo, Hollywood Hulk Hogan."

Crippling back issues or not, The Immortal One, draped in feather boas and dripping in charisma, strutted down the aisle.

"You can love him," I said, "or you can hate him. And there're a lot of fans in the SkyDome who love this legendary figure."

Then we got the sense that nothing was taken from the Hulkster coming back to Toronto. Even though he'd been portrayed on TV as a member of the villainous nWo, in Toronto, at *WrestleMania*, Hulk Hogan was a hero.

"Perhaps the greatest icon in the history of sports entertainment preparing to meet perhaps the future of this industry."

Lawler and I only had to look at each other over the announce table to know this was going to be special. It was one of those nights when nothing was going to plan—in the most glorious of ways. Hogan hadn't even hit the ring yet, and the arena was shaking.

"This is so special, J.R.," The King said. "This is unique."

My announce partner was not wrong. It was on nights like this I was so thankful to have Jerry there beside me, to experience what I was experiencing.

Hogan walked the steps and tore off his T-shirt in classic Hulk fashion. His music stopped and the void was immediately filled with deafening chants of, "HOGAN! HOGAN! HOGAN!"

The Rock was coming into the match as the hero, but Hogan's ovation was like the second coming of the big white father. The fans wanted to give an aging and hurting Hogan the send-off of a lifetime. Sitting there in Toronto, I knew this wasn't Hulk's last day or last match, but it was already the high point of his return to WWE. No one had expected this—Hulk least of all; you could tell by his face.

Ever the pro, Hulkster went straight to work keeping the audience heat alive by simply smiling and nodding to each side of the arena. Small, subtle facial movements from one man in the middle of a huge arena had the place on the edge of their seats.

I immediately wondered what The Rock was thinking, waiting backstage. In wrestling we had an old saying: "There's only so many cheers to go around."

Then The Great One's music hit, and it was time to find out.

There were deep breaths and long strides as The Rock made his way to the ring. The King and I recapped the story leading to the match, setting the table for our viewers, serving up two greats squaring off.

The Rock was all business. Hogan was all business. The Rock's music faded, and both men went to work.

Not with punches or suplexes, but with stillness.

Neither man moved toward the other—which expertly left the space for the audience to amplify their energy even further.

And man, did those people deliver.

I could see in the monitor at my announce table that the WWE cameramen were doing a wonderful job in framing the raucous crowd. I could hear the tremendous passion coming from every seat in the arena.

Hulk barely moved. The Rock barely moved. And yet the scene was electric.

"Many in the crowd chanting for The Rock," I said. "Quite frankly, many in the crowd chanting for Hogan."

Both wrestlers slowly walked to the center of the ring.

"Look at the flashbulbs," I said. "This is a *WrestleMania* moment."

In the middle of the ring, The Rock and Hogan stood and stared at each other. As long as the arena noise was building, both wrestlers knew to hold their positions.

A little move of the head one way for Hulk, and the opposite side for The Rock, and the arena was on their feet. These people were seeing something, feeling something, experiencing something that we all knew was special.

It was wrestling Shakespeare.

"We'll never see Tyson and Ali, we'll never see Babe Ruth and Barry Bonds, but we are going to witness The Rock and The Hulk," The King said as Hogan began to run his mouth in the ring.

The ref pushed between both men and separated them.

It was time for action.

Vince chimed in on my headset: "Let's go with this, J.R.," the chairman said. "Call what you see."

I was ready to do just that. The most insulting thing a commentator can do is try to sell the audience the opposite of what they're seeing.

Hogan and The Rock lunged toward each other and grabbed hold in a collar-and-elbow tie-up. It was in that one move that I could see The Rock being perfect for Hogan. The Great One sold the struggle of trying to move the powerful Hulk—muscles tensed, teeth gritted, The Great One pushed Hogan back—but only a couple of steps before Hulk dug in and reversed course. The Immortal One then threw The Rock backward and the People's Champion launched himself head over heels like he'd just been shot by an elephant gun.

If Hogan couldn't do much, then The Rock was going to fill in the blanks by "creating movement" and making Hulk look superhuman.

Hogan flexed. The Rock looked like he saw a ghost, and the crowd ate it all up with a spoon.

The Rock understood—as we understood, as Vince understood, as the audience understood—that on this night, in this match, Hulk Hogan was the biggest star in the world, and we all swam with that knowledge, together. It was a night when everyone was simpatico.

If the crowd wanted to cheer Hogan, then The Great One was going to give them something to boo. The Rock made subtle changes to his presentation that let the audience root even harder for Hogan, and boo a little louder still at The Rock.

The King and I had worked our whole lives for nights like this. It was the best of what professional wrestling can be. It was storytelling and emotion and passion and skill and experience, and seventy-thousand people who bought every look, punch, grimace, and near-fall.

At the end—when we all thought it couldn't get any hotter—The Rock hit his finishing move on Hogan.

One . . . two . . . and kick-out by The Hulkster!

But not only a kick-out. Hogan took to his knees in a familiar pose. His fist began to shake and his head began to shiver—Hulk Hogan was "Hulking up," and the SkyDome became unglued. This was the act of Hogan becoming impervious to pain, and The Rock sold it like he was seeing his past, present, and future flash before his very eyes.

Hulk punched The Rock three times so the crowd could count along, whipped him into the ropes, and hit the Big Boot under The Rock's chin. The Great One went down like a ton of bricks.

"The end could be near," I shouted, "for The Rock at *WrestleMania X8*."

I was as invested as anyone who had paid to witness this. I was at work, but also a fan. Always a fan.

Hogan dropped a big leg across The Rock's throat, and the People's Champion gagged like a tree had fallen from heaven and landed across his windpipe. I loved watching The Rock work because he was one of the few left who understood that selling is an art form, not a sign of weakness.

"He beat Andre the Giant with that move," I roared as Hogan went for the cover. I wanted to protect The Rock by letting the audience know that if this move could keep the legendary Giant down for three, then there was no shame in Rocky losing.

Except I didn't know the finish. I never knew the finish.

One . . . two . . . AND ROCK KICKED OUT.

"My God," I said. "And Hogan, much like The Rock earlier, cannot believe it."

"He can't believe it," The King echoed. "Neither can these fans."

As Hulk picked up The Rock from the canvas another massive "HOGAN!" chant broke out. Hulk looked for another legdrop but missed. The

Rock instead hit his finisher, the Rock Bottom. But The Great One knew that wasn't going to be enough to keep The Immortal One down. So he hit him with another Rock Bottom. Then, as both men looked spent on the canvas, The Rock kipped up from his back to his feet in one explosive movement.

It was time for the People's Elbow.

"The Rock has reached down to the tune of three Rock Bottoms," I said as The Rock landed the elbow.

One . . . two . . . three!

"The Rock wins it," I shouted.

"Oh my God, J.R.," The King said.

"That was a match for the ages," I replied. "What an emotional ride."

The King was feeling it too. "What an epic match."

I tried to sum up what we had just witnessed. "Man, that was a unique dichotomy of fan support back and forth. But The Rock, with all those Rock Bottoms and the People's Elbow, finally prevailing. The veteran lion got pinned by the younger lion."

Vince chimed in on the headsets: "That was fucking amazing. You did a great job in changing gears out there."

I looked around the SkyDome as The Rock saluted the crowd. If all the people in the seats were lovers, they would have all been smoking right about now.

Vince knew how bad a shape Hogan was in. "Goddamn, we just stole one in Toronto," the chairman said.

But as The Rock was ascending the WWE mountain, Vince's other top star was struggling.

The Three Stages of Going Home

"HE TOOK HIMSELF OUT OF THE GAME. Vince McMahon didn't, J.R. didn't. Steve Williams took Stone Cold and flew him to San Antonio. It would be like John Wayne becoming a coward in a big fight." In the summer of 2002, that's what I said online about my friend Stone Cold Steve Austin. (And to this very day, I still regret calling Steve a coward.)

For the second time in only a few months, Steve had gone home in anger and frustration. He did it on TV days, did it without notifying Vince, and did it without regard for how it could affect the show, the company, or himself professionally.

So I said what I said.

As I look back, I could see the clear path to how this all came to be. I was both understanding of Steve's situation and pissed at Steve at the same time.

If two divorces had taught me anything, it was that strained relationships didn't happen overnight. The break between Steve and WWE had a few different stages—the first of which had reared its head a few months before, on the run to *WrestleMania X8*.

Austin had a match down the card that he didn't really want to be a part of. It wasn't that Steve had anything against his opponent, Scott Hall. It was more that the match meant nothing and was heading nowhere.

"What do you think of this match? You think me and Hall can put together something good?" he asked me.

I replied with a shrug.

"What? You think it's going to be the drizzling shits?"

"Maybe not 'drizzling,'" I said.

I didn't lie to Steve, but seeing how my words seemed to confirm his own fears, maybe I should have.

Steve and Scott were both amazing workers and sharp wrestling minds, but I felt their bodies didn't have the fuel needed to collectively get where Austin wanted them to go. My guess was that they couldn't put together something strong enough to satisfy Austin, who was notoriously hard on himself.

Even though all the backstage gossips wanted it to be true, there was no animosity between Austin and Hall. As a matter of fact, Hall, Nash, and Stone Cold were friendly—they had been for years. The real issue was this match: It had no real purpose, build, or destination.

Vince wanted Hall to win: His thinking was that he didn't want two nWo members losing on the same card, and obviously Hogan was going down to The Rock.

I could somewhat understand the company using Austin to get Hall and Kevin Nash firmly implanted into the main-event scene, as the heel nWo faction wasn't yet running on all cylinders. I'm sure it sounded great in the creative meetings—but the wrestling business doesn't run on paper.

"I don't mind losing," Austin said. "As long as it's the right place and the right time, to make everyone more money."

This was the foundation of professional wrestling: make the conflict compelling enough that people will continue to pay their hard-earned money to see what happens next. Throwing shit out there just to fill time made nobody any real money.

To add to Austin's anxieties, rumors began to surface that Hall was losing his battle with substance abuse again, and he had gone drinking with some fans the night before *WrestleMania*.

Austin wasn't happy, and neither was Vince when he heard about Hall's behavior before the biggest show of the year.

The chairman changed the finish to Austin winning.

Except no one told Austin.

So on the day of *WrestleMania X8*, Austin was angry, Hall was allegedly hungover, and creative hadn't told anyone what was going on.

"I'm drifting," Steve said, pacing around backstage like a caged animal. "They don't have a plan for me, and now I have nobody to draw money with."

He was right: WWE didn't know what was coming next for their biggest star. Austin was holding up his end of the deal, but creative was lacking in their side of the relationship.

Steve knew the WWE model better than anyone: It was a babyface company with one guy on top who drew the money. Bruno Sammartino always had a bad guy to vanquish; Hulk Hogan had a continuous line of despicable heels to overcome. But Stone Cold Steve Austin had no one on the horizon.

"What am I going to do if I'm not wrestling?" Steve asked.

His mostly rhetorical question came out of the blue, but it showed me where his mind really was. Austin wasn't only thinking about this event, this match, this opponent. He was thinking about the end of his run.

Steve had come up through the territory system; bad rings, long miles, and no days off had taken their toll on his body and mind. Even though he was on an unprecedented run with us—and had more money than he knew what to do with—he still thought like a hungry man.

Austin knew before anyone else that the biggest part of his career was behind him. He could sense his body was changing, breaking down, and it was playing on his mind. He was a warhorse, and the passion, determination, and drive that had gotten him to the very top of our business was also slowly destroying him.

"What's going on, J.R.?" Steve asked.

I began to realize that if I didn't talk to Steve every few days, he'd think something was off. "I don't think there's anything to be worrying about here other than bad planning," I said. "Why don't you go talk to the one guy who can resolve those concerns for you?"

I wasn't involved much in the creative end of WWE. I could listen to Steve and give him my opinion, but there was only one man who could put him at ease, and that was Vince McMahon.

"I know what my strengths are," Steve said, frustrated. "And this shit isn't it."

He left, and I went about my business. Later on, I was happy to hear that the boss and his top star had talked about Steve's apprehensions and insecurities. Vince agreed that it made no sense that his biggest attraction had nothing meaningful to do.

Steve and Scott went out there and had their match.

But though all looked calm on the surface, trouble was still brewing. Ultimately, *WrestleMania X8* was the first step in Austin's exit from the company.

Step two came the next night.

Steve and Scott had a decent match—which Stone Cold didn't like—but before long, Stone Cold was pacing again. He showed up for the *Raw* taping and noticed that he was again sidelined to a smaller roll. The script for the show had Steve cutting a promo with no real direction—it was meandering and didn't set up anything new or give a sense of who he'd be matching up with next.

It was filler. Austin knew it was filler. WWE knew it was filler.

"I'm leaving, Jim," he said, dragging his bags behind him. The biggest name in wrestling found himself without a clear creative path. "How can this company not have anything for me?" he asked.

I couldn't answer, because he was right. As a matter of fact, I had never seen someone who was so right make their point in a way that was so wrong.

I tried to talk him out of it.

"Jim," he said, "I've worked my entire career to be in the spot I'm in. I have given sweat, blood, and tears for this company, and they're fucking me around."

Steve was aware, I was aware, and I was certain Vince was aware that WWE couldn't have expanded globally—nor become a publicly traded company—without Steve Austin leading the charge. And yet no one asked The Rattlesnake who he wanted to work with next or told him what the plan ahead was.

I tried to convince Steve to stay and talk to Vince again.

"I've already tried that," he said.

I could see that Austin was burned out and beginning to sour on the company. Steve's straightforwardness could make him seem a lot more complex; his locked-jaw approach to the basics of wrestling booking put him at odds with where the company was heading.

I tried, but he was wound so tight that there was no talking to him. Steve grabbed his bags and went home.

That was stage two. Even though he came back to work a couple of weeks later, Austin's mind was swirling with paranoia, his body breaking down and his tank filled with anxiety.

Stage three came a few months later, when Steve called me the night before a *Raw* taping. He'd heard that he was going to be mixing it up with the rookie everyone was talking about: Brock Lesnar. Finally, Steve felt that he had someone in Brock with whom he could draw real money again.

But then Austin heard the actual plan: WWE wanted Lesnar to beat Steve on TV in an unannounced one-off match.

Austin called me in my hotel room. "They're throwing away a top program on a nothing match," he said. "Just what are they thinking, Jim?"

I hadn't heard the plan.

"You know my thoughts on this without me having to say it," I replied. "Did they give you a reason?"

Austin didn't so much want to converse as to talk. "They've got something big in Lesnar and me. Why are they putting it on free TV?"

I couldn't answer Steve's legitimate concerns.

"Did you ask Vince?" I said.

"I don't want to talk to Vince," came his reply.

I knew then that we were in trouble. If the top star didn't want to consult with the boss of the company, then nothing good was about to happen.

"I'm so sick of this shit," he said. "I'm trying to handle this better than I am, but I can't."

I was worried about my friend. I'd heard the rumors that there was trouble at home. Maybe I should have asked, but as close as Steve and I were, it didn't seem right to bring up his personal life on a business call. We didn't have that kind of relationship; wrestling was our conversation piece. We never strayed too far from wrestling, sports, or hunting when we chatted.

"It's taking longer to get over these injuries, and I don't know how much longer I have left in me," he said. "I don't want to just give away the few big-time feuds I have left."

"How do we go from here?" I asked him.

"When you've stood on top of the mountain and seen the view I've seen, you don't want to see anything else," he said. "I'll call you later."

Vince had already heard of Steve's reaction to the following day's angle; I'm guessing some writer had caught The Rattlesnake's full and frank opinion when it was pitched to Steve. The chairman called Austin and asked him to make contact whenever he got the message.

Steve called Vince at two in the morning.

The next day when I arrived at the arena, I got the same vibe as I had the night Jeff Jarrett was leaving: that giddiness in the air that comes only when there's drama and conflict.

I hate that vibe, but some people seem to live for it.

Then word came that Austin had gone home. Vince already knew (although Austin hadn't told him) and was pissed. The show was in shambles.

I immediately got the feeling he wouldn't be back so soon this time. Vince told me Austin wasn't welcome back in WWE anymore.

I called Steve on his cell; he was on his way to San Antonio.

"They're looking for their next top guy, and I respect that, J.R.," he said. "But they're fucking me around in the meantime, and I don't deserve it."

"I agree," I said. "But this is absolutely the wrong way to do business here."

Steve didn't care at that moment how it looked or how it reflected on him as a professional. He was just leaving, and that was that.

"My issue isn't money," he said. "It's creative. And that's Vince."

I could tell that this wasn't a stunt or Steve's way of looking for Vince to make things right. He meant it. He was allowing the wrestling business to fuck with his thinking, and it was poisoning him.

"I'm not healing up from these injuries as quick as I used to," Austin told me. "I've got money, but I broke my damn neck for that company, and Vince is jerking me around."

The only thing Steve ever wanted since he was a boy was to be a star in the wrestling business. Against all odds, he'd risen up to become the biggest draw in the biggest era that wrestling had ever known—and now he was flushing it away.

And I wanted to help him see that. Steve wasn't the easiest guy to be around anymore, but he was still my friend, and I loved him.

"Stay and fight," I said. "Come and talk to Vince."

"I'm going home," he replied. And I knew he wasn't looking for anyone to follow him, call him, or convince him otherwise.

So what had been a creative issue now became my issue.

"Where's your boy, J.R.?" people asked.

"Can't you control your talent?"

"J.R. can't even convince his friends to do business."

Austin's leaving left me in a tricky spot professionally too. Vince didn't seem to blame me, but the sycophants who wanted my job—and, more important, who wanted the boss's ear—could hardly hide their glee.

To them, the fact that Austin left had proven I wasn't good at my job.

Like any chain of command—and the wrestling business was no different—there was always someone looking to move up. This situation, for some, was the perfect opportunity to weaken my position and convince the chairman that someone else overseeing talent relations mightn't have allowed this situation to arise. I found myself in a bind: Austin's issues weren't anything my office could deal with, yet I'd been left holding the bag.

So, I was hot at Steve for putting me in such a precarious position. What could I tell Vince? That *he* was at fault? I spent day after day, week after week, listening to Austin talk about Vince, and sometimes Vince talk about Austin, and I did what I could—which was to listen and try to advise. But in the end, it was a breakdown of communication and trust between star and promoter.

So I was hot. And I likened my great friend to a coward. Naturally, I'd been given no bullet points or direction from Vince, other than this: "His fans, and WWE fans in general, need to know what has happened."

So I told the fans what was on my mind in a WWE online interview. I spoke in anger, frustration, and not a little pain too. I knew Steve Austin. I loved Steve Austin. And I was mad as hell at Steve Austin.

But while Austin's WWE tenure had ended for the moment, it was a pleasure to watch that kid we recruited from Minnesota; "The Beast" Brock Lesnar would go on to become a true PPV box-office attraction and main-event star not only in WWE, but also in the Ultimate Fighting Championship too.

ELEVEN

TROUBLE IN THE SKY

Get the F Out

BIG WINDS OF CHANGE were running across the WWE landscape. I knew this wasn't the place to work if you could focus on only one task at a time. We'd just finished a show in the UK, and we were flying home to bolster a couple of major strategic pieces of WWE's future. I started our transatlantic trip talking about global expansion with the other executives, but I ended it looking for a missing ponytail among some unconscious wrestlers.

You'd think when you're flying charter instead of commercial, it would be a good day, especially with free food and a fully paid bar thrown in.

The plane on which we were traveling had been gutted and refitted from scratch for sports travelers; all the seats on board were first class, and our wrestlers were served twice the food of a normal passenger.

We had some pretty big dudes sitting aboard the converted 737, and the chairman was adamant that they be fed well and that every food and beverage consumed was to be charged to the company.

Some of the Boys liked the free food part, while others loved the free alcohol part. I didn't think much of it, simply because I didn't think anyone would be so foolish as to get out of line when the CEO of the company and his wife were sitting on the same plane.

Seems I gave some people too much credit.

As we took off, work was being done up front on our newly reorganized talent roster and TV direction, collectively known as the "brand extension." From the wealth of talent yielded by our failed InVasion angle, we had crafted two TV shows on different networks, with brand-exclusive rosters on each. In the absence of WCW, Vince's idea was to build his own competition.

The plan was for more talent to find their way into the spotlight by essentially creating two of everything: two main-event divisions, two midcards, two tag divisions, and so on. We had a lot of talent, but our flagship show, *Raw*, only had so many slots each week in which to try to feature them all. The feeling was that talent who had a hard time getting booked on *Raw* would be free to make their mark on *SmackDown*.

The main concern from the talent was who was going to end up on what brand, since many didn't want to lose their longtime travel partners. The biggest enemy in the wrestling business was the miles—people loved the work but detested the travel.

When word got out that a brand extension was coming, my makeshift office at the arenas was suddenly busy with talent looking for information. People were certain that I knew where they were going and with whom. In truth, I didn't. I didn't want or need to know; in fact, I tried to stay out of the booking decisions as much as possible. My plate was full enough.

I certainly sympathized with their frustration, but I wasn't the guy to make that better for them. The only thing I asked of management was that couples be kept together where possible. Life on the road was hard enough without having your wife or partner on a completely different schedule than you.

And WWE honored that concern more often than not.

"HOW'S THE BEEF, J.R.?" Vince asked.

This was one of those instances where I wished my parents were alive to see how far their boy had come from the farm. My old man would have gotten a huge kick out of his boy flying charter, eating steak and talking business.

The newish brand extension wasn't the only major change happening in the company. While we were in the air, the company as a whole began its changeover from World Wrestling Federation to World Wrestling Entertainment.

The long-standing WWF initials were claimed legally by the World Wildlife Fund, and we had no choice but to rebrand. Vince decided to use the situation to emphasize the entertainment strand in our company DNA.

While our literal identity as a company was being changed across our many avenues of sales, media, marketing, and production on the ground, some of our talent thought it might be a good idea to start some trouble aboard.

"J.R., we need you to come to the back," a production assistant whispered in my ear.

I sighed. We were about five hours into the flight, so I knew it wasn't going to be a good scene back there. I unclipped my seatbelt and walked past the agents pretending they didn't know anything was up. It was like prison rules in WWE sometimes. The agents were mostly former wrestlers, and the Boys didn't like disciplining the Boys. Usually I admired that loyalty, but not in this instance. Sometimes turning a blind eye and letting the madness continue ended up hurting your fellow colleagues much more than it helped them.

This was one of those scenarios.

I got back there and saw Brock Lesnar and his fellow Minnesotan, Curt "Mr. Perfect" Hennig, scuffling in the aisle. Both men thought it would be a good idea to wrestle each other against the plane door at 35,000 feet.

Across the way I saw blood dripping from John Layfield's head. He'd been in a match with X-Pac the night before, and now he was busted open. When I asked how it happened, there were conflicting reports, but seemingly they all involved Michael Hayes.

I went to find Michael and he was unconscious—the result of either a punch from John or just pure partying, depending on whom I asked. As Michael slept, he had been relieved of his trademark ponytail, which was cut off by X-Pac, who was apparently goaded on by Scott Hall.

I uttered the words I never dreamed I'd say: "Where's the fucking ponytail?"

No one seemed to know.

I found Scott, but he too was unconscious. I felt confident that I knew what had caused his incapacitated state. The Bad Guy was in really rough shape, and his pulse was weak, sometimes dangerously so. When I looked up from Scott, I saw Ric Flair doing his familiar one-man parade in the aisle, wearing nothing but his signature robe.

I addressed and soothed one situation after the other; I convinced people to calm down or sit down; I talked to those who needed it; I shouted and scorned. I did my job as best I could.

But I genuinely resented the fact that a kind gesture from the company—free food and booze—was going to result in me having to fire people. As I looked around, all I could see were a lot of well-paid men acting like eighth-graders who'd found the keys to the liquor cabinet. It was bush league, embarrassing stuff. In wrestling, some guys were fortunate, some were unlucky, and some were just plain dumb. It was only the minority, but I knew the chaos they were creating was going to make it back to Vince.

Plus, word had gotten out that one of them had drunkenly attempted to pee on Vince's wife, Linda, mistaking her for the bathroom.

There was no way to cover this up or make it sound better than it was. It was playing out in real time, with the boss right there. Heads were going to roll, and I was the one who'd have to swing the ax. When I went back to the front of the plane, Vince said nothing; he knew it wasn't possible for me to control the behaviors of grown men.

Vince and I met up in the hotel when we landed.

"I hear someone used the seatback as a spittoon," Vince said.

"Looks like it," I replied.

"What are you going do about it?" he asked.

"I'm going to fine the person five grand," I replied. "There were red Solo cups, and he didn't use a one of them." (Shout-out to my friend Toby Keith for the reference.)

Vince nodded. "Also, tell Scott and Curt we don't need them on TV anymore. They're done."

And with that short last sentence, the careers of Scott Hall and Curt Hennig were finished.

I made the calls as instructed; both men understood, because they knew they'd been on thin ice well before the plane ride from hell. Vince wanted Curt to move to the announce table, but Curt felt he had a main-event run or two still in him. Scott was happy to come off the road to try and manage his substance-abuse problems.

I honestly felt like letting Scott go was the best thing we could have done to save his life. On the road, he was constantly in places and around people that weren't good for his health.

As for the missing ponytail, it ended up in a clear bag, nailed to the locker-room door the next day.

The bigger we grew, the more I swung the ax. But I knew that ax blade could be sharp on both sides.

TWELVE

BURNED, HIRED, FIRED . . . AND HIRED

The Fracturing of a Dream

JAN AND I BOUGHT A HOUSE back in Norman, Oklahoma. It was 2003 and past time; I had spent long enough away from my two girls, and I now had grandchildren to consider too. I couldn't go back in time to make myself a better father, but I could go back to Oklahoma to try and be a better grandfather.

I wanted to move back full-time but I knew my job wouldn't allow that, so I contented myself with spending holidays in my Oklahoma house or a few days off here and there. It was the best purchase I ever made for my personal life but the worst I could have made in my professional life.

Vince liked the old Mafia motto: Once you were in, you were in for life.

I mentioned to him that I was looking before we bought, but he was weird about it and didn't want to talk. Then I told him that we got a place, but only as a second home, and he got pretty icy. I knew him well enough to know that something wasn't right.

Pretty soon I would find out the chairman didn't like me planning life outside WWE. But not from Vince himself, of course.

I kinda knew that the writing team liked to see me annoyed—mostly because Vince got a kick out of it, and everyone liked to please the boss. As the company got bigger, I felt the writing was turning more inward, toward what would make Vince laugh or what Vince would approve, instead of what would make the audience care or make the audience react.

The talent seemed to agree.

More and more frequently I was hearing from wrestlers about quality or direction of their individual storylines or the shows overall. I tried to stay away from the creative side of the house whenever possible, but it was my job to raise the talent's issues, and at that moment they were all about creative.

So, much as I dreaded it, I approached the team. Now, I wasn't a saint by any means; once I got going, I called them out repeatedly for not knowing where an angle was going or for being shitty storytellers in general. I definitely could have handled myself more professionally in how I delivered the message, but the message had to be delivered.

Sometimes they handled my advocacy well; other times they didn't. Sometimes I advocated well, sometimes I didn't.

But eventually they wrote a script in which I was literally set on fire and removed from TV, so maybe it hadn't gone as well as I thought. As I watched my effigy cook, I made a mental note to maybe get a little better at company diplomacy. This wasn't a subtle point the writing team was making.

To cover my announce duties, they brought in a sports announcer called Jonathan Coachman. And shortly after being burned alive, I was brought back to TV again.

But this time to wrestle.

I got the call that Vince and creative wanted to put J.R. in the ring again—the place they knew I hated being. By this point I had been beaten up in several interview segments, busted open, fired, rehired, fired, replaced, brought back, and set on fire.

I was at our Oklahoma house when I got the call. Jan was beside me, reading. She could hear the voice at the other end just as loudly as I could. It was Vince pitching the idea to get me back on TV.

"Why are you wrestling?" she asked after I hung up.

"To get my job back," I said.

"Why do you need to get your job back?" she rightfully wondered.

"Well, because they're going to have me lose it in a tag match," I answered.

She was as confused as I was and our audience was sure to be. "Wait," she said. "They're bringing you back from being set on fire . . . to have you lose your job in a tag match . . . so you can win your job back a week later?"

"Yep," I said.

"Why?"

"At this stage," I replied, "who the hell knows?"

I never did understand the allure of having me in wrestling angles. I knew I pulled some good quarter-hour ratings for the company, but it had been drilled into me since I started in the business that my job wasn't to get the audience to care about me, it was to get them to care about the talent.

But Vince thought it was funny to watch a nonwrestler wrestle. So it happened. But a curious phenomenon was building in response: The audience wasn't going along.

The more WWE tried to humiliate me, the more the audience rooted for me. Vince tried several times to bring in new commentators to take my place, but the audience rejected them with their boos and passionate online feedback. It never took long before Vince himself became frustrated at the new guys' varying abilities to sell the story he wanted sold in the way in which he wanted it sold. I began to realize that, while I kept being taken off TV so WWE could try something new, I was always brought back because the newer version never worked out.

It was like Vince wanted me gone but couldn't understand why there was such an attachment between me and the WWE fans. So he'd do something else on TV to try to humiliate me, only for the audience to become more invested in me, more protective. WWE had been playing hot potato with me so much that I could tell the company wanted to move me out for a younger, more "TV-ready" face.

Thing is: What I was doing on the air for the company wasn't reliant on my face, it was reliant on my voice. And in that voice was the kind of passion and experience that WWE couldn't teach—certainly not overnight, anyway.

I didn't blame or wish ill on any of the guys who were brought in—they were just trying to make a living in the wrestling business, same as me. But the WWE fans told Vince time and time again that it was my voice they wanted out there. The people didn't care that I sounded so southern or that my face sometimes drooped or that I was getting older. They wanted the voice that talked them through the biggest boom period in wrestling history, the voice that was stamped on some of their fondest memories. They wanted to hear someone who knew the business inside out and could make a call on pure instinct and passion. They wanted fire in their calls; they trusted me to let them know if something special was unfolding or if something was "bowling-shoe ugly."

I was a fan. I was honest. I loved to call what the people loved to watch.

I understood, of course, that I wasn't going to be around forever, but the succession plans were far too premature for my liking. These new guys weren't being groomed to take my seat eventually. They were being brought in to do it now.

Thank God for my new home, my wife, and my family. And my Oklahoma Sooners. Home games were such a hit in my house that Kevin Dunn—who was not only the executive producer of WWE but also a close confidant of Vince's—brought his sons down and stayed overnight to see a game. Vince used to say that Kevin and I were his number one and number two in the company. I'm not sure which was which, but I'm guessing we each thought the same. It was only when Kevin and I were outside having a cocktail that it hit me what Vince was trying to do to me.

"He doesn't like to be left, Jim," Kevin said. "Maybe you don't realize how important you are to Vince."

"Did he say that?" I asked.

"He's not going to say it to you," he replied. "But you wear a lot of hats in there to keep his company running smoothly. He depends on you."

"I'm not going anywhere anytime soon," I said.

Little did I know.

Into the Sunset, Quietly

I GOT A CALL saying that Stone Cold was in the hospital in Seattle. It was the night before *WrestleMania XIX*, and Steve was one half of the upcoming main event, the capstone of a historic trilogy with The Rock.

It was also slated to be Austin's last match, and a way for him to leave the business the right way. Austin knew in his heart that he didn't want to end his run on a sour note, so a return to face Rock one more time was the perfect way to say farewell.

Nobody had ever generated enough interest or box-office revenue to even attempt offering the same pairing three times, but Steve and Dwayne were a different breed—1 and 1A in the business—who had created a perfectly planned storyline. For his last time out there, that's *what* Steve wanted and *who* he wanted to do it with.

Over the years a healthy and respect-driven rivalry had built between The Rock and Austin. It never went anywhere destructive or harmful—it was more iron sharpening iron. I applauded the fact that they wanted to compete because they knew if The Rock and Austin took a day off, someone else was going to make ground. Neither man wanted that; both wanted the spot. Never—not once—did either of them come to me and complain about the other guy. They were both alpha males and stand-up men.

The fact that Steve wanted only one man to share the ring with on his way out spoke volumes about the level of respect both men had for each other. They were students of the game, who knew the effect they had both on each other, and their legendary careers.

The Rock would continue his journey, and Austin would bow out. The

Rattlesnake's injuries had become too much to manage, and Steve didn't want to be out there in front of the people unless he was able to give them everything.

THE CHAIRMAN AND I got to the hospital as quickly as we could. It comforted me to see that Vince was as worried about my friend Steve, the man, as he was about his history-making main event. Austin and Vince had outpaced just about every record in wrestling together and built a unique relationship that went beyond worker and boss.

"Did they tell you what's wrong with him?" Vince asked me for the tenth time.

"They did not," I replied.

I was sure he would ask me the same question again before we got there, and he did.

When we arrived outside Steve's room, he was embarrassed to see us; he had no idea we were coming. "Aw, shit," he said when both of us walked through the door. "I don't want no fussing, and I'm going to be fine."

The Rattlesnake wasn't a high-maintenance kind of guy in that regard and he hated being a burden. He was a perfectionist and a pain in the ass sometimes when it came to his work, but as a person he never wanted to be a liability.

He folded his arms and couldn't quite look either of us in the face—being in a vulnerable position wasn't something Austin enjoyed at all. "I drank too many of those goddang energy drinks and they did something to me," Steve said, almost annoyed at having to explain himself, even though no one had asked. "I'm going to be fine; I'll be there tomorrow."

"What did the doctors say?" Vince asked.

"Not much," Steve replied. "I thought my damn heart was going to explode."

Vince went to find out more.

It was odd to see Steve in a hospital bed without something broken or torn. He wanted to look his best and be his best, so he completely overdid his diet and training. But he was also fighting severe panic attacks. He was anxious about bowing out and about how to give the people the Stone Cold they knew and loved one last time.

Anxiety wasn't a term Austin wanted to use, sitting there in a Seattle hospital in an ass-less gown. He did overload on caffeine and he did train himself into the ground—he did go too far with too much in too short a period of time—but it was all driven by the sheer panic of not being perfect. And it scared him when it all caught up to him and his body began to react. No one can live on caffeine, energy drinks, anxiety, and no sleep. Not even Stone Cold Steve Austin.

"I need to get out of Dodge," he said. Steve's head was down; I could tell he was emotional. "I'm damn near afraid to look anyone in the face," he said.

Well, now I had to hide the fact I was emotional because he was emotional. Neither of us big tough bulls were going to cry. Okay, there was only one truly tough bull there, but if he wasn't going to show a softer side, then neither was I, goddamnit.

"I'm emotional too," I said to him. I cracked easily.

"You are?" Steve asked.

"Yeah," I said.

"You big baby," he said.

There was a manly pause; the kind guys have when they're worried about something but can't say it.

"Okay, then," I said.

"Okay," he said.

I tried to think of something to say. "Okay," I muttered.

"Yep," he replied. "Exactly."

Through the glass in the door, I could see Vince in the hallway talking to a doctor.

"I just want to make sure the people see me at my best," Steve said. "I don't want to go out stinking up the joint."

And in that second, I saw the mental anguish that perfectionism brings to a person. Steve was a handsome, jacked-up dude in his thirties with a bank full of money and all the fame he could handle—yet he couldn't shake the feeling of not being good enough. It was just as debilitating as his bum neck or bad knees.

The perfectionist attitude that had propelled him to the top of the mountain was now beginning to turn on him.

"We'll deal with tomorrow when that comes," I said. "Let's get you healthy."

THE NEXT DAY when I came back for him, he was looking better, but his head was still down. He had slept, and they had pumped fluids into him, but his mind was still gnawing away.

We got in the car and left the hospital. Austin wasn't a sociable creature on the best of days, but today he didn't want to see anyone or anything.

"Do you want me to say something on commentary?" I asked him. "About this being your last match?"

"Hell no," Steve replied. "We don't want to depress the people during the show. I'll ride off into the sunset quietly."

The biggest money draw in wrestling, the man who had changed the meaning of "WWE Superstar," was asking to retire without fuss. It was the measure of the man, the guy I knew behind the persona of Stone Cold.

"I want to go out on my back," he said. "The Rock did the honors for me in our last two matches, I'd like to do right by him."

Austin understood the traditions of the business: that when you leave, you leave it better than you found it. No one could say that Steve Austin didn't leave WWE in better shape than he found it.

"I'm feeling sick, Jim," he said. I knew he didn't want me to answer him back; he just wanted to say what was on his mind to a friend who would listen. "I don't know what I can do in this match. I don't know what my body has left in it. You think I can get this done with my neck and knees the way they are?"

I nodded. I knew he could do just about anything he wanted.

"Vince isn't closing the show with you guys," I said.

Steve breathed a huge sigh of relief. And in that second, I knew he really was done. Any other time, Stone Cold Steve Austin would have challenged the boss about not being on top of the card. But this time, this day, Steve knew Vince was trying to help calm him. The chairman was taking the pressure of closing the show with a bang off Austin's shoulders.

Not only didn't the fans know this was goodbye, but most of the people in WWE didn't know either.

At thirty-eight years old, Steve was retiring from a physical sport after a physical career. It wasn't the money that had gotten him into wrestling, and it sure wouldn't be the money that could lure him back.

"WITH THREE ROCK BOTTOMS," I said as the match finished, "The Rock has defeated Stone Cold Steve Austin at *WrestleMania*."

The mat was stained with Stone Cold's blood. His body was flat as The Great One sat next to him. It was the end of a battle, a rivalry, and an era.

"You are looking at, ladies and gentlemen, two of the greatest, when it's all said and done, that this business will have ever offered you. They gave you everything they had here tonight."

The Rock stooped down into Austin's ear and talked to him as Stone Cold stayed flat on the mat. It was a sign of respect. The Rock stood, saluted the crowd, and gave Stone Cold Steve Austin the ring to himself. Usually the victor stays for the applause, but this wasn't a usual circumstance, and The Rock was a traditionalist at heart, having been raised in the business. He wanted Steve to have the ring.

"This was a night that I know in my heart I will never forget as long as I live," I said as The Brahma Bull walked the aisle back through the curtain.

Austin rolled to the outside, and the crowd began to chant.

"That's one proud man," I said of Stone Cold as he limped toward the back. "He gave us everything he had, every fiber of his being. He laid it out there tonight."

I was trying hard to stick to Steve's wishes—to not say that this was it—but I wanted the world to know just what I thought about him as he walked up the ramp. My true emotions were trying to bust out, but I just wanted to do the best job I could to see Steve off.

Nearly sixty-thousand people in attendance, and one million more around the world, watched as Austin walked off the stage and took in the sights and sounds.

"Austin is saluting these fans here at *WrestleMania*. There's only one Texas Rattlesnake, and there'll never be another like him," I said.

There was one more amazing match left on the card, but I couldn't wait to get backstage to see my friend.

"How are you feeling?" I asked.

"Relieved," he said. "There's a weight off my back, and I can ride off in peace."

If ever any man in this business had earned his retirement, it was my friend, Stone Cold Steve Austin.

THIRTEEN

THE CORPORATE AX

Moving in a Different Direction

I GOT MY FINANCIAL AFFAIRS IN ORDER; I looked over my life and was happy with what I had achieved. My health was failing, and I knew instinctively it would be bad. Both my parents had died in their early sixties; I wasn't designed for longevity.

By 2004, my stomachaches were becoming so painful that I began to self-medicate with pain pills, Xanax, and Crown Royal, which I was drinking like Snapple. It was a stupid decision, but it was the only way I could think of where I didn't have to tell my wife or my boss that there was anything wrong.

That combination usually helped during the day, but at night I was overusing Ambien to sleep. My existence soon became miserable, as I veered between exhaustion, pain, stress, and drunkenness. I was scared stupid, and I didn't want anyone at work to know.

I had already suffered two bouts of Bell's palsy and a number of humiliating "firings"; I didn't want to throw this up on the table too. I already felt the ax above my neck, so I was sure this would be the thing to push me over the professional cliff. Turns out I had already been pushed—I just didn't know it yet.

Whatever management's feelings about my appearance and vitality as an announcer, in my administration role I knew I was doing good work. My team and I had built the most successful roster in the history of WWE—and we had a whole new crop of future main-eventers and Hall of Famers in the pipeline. But this was the wrestling business, and new was always better, even if it wasn't right.

I'd heard rumors that my time in talent relations was coming to an end, but not one single word was mentioned to me before Vince said, "I'm moving in a different direction, J.R."

We were backstage in a makeshift office just before our TV taping was to begin.

"Different direction?" I asked.

Vince nodded. "I want you to go down to the locker room and introduce Johnny as the new head of talent."

The Johnny he was talking about was John Laurinaitis, whom I'd hired from WCW. Johnny Ace, as he was known in our business, was my number two, and he had clearly set his sights on my job.

"Okay," I replied.

Vince, being Vince, moved on to some other piece of business, and that was it. The chairman had made his decision—no discussion, no feedback, no explanation. I was simply out. I didn't know what I'd done—or didn't do—to be pushed aside; I didn't ask, either. As usual, I wanted to be seen as the strong, silent type; or maybe I was afraid of the answer.

Vince talked constantly about respect in the wrestling business, and I, like a fool, bought it. Seemed to me, at that moment, that respect only flowed one way. I didn't even get a thank-you.

But, as always, I did what I was asked to do, and I introduced John in his new role. Even though a lot of the Boys side-eyed the decision, I kept my mouth shut; no one would see how much it broke my heart. My official line was, "Vince wanted to make a change, and that's what's happening."

It didn't really hit me until I saw a statement posted on WWE's website to make the change public and permanent:

> Jim Ross takes on Business Strategies position, John Laurinaitis to head WWE Talent Relations. Jim Ross (J.R.) has moved to the new role of Executive Vice President, Business Strategies. In this role, Jim will work closely with Vince McMahon, WWE Chairman, as an advisor on WWE's core business, as well as new business endeavors. He will continue as the famous "black hat" announcer on WWE *Monday Night Raw*. John Laurinaitis has been promoted to Vice President of Talent Relations and will assume all the responsibilities of the Talent Relations Department.

It was the first time I ever felt ambivalent about my overall place in WWE. I still loved the business, and I knew I had so much left to give, but I was worn down from the constant politics of simply working there.

I was also physically hurting from the anxiety of having to look over my shoulder all the time, wondering where my next humiliation was coming from or what would happen to my job.

But I wanted to tough it out. I wanted to be who my father expected his son to be. I wanted to be the man whom I thought Jan would respect more. I wanted to be the good soldier whom Vince hired.

THAT MEANT HELPING JOHN in my old role because I believed that would help the company. I gave him every piece of information I had, all the knowledge I had collected over the years.

He asked me to continue doing the payroll because he "hadn't the time." I felt stuck: If I didn't do it, people wouldn't get paid, and I certainly didn't want to go to Vince and make it look like I was ratting on the guy who took my job.

So I just put my head down and continued to do payroll. I'd do all the numbers and FedEx them to John, who'd "make changes" and submit them to Vince. In truth, there were very few changes made; Vince was getting my payroll and paying Johnny for it. I knew it wouldn't be long before Vince found out himself. John didn't know the numbers, and Vince generally liked to drill down into the reasoning behind certain payments.

"You still doing payroll, J.R.?" Vince asked me after a couple of months.

"Just helping out," I replied.

"What the fuck is Johnny doing?"

"He's just finding his feet," I said.

"Don't do it anymore."

"Well, okay," I said. "But I didn't want us to be late on people's money."

"That payroll will be done," Vince said. "I'll make sure of it."

And he did. No one was paid late, and the last part of my talent relations job was handed over. It was framed later like I'd been given a promotion; they even came up with a "Senior VP of Business Strategies" title for me to move into, but I was never even told what the head of business strategies does. I had a sneaking suspicion it didn't matter. It was simply etched on a door that led to a big new office. The second I walked in, I knew I'd never feel comfortable there, because to me this was the retirement home, built to keep me away from the real work that I loved.

I did use the quiet of the office to think, though. My phone wasn't ringing and my doorway wasn't busy; I didn't have the pressure of payroll, nor the headaches of talent issues; I wasn't scouting anyone or negotiating a deal.

And I hated it.

I got in my car and went home instead. I wanted to see Jan and get her take on what was happening. "You remember that meeting you once had with Linda McMahon?" my wife said.

"What meeting?" I asked.

Jan replied, "When Linda thanked you for all you do for Vince."

"Yeah, I remember."

"What did she say just before she left?"

I knew where my wife was heading. "She told me not to get too close to the flame."

Jan put her hand in mine and said, "That was a warning, sweetheart."

The trappings of an office and a fancy title were never the appeal. If the company didn't have any use for me at headquarters in Stamford, then I wanted to go home.

My real home: Oklahoma.

FOURTEEN

THE OUTHOUSE

From the Farm to the Garden

"J.R., HOW WOULD YOU LIKE TO MAIN-EVENT IN THE GARDEN?" Vince asked. Hunter needed a little something extra in the run-up to his match with Batista in 2005, and the chairman thought I could help out.

By "help out," I mean get my ass beat. But it was the Garden, the venue I had grown up dreaming about, and if my entrance fee was an ass-kicking, then I was happy to pay that tab. It wasn't a "comedy" angle, wasn't a "laugh at J.R." angle; it was an old-school, blood-and-black-eyes angle. It was the kind of stuff that excited the younger me when I listened to Skandor Akbar talking about wrestling in the Garden. Back then I was just breaking in as a referee, and the only way I figured I might get to MSG was to officiate a big match, not *compete* in one.

It's hard to explain to anyone outside of our business just how romantic it is to see your own blood, midring, in the most famous venue in the world.

As much as I hated to "wrestle," the Garden itself made me look forward to it.

"We want Hunter to be a bully," Vince explained as he put on his gravelly pitching voice. "We want the audience to hate his guts for what he's doing to J.R.—just despise him."

"What's he going to be doing to J.R.?" I asked.

Vince paused. "Well, he's going to beat the shit out of you."

"No, I get that. But what kind of beating should I expect?"

"A good one."

"Good for him or good for me?"

"Well, it's probably not going to be good for you, Jim," Vince replied.

That made sense, I suppose. The aim of the game here was to make Triple

H look like a dastardly heel who luxuriated in beating up an out-of-shape older man.

I said, "I want to get my own color out there."

Vince nodded.

I felt a man had to have some pride. If I was main-eventing Madison Square Garden, I was going to cut my own damn forehead doing it.

Backstage on the night, my dander died. When you're a week away from getting punched you can run your mouth. When you're an hour away from being punched you shut your mouth and pray.

Good ol' J.R. was praying.

"You okay, Jim?" Hunter asked.

I nodded.

"You're okay with getting your own color?" he asked.

"Oh yeah," I said.

Triple H nodded and left. "See you out there," he shouted back.

Arn Anderson, an all-time great performer who now produces backstage, broke a piece of razor blade and taped it to my wrist supports to hide it.

I wore black jeans; it's easier to hide fear with black. I put on a white T-shirt and my Oklahoma Sooners jersey over that—all part of the plan.

Time came quickly. I was ready to main-event in my childhood church. My music played and I came through the curtain; my nerves were gone. I was just thrilled to know I had made it to a place that so few of my colleagues ever got to. I was suddenly keenly aware of all the talents on all the car rides, all the small payoffs in all the territories—every one of them was hoping for what I was experiencing: to walk that aisle in the most famous arena in the world.

The man in me didn't feel worthy, but the boy in me was blown away.

I took an extra few seconds to look around and soak it all in. Jan was in the crowd; I could see how happy for me she was. She also didn't know what was about to happen. I usually told her everything, but I didn't want her worried about me unnecessarily, because even though I knew what was waiting for me, I also knew *who* was waiting for me.

Triple H is a pro's pro and he knew exactly how to maximize my value to the story without taking advantage of me or my inexperience. If anyone was going to take the best care of me in the middle of an ass-whooping, The Game was that very man.

The bell rang, and The Game offered to shake my hand—a classic heel move. I refused, making me look somewhat tough for two seconds, before the mauling began.

I got in one shot but was then whooped unmercifully. On cue, the referee stepped in, and Hunter backed the official into the corner to argue his position. This took the focus from me so I could juice, brother. My time was now. Out came the blade, I did my business, and then lay there waiting for the crimson mask to appear.

Triple H picked me up off the canvas and surveyed my handiwork as he punched my face.

"Okay, J.R.," he whispered. "Here we go."

Triple H had made his own blade, knowing that I was a rookie at this—but I knew what "here we go" meant.

Hunter was going to finish the job on my forehead, as I hadn't struck oil myself. I had tried, I felt I had gotten in there enough to produce the magic color. But when you've never sliced your own forehead before it's hard to tell what's the optimum amount of blade and pressure to get you where you want to go.

Like a good doctor, The Game was so precise he made it feel like nothing more than a bee sting. I didn't even have time to think before I felt the warmth of my own blood streaming down my face.

What a weird and wonderful business I was in: Another man had cut me open out of respect, to make sure that I could walk back through the curtain having upheld my end of the deal. It was like being in a normal job where one guy helps another get his job done to complete the task in hand—except mine involved a sharp blade and my own blood.

Hunter had helped me with my job, and now he went about his own. Every punch he threw I felt, but none of them destroyed me. The Game did exactly what he needed to do to make the people hate him. *Boom! Boom!* More punches to the head. I was falling on the ropes. He took my belt from my jeans and whipped me with it. He wrapped it around his hand and went to work some more on the open wound. He tore off my beloved Sooners jersey to reveal a crisp white T-shirt underneath—because nothing underlines violence more than blood on white.

I was bleeding like a stuck pig.

And then, mercifully, my beating was over. Triple H's real opponent, Batista, made the save. As I lay on the mat, I listened for the crack of a steel chair as The Animal laid out Hunter. Batista then grabbed my wrist and dragged me over to an "unconscious" Hunter. My arm was draped over The Game and one . . . two . . . three! I had beaten the multitime World Champion in the main event at Madison Square Garden.

I couldn't wait to get backstage and bask in the glory of being through a war with the Boys. I was battered, bloody, and happy.

Unlike Jan.

I hadn't told her what was going to happen, and she was worried out of her mind. From her point of view, her untrained, overweight, fifty-something husband had just been assaulted on live television.

The athletic commission doctor wanted to give me four stitches, but I knew Jan wanted to get out of there. She couldn't wrap her head around how this was okay, that grown men would do this for money. She didn't come from the wrestling business, but she had grown to love it—except on this night.

"I want to go, Jim," she said.

I think she might have been afraid of blowing, and saying the wrong things to the wrong people. I could totally understand: She was protective of me.

The doctor glued me shut, and Jan had a car service waiting. For the first time in our marriage, I could see she didn't like what I did for a living. She was shaking; we didn't talk all the way back to Connecticut.

I should have warned her. I had wanted to prove I was a man, but I didn't want to worry my wife. I was caught between my two strongest desires: to prove my manliness and to protect Jan from everything bad.

No, I'm Good with It

I COULDN'T HIDE IT ANY LONGER: Jan finally made me tell her what was going on with my stomachaches and sleep troubles.

I was walking around WWE feeling like someone was trying to put a bullet in my career. After being fired, hired, humiliated, and relieved of duties, my ego was fragile—but my health more so.

I was worried that even though I wasn't needed at WWE corporate headquarters, if I tried to move home to Oklahoma, it would seem like I was cashing out my chips.

"Honey," Jan said, "if you want to go home, we'll go home."

I knew she'd follow me to the ends of the earth if she had to.

After months of debating, I decided the fancy new office I was given after being "promoted" out of talent relations was useless to me. It looked good but meant nothing. After decades on the road, I wanted to be closer to my friends and family, closer to my doctors.

I just needed to tell the chairman my plans.

As I was now primarily an announcer, I asked Vince if he had any issues with me moving back home to Oklahoma. I knew there was some precedent, with newer announcers like Michael Cole not living in Connecticut, and older names like Gorilla Monsoon, who was never situated there in his time either.

"If I'm primarily going to be just an on-air talent moving forward, then I could get to wherever the company needed me from home," I said.

"It's fine," Vince replied. "I don't have a problem with it."

"So, you're sure?" I said.

"J.R., I don't want to talk about it anymore," the chairman replied. "I said I'm good with it, so go home."

Something was awry. I knew by his tells that he didn't like talking about me moving, but I took him at his word.

Jan and I moved to Norman, Oklahoma, and I set up my home office for any WWE business that might need it. The joy of being home almost made me forget the agony I was in. Everything was clicking into place and I began to ease into the administration-free life that WWE had chosen for me.

Jan and I were enjoying our new home, with family around and meals by the pool. I even made an appointment with a specialist to find out what was causing the crippling pain in my stomach.

I was sure being in Oklahoma was going to be good for me mentally and physically, but I'm not sure the chairman felt the same.

"We're going in another direction, J.R.," Vince said.

We were in Waco, Texas, at a TV taping, and Kevin Dunn was there too.

"What does that mean?" I asked.

"We're taking you off TV," Vince said. "You finish up tonight."

"And you're telling me this now?" I replied. "I have to do two hours of live TV with this on my mind?"

I felt ambushed, even though there were always rumors about this guy or that guy replacing me.

"Can I say goodbye?" I asked.

"No, say nothing," Vince replied.

The boss's rush to move me from TV led me to believe that there was already another plan in place.

I nodded and walked for the door. "I gotta tell you, Vince," I said. "This is completely unprofessional that you're telling me my career is over and then putting me on the air."

Vince had reached out to Ultimate Fighting Championship's Mike Goldberg to replace me on commentary. Mike was great at his job in the mixed martial arts world, but he wasn't a wrestling fan and didn't know the first thing about our business. Still, Vince wanted him to sign and go on the air immediately—taking my seat.

I only knew what WWE was doing because I was kept in the loop by an old friend, Marc Ratner, the executive director of the Nevada State Athletic Commission. Marc was also a friend of Mike Goldberg's.

It felt like a punch in the gut, being told by an outsider what was happening to me in my own company.

"I told Mike," Marc said to me over the phone, "that replacing J.R. isn't a good play. The WWE fans would hate him for taking your place."

I appreciated Marc's call, but I was still steaming.

In the end I heard back that Mike Goldberg didn't sign. He didn't like the cloak-and-dagger approach, and he wanted to stay connected to his MMA roots.

It didn't matter, because Vince had decided to take me off TV anyway—and he was going to use most of his family to do it.

Showtime quickly came, Vince's music hit, and out strutted Mr. McMahon. The week prior, Stone Cold had attacked the whole McMahon family, and now the patriarch was looking to take his bad mood out on somebody else.

That would be me.

"Who deserves to be fired here tonight?" he asked. "I'm not gonna blame Austin, and I'm not even going to fire Stone Cold."

No, that would be me.

After telling the audience they were fired, Vince summoned all three who were at the announce position the week before to join him in the ring. He said it was bad enough that neither The King, Coachman, nor I never went to help him or Shane, but he was appalled we didn't make the save for Stephanie or Linda McMahon.

Coachman groveled, while The King was more measured in his apology, but both men were forgiven by their benevolent boss and sent out of the ring.

That left just me and the boss.

"J.R., looks like I can have myself some fun here in a minute," Vince said.

He wasn't kidding.

I reluctantly apologized, but that wasn't enough. The chairman called out his daughter, Stephanie McMahon, to make sure she got in on the act too. "Ladies and gentlemen, the most beautiful woman in the whole world," Vince announced as his only daughter walked the ramp.

Steph got into the ring. "J.R., apologize to me," she demanded.

Vince whipped the microphone from her hand and got in my face. "I'm not asking you to get on your hands and knees," Vince proclaimed with a smile. "Although that might be the next step."

The chairman was clearly having fun at my expense. I couldn't help but lament the waste. The whole point of an angle like this is that the good guy gets his revenge in the end, and I sure knew that wasn't going to happen. All of this time on the air with the main bad guys could have been used to build up someone backstage instead of spending it on an old announcer on his last night.

"The floor is J.R.'s," Stephanie said. "Apologize or get fired."

She put the mic in my face. "I'm sorry your momma got Stunned," I said, referencing Stone Cold's finishing move, the Stone Cold Stunner.

Steph wasn't happy with my reply. She slapped me across the face, and I fell to my hands and knees. I got up, looking pissed—because I was pissed. I didn't mind doing whatever was needed if it was going to benefit someone. But this wasn't doing shit for anyone.

Vince called his son, Shane, out, while I stood there like a dumbass holding my face. Instead, Vince's wife, Linda, made her entrance.

"My God, you look lovely tonight," Vince said to his wife as she stepped through the ropes. "This is really no place for you. Steph and I have got this. No need to get your hands dirty."

Linda meekly took the mic. "Well, Vince, as your devoted wife—and Steph, as your mother—I just simply cannot let the two of you continue this way."

The audience sighed, hoping it was over. But I knew we still had one more piece of business to take care of.

Linda continued, looking at Vince: "The only way to garner respect from people isn't by yelling and screaming. It's by taking action."

Mrs. McMahon stood between me and Vince and linked my arm. "So, J.R., on behalf of the entire McMahon family . . . you're fired."

The audience couldn't have hated this more. Linda was turning heel on good ol' J.R. for no other reason than that it didn't matter. I walked to Vince to plead my case, but Linda kicked me right in the family jewels. No cup: I was tough that way.

Down went J.R. again, with the sound of the McMahons laughing in my ear.

I knew Linda was getting nothing from this; she had already apologized profusely to me before the show, and she seemed genuinely upset at the thought of having to hit me at all. I assured her that it would be fine, but I could tell she wanted nothing to do with this. (Years later, that kick came back to haunt Linda a little when she moved into political life and her opponent replayed the kick in an ad to embarass her.)

But there I was, on live TV, holding my junk as Vince clapped like a seal.

"You're fired, J.R.," he shouted again, 'cause he's subtle that way. "You heard it: You're fired."

"You're Gonna Want to Watch"

I WENT HOME FEELING LIKE SHIT.

I was off TV, out of talent relations, in pain, humiliated, drinking too much, taking too many painkillers and sleeping pills. I knew, by 2005, that I needed to make some changes in my life.

I had ridden out another couple of weeks since being fired on TV, but Jan couldn't stand to watch me in so much pain anymore, so I finally went to my GP and he checked me out.

"Jim," he said in that voice doctors use when they want you to listen carefully, "we need to check further."

Jan and I drove to the hospital ourselves; she could tell that I was nervous.

"Is this why you've been acting weird lately?" she asked.

"I don't want to know what it is," I said.

"We're going to figure this out together, no matter what it is."

I'd been keeping it in for so long that finally just acknowledging I was worried felt like a load off my shoulders. Still, I was dreading the actual news. I knew that the kind of pain I was in, for as long as I was in it, couldn't be good.

In the hospital, I ended up in the ICU almost immediately. "Mr. Ross, we need to fix this now."

"Fix what?" I asked.

"We can see serious damage to the colon, and we need to take a further look immediately."

I held my wife's hand as my whole world began to collapse in around me. I was a fatalistic person; hearing the specialist just confirmed all my own worst thoughts. I had tried to be the man my father raised and tough it out. But in the end, my body was closing down, and no amount of toughness was going to make it better.

I needed to get opened up, and it needed to happen immediately.

"Shane called," Jan said. "He's been asking for you."

"McMahon?" I asked.

"He wants to know if it's okay to update their website with how you're doing."

"That's fine," I said. "Nice of him to call."

I took the daunting ride to the operating theater with Jan by my side. I looked up and saw how strong she was. There was no doubt in her mind that we were going to end up better than ever. Just watching her composure settled me; her faith steadied me and her love reassured me. This thing that I'd been running from, that I'd been scared by, I could finally face it head-on because my wife was there with me.

And out I went—unconscious and into the unknown.

Diverticulitis had destroyed thirteen whole inches of my colon. The surgeons cut, inch by inch, until they were satisfied that they had gotten all the affected area. Because the damage was so severe, I had been poisoning myself with waste finding its way into the bloodstream. The accumulative damage was so great that I was less than thirty days from death by the time I'd found my way to the hospital.

I spent eight days in the ICU before they'd let me go home. But home I went.

"SHANE SAYS THAT ALL THE FANS ARE ASKING FOR YOU," Jan said as she tucked me in. "Your being in the hospital was a huge story online, and the fans are flooding the company with well wishes."

It felt great to be home, and even better to know that I meant something to the fans and the company. Word was that WWE was going to give everyone an update on *Raw* that night.

I heard my home phone ring and Jan answer; she came through with a huge smile on her face. "It's Vince," she said.

I was in my reclining chair, as any other position on any other piece of furniture was too painful. I spent weeks in that position before I was well enough to move around freely.

"Hello?"

"Hey, J.R., you're gonna want to watch *Raw* tonight. I've put something on there you'd like to see."

"Okay," I said, intrigued.

"Well, okay then, you really should watch," he said, hanging up.

Vince didn't seem interested in any updates on my health. He just wanted to make sure I was watching TV later that night.

I checked my cell phone, and it was loaded with texts from everyone in the business. I felt like a kid who was recovering comfortably at home after a scare. But more than that, I felt loved and appreciated—and out of my mind on pain medication.

Raw started, but I knew I wasn't going to be able to stay awake. My eyes were rolling an hour in. They announced on that air that the update on J.R. was going to close the show.

That's when small alarm bells began to sound in my mind.

"You're the main event," Jan said, smiling beside me.

I hadn't the heart to tell her that there was no way they were putting me on last without making something of it.

"I wonder what they're going to do," she said.

I smiled back, my guts twisting a little. I knew my daughters were watching too.

I couldn't fight it any longer and fell asleep.

I awoke to see Jan upset across from me.

"WHAT'S THE MATTER WITH HIM?" Jan asked, with tears in her eyes.

"Who?" I asked, already knowing the answer.

"Vince," she replied.

I'd missed the whole thing but I watched a replay.

My segment opened with a shot of a medical facility, and I knew by the setup that we were about to get one of WWE's classic "comedy" bits. Into the operating theater we went, and there was my black hat on a dummy on the bed.

"All right, J.R., time for your colon surgery, and we're going to get to your blockages—there's no doubt about that," Vince said, dressed in surgical gear. "We have a crack team here. I'm Dr. Heinie," Vince said, introducing himself. He then pointed to a blonde actress who was standing beside him in a tight nurse's uniform and push-up bra. "This is Nurse Slobberknockers," the chairman of a billion-dollar company said.

They pulled back my surgical gown and a plastic ass was exposed in the air, punctuated by gas noises. This was Vince's favorite kind of comedy. They piped in some of my wrestling calls while the chairman checked to see if his stethoscope worked on the nurse's chest.

I couldn't look at my wife, even as she tried to catch my eye. I was afraid of my reaction.

Vince proceeded to listen to the ass and heard a toilet flushing.

"Okay, this is going to be severe, J.R.," he said.

You don't say, Boss.

For the next five or six minutes I watched in silence as Vince pretended to pull implements from my ass on live TV. A football, an owl, a hand, a goldfish, and on and on, until Vince pulled out a mannequin head that was meant to be me.

"Hey, J.R.," Vince said into the camera. "I think we've solved the problem: You've got your head up your ass."

The chairman then pushed my body from the operating table to make room for the rubber-clad nurse to lie down. Vince kissed the nurse's cleavage as the Oklahoma fight song played out the scene.

I turned it off and wanted to cry. I was beaten down, medicated, sore, tired, vulnerable, and now humiliated, again.

"Whenever we meet him, he's nice to us," Jan said. "Why does he do this to you?"

Truth was, the chairman wasn't like anyone I knew. He could be cold and spiteful and an asshole without much effort.

Someone in creative had stuck me good with this skit, but Vince was relishing every word and every chance to kick me further. His eyes were alive, and his face was painted with joy.

"He's like Michael Jackson," Jan said. She was even more angry than before. "He's built his own bubble around himself and has no idea how to live outside of it."

As much as I was hurting, I felt twice as bad for my wife. She had no idea why they'd close the show just to hurt me, to further humiliate me. I had no answers for her. I didn't know why they'd do it to me either.

"The fans will hate them for doing that to you," she said.

"Vince doesn't care what people think," I replied. "Vince talks about respect all the time, but he has no idea what it means."

As much as I nearly fell into my default mode of trying to analyze and explain Vince, I caught myself. "He's a strange cat, and I doubt even he knows why he does what he does sometimes."

I lay at home, my phone lighting up with messages from people disgusted by Vince, but I didn't want to talk to anyone. I was relieved to get my health scare sorted and to be at home with my loving wife, but everything else just felt like a mess.

FIFTEEN
SMOOTH SAILING . . . FOR NOW

A Neutral Show

"J.R.?"

"Yeah?"

"It's Kevin."

I was on my patio. It had been about eight months since Linda McMahon kicked me in the balls and Vince fired me on live TV. Kevin Dunn, WWE's executive producer, board member, and Vince McMahon's confidant, was on the phone.

"Hey, Kevin."

"We need you to come back," he said.

"When?"

"Well, *Saturday Night's Main Event*, on NBC."

My heart began racing a little with excitement. This was a big assignment in the company, as WWE hadn't produced a *Saturday Night's Main Event* with NBC in almost fifteen years.

"Okay," I said.

"Okay?"

"Okay."

Kevin hung up; there wasn't much more to say. They asked, and I agreed. I was still under contract with WWE, but they had just decided not to use me on TV. Instead I was a "consultant."

Jan popped her head out the door.

"Was that them?" she asked.

"Yeah," I said.

She smiled. "Told you they'd call," she said, before going back into the house. Jan still found it hard to talk about WWE, but she knew I was miserable without doing what I loved to do.

I took a little time to think: to weigh up all my options, what I wanted to do, and what I felt I had left to prove. Fact was, there were plenty of terrible jobs out there I could go do. But my dream job was still open, and despite WWE's best efforts to replace me, they were finding it hard.

I still wanted to be the voice. Maybe it was my fragile ego, or maybe it was the two ex-wives and current lifestyle I liked for Jan and me—but I was willing to go back.

I got into bed that night and made peace with the knowledge that my walk to the pay window every month in WWE might be scattered with indignities. But as in any sometimes-dysfunctional relationship, I convinced myself that it would be better this time.

Jan was awake too. "Why do you think they're bringing you back?"

"Vince didn't like the other guys he brought in."

"But why now?" Jan asked.

She was right: Why this event? "Well," I said, "this is NBC, and I know Dick Ebersol was as puzzled as anyone when I was taken off the air."

Ebersol was the guy who hired me for the XFL and was a huge fan of my work; he was also a major executive at NBC and a longtime friend of Vince's.

"You think Dick said something to Vince?" Jan asked.

"That I'll never know," I said. "Vince never says if he makes a mistake."

I could tell my wife was a little anxious about me going back. She'd seen a lot of stuff that had upset her and a lot of stuff that had upset me.

"You don't have to go back, you know that, right?" she said. "We can make some changes. I just want you to be happy."

"Going live makes me happy," I said. "The other stuff not so much."

"If you're sure." Jan reassuringly patted my hand and turned around to sleep. "It will be interesting to see how they announce it."

My wife was right: WWE and Vince needed a reason for bringing me back that wasn't anything to do with them being just plain wrong. The angle they eventually took was that this was a neutral show, in which *Raw* and *SmackDown* Superstars were both on the card, so only a voice that wasn't on either show would make sense. Even though my partners were Jerry Lawler, who was still on *Raw*, and Tazz, who was on *SmackDown*.

But I was a businessman first. The details of how to get me back on-screen didn't matter, as long as I was back. I loved being live on the air more than anything else in the world. All the politics, childish pranks, bad writing, and professional maneuverings couldn't touch me once I was let loose to talk to the world.

I was honored WWE had come to me with such a high-profile job. I was proud they had put the responsibility into my hands.

And I missed commentating.

There was only so many times I could "consult," while I was off the air, before my mind started to wander back to calls I'd make or pictures I'd paint if I was back on the air. The habit of describing the action that I had picked up with my father as a kid never left me. And I hoped it never would.

So I went back to work again.

Backstage, one of the bigger hugs I got was from Stephanie McMahon. She told me just how happy she was to have me back, and I knew she meant it. She embraced me a second longer—and with a tiny bit more force than usual for a passing courtesy.

And then there were the Boys.

Wrestlers up and down the card were happy to see me. I wasn't their boss anymore, but I'd helped bring in almost everyone there, giving them their first contracts and opportunities. It felt like that brotherhood we talked about all the time was real. I was returning back to my road family, who embraced me fully.

WHY I WAS BACK WAS NEVER DISCUSSED; it was just business as usual. Everyone involved in the production end of the show knew that Jerry, Tazz, and I would be seamless out there. My old dance partner and I had been separated, fired, left, returned, moved, and reshuffled a million times before. We knew this game better than anyone, and we could effortlessly roll back together when needed.

I was adamant that I didn't want to let any more negativity into my life. I was healthy, I was happy, and I was back doing what I loved to do: talking to the people at home.

"Welcome, everyone, to *Saturday Night's Main Event*! The historic Cobo

Arena has been sold out for weeks, as WWE returns to *Saturday Night's Main Event* on NBC, after almost a fifteen-year absence."

Triple H's music blasted out on cue, and we were off and running. Commentary, production, and talent were all working like seamless cogs in a giant crazy wheel.

"Hello, everybody, I'm Jim Ross, and it's nice to be back on WWE television." I felt The King pat me on the back as that sentence rolled off my tongue. "A Boomer Sooner welcome," I said. "I'll be working tonight with Tazz, who will be calling the action of *SmackDown*. And representing *Raw*, of course, is the one and only Jerry 'The King' Lawler." I could feel the electricity, the goodwill, the excitement around me. "What a night here in Detroit for *Saturday Night's Main Event*."

Tazz chimed in: "We're all fired up. Hey, welcome back, J.R."

It felt great and natural to be out there again.

I got the impression that WWE's plans were for me to come out and call big matches and big events from time to time, but my sole intent was to prove just how good I was. I didn't care whom they hired, from what background or what age, shape, height, or accent. No one loved this business like I did. No one knew this business like I did. No one had the passion for this business that I had. And all of those things resonated with our audience. They could hear my love for what I was watching; they could connect with it, feel it while they were seeing it.

I knew in those first two minutes that I was doing what I loved to do most in this world.

My Highlight Reel

DONALD TRUMP WAS BODY-CONSCIOUS, to say the least. He arrived at our TV taping almost as fixated on the guys' bodies as on the women's. *Almost.* After a few minutes of walking around among the tightest, most ripped, tanned bodies on planet Earth, The Donald was suddenly wearing a large, heavy overcoat, even though he was clearly too hot.

We were on the build toward *WrestleMania 23* and the "Battle of the Billionaires" between Donald Trump and Vince McMahon.

Backstage, Trump's eyes were wandering, and because of WWE's new policy of hiring *Playboy*-type models for the women's division, there were plenty of places for The Donald's eyes to wander.

"I like passionate people," he said to me as he watched the Divas walk around backstage. He said it loud enough for them to hear. Trump was like a kid in a candy store at WWE. Everything in our world seemed to suit him—except the need to fight. I had seldom seen a WWE guest who was as nervous about getting physical as Donald was.

"You're going to look after me? You sure now, Vince?" Trump asked.

"I'll bring you through it," Vince replied.

"'Cause I don't want to look like a loser."

Vince laughed. "You won't, Donald, I'll make sure of that."

Vince was going to break out all the smoke and mirrors to make Trump look good. He'd add match stipulations and a special guest referee, surrogate wrestlers, even drop money on the fans. And those Divas that Donald liked so much—they would walk him to the ring.

With all the hype, I knew the path to *WrestleMania 23* was going to be an interesting one, but I had no idea just how personal and fulfilling it would be for me and my family.

It was in Chicago that they announced me as the last entrant into the Hall of Fame, Class of 2007. Kevin Dunn had told me the night before that it was going to happen, just as I was heading to happy hour.

"You're going in, J.R.," he said. "Congratulations."

It was a big deal for me. I was going in with some of the true greats in our business: The Sheik, Mr. Fuji, Nick Bockwinkel, Mr. Perfect, my longtime friend Dusty Rhodes, and my broadcast colleague, Jerry Lawler. All of these men had blazed their paths through our business, all had been wrestlers, all had been champions—except me. I was a wrestling fan who'd lucked into, and worked damn hard at, becoming an announcer whom people might like to remember fondly.

I was honored at the thought of sharing the stage with those men.

The next night, live on *Raw*, they announced my induction on the air and played a highlight reel on the arena screen and for the fans at home. I had known it was coming, but I wasn't prepared for the reaction. The applause grew so loud that I felt compelled to stand and thank the fans in the audience.

As I tried to sit down before the live camera came back to our table, The King grabbed my arm and kept me standing. "Vince told me to not let you sit back down," my partner said. "This is classic."

So I kept standing, and they kept cheering; I was completely caught off guard. I'd hoped some people might consider my career Hall of Fame worthy at some point, but wrestling was a star-led business, and I was just a commentator.

"There's just nobody better than Jim Ross," Steve Austin said to finish the emotional video package.

I couldn't see the fans' faces anymore because my damn eyes were watering so much.

"Ladies and gentlemen," The King said live over the microphone. "The newest member of the WWE Hall of Fame, good ol' J.R., Jim Ross!"

Sometimes it's only when you look back that you see the best moments of your life, but there in Chicago, in real time, I knew I was living one of mine. All the calls, all the matches, all the miles, all the humiliation, all the triumphs, all the money, all the heartbreak, the missed birthdays, the marriages at which I'd failed, all the times I called Jan to tell her I couldn't come home, all the fighting with Vince, all the good times with Vince . . .

It was all worth it.

It all meant something to the people in the arena, and it all meant the world to me. They sounded like they liked me, and for once, I liked me too.

As the cheers turned into chants of "J.R.!" I kept standing, and the people kept standing too. I waved, took off my hat, wiped my eyes, and they kept applauding. The longer it went on, the more I tried to control my tears, but I couldn't. There was nothing more validating than being told by the fans in a brutally honest big market like Chicago that you were worth something, that you had done something with your life that other people held so dear.

"You know whom you're going to get to induct you yet?" King asked after the show; he was working on getting Justin Timberlake to be his inductor.

I knew exactly whom I wanted to induct me.

"Hell, Jim, I'm not going to write nothing," Austin said when I asked him. "I just want to talk about you from my heart."

"I hope you don't write a speech," I said. "You've made a few dollars coming up with stuff on the microphone, and I was hoping you'd do that."

"Damn right I will."

I could tell it meant something to Steve to be asked, and it meant everything to me that he accepted.

On the night of the induction, I saw William Shatner backstage, looking a little nervous. As it turned out, The King couldn't line up dates with Timberlake, but, being the legend he was, he was able to arrange for Captain Kirk to come along and be his inductor instead.

"What do you mean there's no teleprompter?" Shatner said to a production guy as I walked past.

I had a feeling my guy wouldn't care.

It was showtime. Austin walked out, and the crowd went nuts.

"I'm out here tonight to help bring into the 2007 WWE Hall of Fame a very good friend of mine who has helped me out so much in my career. When I thought about what I might want to say, I've been thinking about it for some time, and I didn't really feel like writing anything down. I don't like doing that. I just wanted to come out here and start talking about Jim Ross. When I talk about Jim Ross, I'm going to bring out a guy who's probably . . .

well, he is one of the greatest announcers of all time. When I say 'one of the greatest announcers of all time' I'm not just talking about our business. I'm talking about any business. Whether it's Major League Baseball, professional football, college football . . . I mean the greatest of the greats to announce. That's what I think about Jim Ross. But let me be more specific and talk about WWE—or professional wrestling, sports entertainment, whatever we care to call it. He is the best of the best. When I say that, I say that with all due respect to Gordon Solie and every other announcer who's ever called a match. But tonight is the Hall of Fame and I'm calling it like it is. I'm calling it like I see it. I'm calling it like I believe it: Jim Ross is the best ever in this business."

Steve, off the cuff, was captivating the thousands in attendance. The more he progressed, the more nervous I got. I had no idea how I was going to follow one of the best of all time with my own speech.

Austin finished by saying: "I wanted to tell Jim just what he meant to my professional life, and my personal life. I say, 'Jim, I love you.' I told him that because I do."

They played a video package, and Steve invited me to the stage. I was already overwhelmed.

As I walked the steps onto the stage, everyone was standing—but out of all the faces looking back, the only one I could see was Jan's. Her eyes were full of tears, and her face was full of pride. After everything we'd been through, I suddenly realized that it must have been so cathartic for her to see and hear what it all meant.

I know it was for me too.

I started my speech. "Thank you, J.R.!" the fans chanted as I tried to stay on message. I was afraid that if I looked up I'd cry; it was that simple. But when I glanced up and saw my wife, my family, my peers standing again for me, and the fans chanting in the background, I couldn't help it. I wept.

I addressed the crowd as best I could. I tried to keep it brief, but it didn't end up that way. I had a couple of things on my mind, and I was happy to be exactly where I was, on a great and wonderful night.

It felt so ironic that, on WWE television, they were chipping away at me, trying to make me mean less to the people so I would become easier to replace. On this night, in front of these people, it felt like the more the company tried to keep me down the more the people got behind me.

Unfortunately, those battles at work had affected me at home, and I wasn't the easiest guy to live with. I was already a workaholic, but with my head on the chopping block I felt I needed to do more than ever just to stay alive professionally. My wife, looking radiant, had dealt with my shit and WWE's shit with grace and class, and as I spoke, I couldn't stop looking at her.

She was my world, and I was letting my job take me from her far more than it needed to. She would never say it, but I knew that all the bad times I went through were affecting her just as much as me. TV is TV, and wrestling is wrestling, but the family struggles in our business were real. You're either at *WrestleMania* or the local bingo hall; the boom-or-bust cycle in our business is especially merciless.

I soaked up every second, every chant, every good word, every thank you, and every time my Jan wiped her eyes. This night, at the Hall of Fame, with my Angel watching, I really felt like I had won.

SIXTEEN

SMOOTH SAILING IS VERY MUCH OVER

Blogging and Drafting

EVERY YEAR WWE HAD A DRAFT, in which Superstars would be traded between *Raw* and *SmackDown* to freshen up the creative opportunities and build new matchups. Word had gone around that this time WWE was going to include the announcers and referees as part of the talent pool for the 2008 draft.

The worst thing I did was open my mouth and say I didn't want to go to *SmackDown*. I should have known Vince would see it as a public challenge, and he'd make happen the one thing I said I didn't want to happen—me leaving the announce team on *Raw*.

I said:

> I can't speak for The King, but I am personally not interested in leaving *Monday Night Raw*. I hope that I didn't just jinx myself. Working regularly on another broadcast would feel strange at this stage of my game.

And:

> If you are like many wrestling fans, including me, and like surprises, then Monday night is certainly the night for you. I would wager a case of J.R.'s BBQ sauce that virtually no talent knows for sure what fate awaits them come Monday night. Indeed, speculation is running rampant regarding Monday's Annual WWE Draft, but that's all it is or can be at this point . . . speculation. I was asked by a WWE fan in the DFW Airport on Friday afternoon if I thought any

> of the announcers would be drafted and I answered "No" because at the end of the day does anyone truly care who announces what brand? And the same goes for the referees. I would be shocked to see any draft pick wasted on an announcer or a referee, as WWE fans want to see major Superstars change addresses and begin new rivalries along with making fresh matches.

These public thoughts were quickly brought to Vince's attention.

This highlighted for me the biggest change I'd seen in the boss since I came to WWE all those years before: his propensity for being goaded by others. Now, Vince has always been his own man with his own brilliant mind—but when I first came to his company, he was firm in his vision and concrete in its implementation. But somewhere along the way, the chairman amassed a circle of sycophants who learned what to say and when to say it if they wanted to get their way.

My blog post wasn't brought to Vince because anyone believed it to be a problem; it was brought to Vince because someone believed it to be an opportunity to steer the boss into messing with good ol' J.R. again.

The night before the draft, I asked Kevin Dunn at the Hyatt hotel bar if I was going to be moved from *Raw* to *SmackDown.*

"Are you kidding? You think we're stupid enough to break up our Madden and Summerall?" he said, referencing the most respected commentary duo in NFL history.

Even though we were all kept in the dark, Kevin was very much part of the inner circle—Vince's right-hand man—so I believed him. I knew Vince liked change for change's sake, but I felt fairly confident that he wouldn't tinker with one of the few parts of his show that was working—there were many other parts that needed his attention.

I should have known better.

Live, on the air, a cameraman was told through his headset to kneel in front of me and get my face good and tight on the screen. By this point, WWE had spent years trying to keep the camera *off* my face, so I knew that the camera wasn't so much for the audience at home but for the chairman in the back.

As they cut to my shot, they flashed a graphic underneath that said I was moving to *SmackDown*. I was shocked, and I started shaking my head in front of the world. I couldn't understand why it was so difficult to just let me do my damn job.

I felt betrayed—again—by Vince, who I knew was backstage having a great time with all his sycophants, laughing as they took me from the team that had guided the company through its highest-rated years.

And it wasn't the transfer to *SmackDown* that I was hot at—it was the ambush that truly got to me. It felt like nobody backstage really got how much my job and my profession meant to me and my family. I wished I could just take my check without getting my pride and integrity battered every time the boss decided he needed entertaining. If I could just stop caring so much, I knew I mightn't have gotten as sick as I did.

"You want a ride to *SmackDown*, J.R.?" Vince asked when I got to the back. The "ride" was the WWE corporate jet.

"No, I don't," I said. I didn't want to be around Vince at all, and I needed some time to call Jan.

I was reluctant to tell her, because she'd already heard it so many times over the years: me on the other end of the line, with the fight drained out of me.

"I'm thinking of quitting," I told her. Just the word "quit" felt wrong coming out of my mouth. My father had raised me to never do such a thing, no matter the situation.

"I'm okay with whatever you decide," she said. "I just want you to be happy—and working there isn't making you happy, honey."

"I've no suit. I can't wear the same clothes on TV two nights in a row," I said.

The *SmackDown* taping was the next night, and I needed to get there if I was going, with no time to go home and repack.

"You gonna go to *SmackDown*, then?" Jan asked.

"I can't let them beat me," I said. "I don't think I could live with myself if I let them push me out."

"I'm with you," she said. "Whatever you decide is best for you, I back you one hundred percent."

I looked at the clock in my hotel room: It was morning. I'd been on the phone all night with my wife.

With little or no sleep, I wrote on my website:

Some postdraft thoughts . . . As many of you know, I was "drafted" to *SmackDown* Monday night in the random lottery. Obviously, that means I will be leaving *Monday Night Raw* and my longtime partner, Jerry Lawler. I am not happy about this surprise development. I also contemplated calling it a career Monday night and not going to Houston to tape *SD.* After speaking with my wife and thinking on this matter until 6 a.m. Tuesday morning, I have decided to do the right thing for the fans who care and the talent who care and begin my new assignment. It has been explained to me that the WWE's *SmackDown* tenure on My Network is a high priority within the corporation. Allegedly, my presence is needed in that effort. Many are speculating about when I learned of this development . . . the same time those of you were watching at home. I should have detected something with the demeanor of certain individuals either thru their plastic, poker faces or the perceived smirk that I thought I might have seen on some of their faces during the day. As far as going to Connecticut each week to do *SmackDown* postproduction, that's not going to happen. Either Mick Foley can handle it or WWE can install a DSL line in my home to facilitate the work. I will miss working with The King as the wrestling biz is one in which a guy can count his legit friends on one hand . . . even after a 30-plus-year career. King has been like a brother to me . . . albeit an "older brother." ;) We will remain friends no matter that our team has been corporately imploded. I believe that I have been strongly loyal to WWE no matter the hands that were dealt to me over the years. In my tenure there I have earned a good living, of which I am thankful. I will fulfill my commitments that I have made because unlike many in the business, my word is still my bond. I can't predict how long my *SmackDown* tenure will be, but I can promise that no matter how long or short it is, I will do my utmost best while sitting at ringside. I am not the kind of man who will "phone in" a damn thing. My sincere thanks to all of you who have supported me on *Raw* over the years. I hope I was able to provide you a memory or two. Hopefully, we can create new memories now on *SmackDown*. Based on my professional experiences, I look at each broadcast as potentially my last, which helps keep me motivated. So with that said, we begin another chapter in my crazy life in the unpredictable world of 'rasslin'. I still plan on attending *Raw* in my home market of OKC next Monday and I hear that tickets are still available. Anyone have any extras? Boomer Sooner! J.R.

A few hours later, as I waited for my delayed flight to Houston from San Antonio, I updated my thoughts:

Upon further review . . . Changes in one's life take some adjusting to, especially at my stage of the game. This week I received an unexpected change in my professional address. Within hours of writing an emotional blog, I am positively moving on. I am going to do all I can to make *SmackDown* the best program WWE produces. Working side by side with Mick Foley should be fun. It will be entertaining, I assure you. Mick is a great friend and a man I greatly respect. The *SmackDown* roster is loaded with exceptional talent and WWE wants the brand to grow, and I intend to do all that I can in my role to facilitate that growth. The abruptness of the "trade" shocked me. I most likely responded in a nonprofessional way in the eyes of some fans. That's their prerogative and each has the right to their opinion, as do I. Not to be a cliché, but wrestling has been great to my family and me. I owe it to the business to "man up" and to kick ass on *SmackDown*. That's my plan. My emotions are what they are and I will not apologize for my candor or honesty. My feathers were ruffled . . . poor me. I still bring bona fide passion to every broadcast and fully expect to deliver come showtime. As I write this, I am in the midst of some travel delays, but I will definitely be in Houston and will be looking forward to "business picking up." I will practice what I have preached and I feel that after sleeping on this major change all things happen for a reason. Life is good. My tank has been refueled. Let's have some fun. For those of you that were offended by my earlier rant I apologize. For those that think ol' J.R. can't get the

> job done, I suggest you sit back and watch. I wish my good pal The King and Michael Cole great success, but my professional priority is to help *SmackDown* kick ass. In more ways than one, "the game is on." Boomer Sooner! J.R.

When I got to Houston, I bought a last-minute outfit at the Men's Wearhouse there. I got to the arena, and the writing staff was euphoric. Vince was looking for me, of course.

It was unusual for me to get to a venue midafternoon on the day of a show, so I'm sure some people were wondering if I'd come in at all.

"I'm disappointed in you," Vince said.

"Well, that's funny," I said. "Because I'm disappointed in you too."

Vince had clearly seen my blog posts. Out of respect for him and our relationship, we kept it cool and private.

"It's just business, J.R.," he said.

"What business wouldn't have been done if you'd just told me?" I asked.

Vince couldn't answer. "I wanted to keep things under wraps."

"Who do you think you're talking to, Vince?" I replied. "I've been keeping things under wraps here since the day I walked in."

I could see the chairman begin to dig in his heels. "Well, that's the way I decided to do it. We needed to see your real reaction on the air," he said. "And it's not just you, J.R. I've ruined my son-in-law's life by moving him to *SmackDown* too."

Triple H was now Vince's son-in-law, having married Vince's daughter, Stephanie.

"Was Hunter told he was moving?" I asked. "Did you give your son-in-law the courtesy of letting him know?"

"His life got changed around too," Vince said, expertly avoiding my question. "He's been drafted to a new show, just like you."

There was no point in trying to get Vince to see my point of view. The boss had made up his mind. After all, this was the sixth or seventh time I had been removed from the *Raw* booth. Why was I so surprised?

"I'm here to work," I said.

Vince put out his hand and I shook it, but I knew—and maybe he did too—that nothing would ever be the same between us. I was tired of being the butt of WWE jokes.

I found out a couple of days later that Triple H wasn't going to be on *SmackDown* after all, as Vince had changed his mind and wanted Hunter to remain on *Raw*.

After years of having Vince's trust, being his sounding board, and helping build WWE into a behemoth, I was now firmly on the outside. Guess the boss did mind my moving back to Oklahoma after all.

Leaving and Returning

MICK FOLEY IS KIND, smart, and articulate, a natural storyteller. His in-ring career in WWE was over, so he seemed like a slam-dunk for the commentary booth. If there was anything I was looking forward to on *SmackDown*, it was sharing commentary duties with Mick.

I did everything in my power to squelch my bitterness, trying to look at the positives of moving positions—the main advantage being I would be home more on the days my beloved Sooners were playing.

I wanted 2008 to be about more than just WWE, so Jan and I opened two BBQ joints in Oklahoma. I was beginning to think about life outside of the company; I was determined to not let the wrestling business and all its machinations have such a walloping effect on me.

Mike Adamle, my latest replacement on *Raw*, lasted a month before Vince got fed up with him and moved him into a different on-air role.

At *SmackDown*, Mick and I worked hard on our timing and chemistry. We both felt we had something to prove—Mick as the new guy and me as the old guy—and it pushed us to get better as a team.

But it wasn't long before I couldn't help thinking that Mick wasn't going to last either.

"How do you do it?" he asked me one day at the announce table.

"Do what?" I said.

Mick's face was genuinely pained. "Take this amount of abuse," he said. Vince's style of producing his announcers was really starting to get to Mick. "I've never been spoken to like that before," he said. "Vince is talking to me like he has no respect for me. Like I'm nothing."

I could feel Mick's hurt.

He continued: "He never once spoke to me like that when I was talent. I had no idea this is what commentating would be like."

Foley's contract was coming up, and I knew he had his eye on the door.

"Maybe you should talk to him," I said. "Vince might not know how you feel."

"I did talk to him," he replied. "He told me that he wouldn't do it anymore, but since then he's only gotten *worse*."

A few months later, Mick didn't renew his contract with WWE, so former ECW champion Tazz came on board as my partner instead. "The Human Suplex Machine" was also a retired talent who transitioned over to being a great announcer. He understood naturally how to use his voice to maximize the story that was being told on-screen.

I had really enjoyed working with Mick, and now Tazz and I were getting something going too, until I saw the same look on his face that I had seen on Mick's.

"Is he always going to be like this?" Tazz asked, talking about Vince.

"Maybe you should talk to him," I said.

"I did," he replied.

Tazz left about eight months later to join Mick at Total Nonstop Action Wrestling—or TNA—a new wrestling company with national TV, owned by the mega-rich Carter family out of Texas.

There was change in the air—and not the planned kind.

"J.R., we're going to make a change," Vince said when the Tazz news came out. "I'm going to move Todd Grisham to lead announcer on *SmackDown*."

Todd was a bright young talent who was expected to replace me on *Raw* in the fall of 2007—until the sustained ovation that I received in Chicago after my Hall of Fame announcement gave me an unlikely reprieve.

"Okay," I said warily.

"So I want you to be the color guy for Todd."

"Color guy?" I said.

"That's what we need," Vince replied.

The lead announcer is the point guard, who speaks first and opens and closes each segment. It's his or her job to provide the primary narrative upon which the analyst should expound. In old-school parlance, the lead talent does the ongoing play-by-play, while the analyst provides color.

Vince wanted Todd to steer the ship while I provided sound bites.

"Okay," I said to Vince. "Whatever you need."

This further demotion just underscored for me how the company viewed me and my worth. It was no surprise after all the times they tried to move me on.

I TOO WAS NOW THINKING about my own contract. Just how long could I keep fighting to protect my job in a company that was clearly trying to replace me time and time again?

Todd and I got along great; he is a very bright man who loves what he does. He knew I didn't have a problem with him doing this job whatsoever, and we even had some laughs on the road between shows.

But I couldn't shake the sense of dread.

And it caught up with me again in fall of 2009.

On a plane, no less.

I had boarded my flight from Oklahoma to work the *SmackDown* taping in Atlanta. I was looking forward to it because The King and I were to be reunited for just one show.

Not long into the flight, my facial muscles lost their grip. I got numbness, then a migraine. I began to quietly try soothing myself, thinking I was having a stroke. I tried to calm my breathing and heart rate while I looked for a flight attendant. We were over an hour away from our destination of Atlanta, and I was terrified I wasn't going to make it.

Even though it felt different from the other two earlier bouts, I came to realize that it wasn't a stroke I was having but another attack of Bell's palsy.

We landed, and I knew the WWE doctors were in Jacksonville with the *Raw* taping, so I texted one of them the first second I could. He immediately prescribed me Prednisone and other anti-inflammatories that shut down the creeping effects of Bell's palsy and help start the healing process.

I scrambled out of the plane and hurried through the airport. Some fans called my name as I rushed past with my head down. I got a car service and headed straight for the local CVS pharmacy where I got the pills I needed.

I stood outside the drugstore and called Vince.

"J.R., I just heard what happened. Are you okay, pal?" he asked.

"I can work," I said.

"No, let's get you home," the chairman replied.

I wasn't in much of a mind to fight back, so I went to my hotel and waited for WWE to contact me with new travel arrangements.

When I got home, I saw my neurologist in Norman and had a long consultation and some testing. He diagnosed me, as expected, with full-blown Bell's palsy. It was on the right side of my face, and it had adversely affected the vision in my right eye more than previous bouts. He was concerned about the cornea in my right eye being damaged, so I had to use an eye patch and a ton of artificial tears, and I had to tape my eye shut at night to sleep.

Jan let me know that the fans were asking about me online.

I wrote on my website:

> My timeline on returning to work is unknown as I write this. I wanted to be a part of WWE *Bragging Rights*. I think it will be a fun and unique show that will be showcasing some new talents in key bouts. How well they perform is up to them, but I hope that they take advantage of their opportunities no matter their roles. It's easy to "get lost" in a seven-man tag, for instance, but it is up to every man in the match to make their presence felt. Quality of minutes is just as important as quantity of minutes. For those fans that think that this is the end for me or the end is near, I suggest you rethink your position. I still love to play the game. I am an old-school guy who still loves calling wrestling matches and sitting at ringside soaking up the adrenaline from the fans.

In truth I wrote that last part to myself. I was losing hope and slipping into a deep depression. There was no cause and no cure to what I had, and it was like a curse hanging over me every minute. I couldn't stop thinking if today would be the day I got another attack that rendered my facial features even more paralyzed.

I knew we were okay financially. Jan and I had saved well, invested well, and we were under no pressure to buy the groceries. It was perfectly obvious that I was slipping out of favor in WWE, and with this latest health scare I couldn't stop my mind from thinking the worst.

"Someday you're going to have to realize that this job isn't your life," Jan said to me. "If you make WWE all we have, then we have nothing."

Wrestling was my mistress, but she didn't always love me back.

I knew from experience that I was about to go down a dark hole: weeks of blacked-out rooms, solitude, no stress, electrical stimulation, depression. It was all coming my way.

But I had Jan.

"Don't take everything so personally," she told me. "Look at what we have and how lucky we are."

I'd almost had enough, but she was helping me through. I was so depressed that if I didn't have her I would have done something stupid.

But my wife carried me through again. She wasn't afraid of anything, and it's hard to stay down when you have a woman like that waiting for you to get back up again.

So I did.

I fought.

Again.

SEVENTEEN

DOWN THE HOLE, SEEING LIGHT

Under No Circumstances

BY 2010, MY CONTRACT WAS COMING UP. I'd been out six months; the effects of my latest Bell's palsy attack were lingering longer than I'd hoped. Professionally, I wanted to be back on *Raw* with The King, but I knew chances were slim, so I began to look around for what else there might be.

Personally, I was sick of being sick, so I changed my diet and training regimen. I had grown up a country boy, where everything was fried, so it was quite the task for me to break old habits and make the changes I should have made a long time before—but I did it. I began eating healthier and working out regularly.

I was feeling better, both mentally and physically, and I was determined to put all the bad, bitter shit behind me. My wife carried me through the darkness again, helping me find perspective on where I was in life and where I wanted to be.

When asked in press interviews, I talked more openly about my contract and that I'd met with mixed martial arts companies and other sports brands who were interested in my services. I wanted WWE to know that I could take my skills into other arenas if the right offer were to come along.

I didn't necessarily *want* to leave WWE, but if I had to, I'd be ready.

I met up with Vince in Stamford, and we shook on a short-term deal that would extend my services past that year's *WrestleMania*, where we'd have more time and space to figure out exactly what to do.

"We want you to call something at *WrestleMania*," Vince said. "And we'll figure out the rest after that. How does that sound, J.R.?"

I was fine with it. I had reached a place of acceptance, and I was happy to wait another couple of months to hammer out a longer deal. Plus I was excited to get back to *WrestleMania.*

When word got out that I'd met with Vince, friends in the company called me regularly with rumors they'd heard; some days I was definitely involved in *WrestleMania*, and others I wasn't mentioned at all.

I had kinda gotten used to being on the fringes of the company by now. I'd gone from the center of the action, making decisions, building the foundations, helping WWE to become a global brand, to waiting by the phone to see if I was coming in to call a match.

I'm not going to lie: The velocity of my fall from grace was humbling and painful. Like a lot of men, I saw myself mostly through the lens of my career. When *it* was doing well, then *I* was doing well; and when it wasn't, I was hard to live with.

Some days I couldn't feel anything, even if I wanted to. Other days I felt everything all at once. Being at home and battling the effects of my illness was playing havoc with my mind.

But then I got the call.

"Bring your tux," Kevin Dunn said. Those three words were like music to my ears. I had spent a long time feeling worthless as I battled back from my illness. Although I wished it wasn't the case, being needed made me feel better about myself.

I hung up and walked into the kitchen where Jan was making dinner. "Hope you have something nice to wear," I said.

She turned around, surprised. She hadn't heard this kind of upbeat tone in my voice for months. "Why?" she asked. "Are we going somewhere?"

I got a little emotional. It could have been my illness, but I'm fully sure it was relief. "They want me to bring my suit for *WrestleMania.*"

Jan hugged me close.

Besides my own health battles, around that time I had also lost some dear friends: Steve "Dr. Death" Williams, two-time NWA world heavyweight champion and fellow Oklahoman Jack Brisco (brother of WWE scout Jerry), and one of my first mentors, Skandor Akbar. It was a tough, tough time.

"Vince wants me to work Shawn vs. 'Taker," I said.

Jan gripped me even tighter; my wife knew what getting the call meant to me.

"Shawn and 'Taker asked for me," I said. "Vince approved it, and Kevin just called."

"I'm so happy for you, honey," Jan said.

My wife had seen me slip down lower than she'd ever witnessed before. This one call, and all that it meant, was like someone throwing me a lifeline.

"It's such an honor that the Boys want me to call their match," I said.

Jan looked me right in the eyes. "I wish you could see yourself as they all see you, sweetheart," she said. "You can't let your worth rise and fall based on your airtime."

Her words hit me hard. She was right, as always.

I ordered my tux, our travel was arranged, and Jan bought a brand-new outfit. After months of illness and losing friends, I was ready to make my way back into the world, back into the business I loved.

My dark fog lifted, and I began to feel human again.

THE DAY BEFORE *WRESTLEMANIA XXVI*, I checked into the hotel with my tux over my shoulder and a pep in my step. I had been involved in several *WrestleMania* shows by then, but the scope and grandeur of the event never got old. It was the Super Bowl of our business, and every single person in the company wanted to be a part of it somehow. I was no exception.

As Jan and I walked to our room, we could feel the buzz building. WWE had rented most of the hotel, so around us costumes were being finished and makeup tested; giant production cases were wheeled in, along with miles of cabling and monitors; there were interviews, nervous excitement, hugs, smiles, worry, nail-biting, happy-jumping, reunions, perfume, the clacking of high heels.

And Jan. Looking proud, looking beautiful, looking happy.

I felt sorry that she'd had to see me so down for so long, but now I was bursting with pride that she'd watch me walk that ramp once more to call the final match in Shawn Michaels's long and illustrious career, as he faced another WWE legend in Undertaker. Shawn had been with the company since the late 1980s, and Undertaker had been there since 1990. The match truly had that rare *WrestleMania* aura around it.

"This is one helluva honor," I said to her as we waited for the elevator.

Everyone was shaking my hand and patting me on the back. I squeezed Jan's hand a little tighter. She looked at me, her eyes sparkling.

"Are you working the show tomorrow?" people asked.

"Yep," I replied. "'Taker and Shawn."

Everyone seemed genuinely happy to see me.

I saw Kevin in the bar as we passed, and I waved to him. He signaled for me to join him.

"Let me get my bags settled and I'll be right down," I said to him from the doorway.

Jan couldn't wait to get to the other wives and girlfriends. This was one of the highlights of her year, getting dressed up and joining the other families. "I'll see you soon," I said as we parted.

"Honey," she said. I stopped in the doorway. "I'm proud of you."

My eyes filled a little. Hers too.

I walked into the bar and said hello to some colleagues before sitting down beside Kevin. "I got some bad news," he said. "We're not going to use you."

I looked for the hint of a smile, a sign he was joking. "What?" I asked.

"Yeah."

"I brought my tux like you asked me to," I said.

Kevin looked me in the eye. "We don't think you're healed enough," he said.

My stomach sank and my guts twisted. "I brought my wife, Kevin, I've . . ."

"Sorry, J.R. We won't be using you tomorrow."

The conversation was that short; clearly, there was no bartering to be done or middle ground to be found. It was a decision made about me, without me.

I got a look at myself in the mirror behind the bar after Kevin had left. The hardest thing in the world for me to accept was that I was being rejected for *me*—not the quality of my work, but my appearance. It was literally the one thing I could do nothing about. No one would be more excited than me if I could regain my ability to smile. But it was out of my hands.

When I got back to my room, Jan was still out mingling. I sat on the bed, trying not to let it get to me too much, as I didn't want to trigger anything that might bring on another bout of Bell's palsy.

The door opened, and I could tell by Jan's face that she'd heard. She got on the bed and hugged me, even tighter than before. She didn't say anything, and neither did I.

Something clicked in me there and then; a callus came over the part of me that loved WWE and loved the business. I couldn't keep allowing myself to be vulnerable and hurt this way. I had to protect myself from the heady highs and the hellish lows of my career.

"There's none of this I can change," I said.

"I know," Jan replied.

"I gotta start looking out for myself."

NEXT DAY I SAW SHAWN AND 'TAKER, who were both angry on my behalf.

"We tried," Shawn said. "Both of us."

'Taker was particularly pissed. "I'm sorry, J.R.," he said. "We both went to bat."

"We were told under no circumstances was it going to happen," Shawn said. "Vince didn't want to hear about it anymore."

I put on my coach voice—I didn't want my issue to become their issue, especially on such an important day. "I'm rooting for you two guys," I said. "Go out there and steal the show. I'm sorry I won't get to call it, but the important thing is the match."

I knew how paramount it was to two old-school guys like 'Taker and Shawn that their story be told right. We all three had started out around the same time, and we all three had the same approach to the business. They were emotionally attached to me calling their match. I had been ringside for their previous encounter at the last *WrestleMania*, so they wanted the symmetry of me calling this one too.

But Vince wasn't giving in.

"I don't know why this isn't happening," 'Taker said before he and Shawn left for the arena.

The biggest kick in the gut was watching the team buses pull off for the arena without me. I tried to suppress the visceral shame, but I felt like I was drowning in it instead.

At the stadium, Jan and I watched the show from a box. People were avoiding eye contact with me—a total 180 degrees from the day before.

"I don't get it," I whispered to Jan. "It's not like I'm so disfigured that I'd scare the children or anything."

"Don't look for logic where there is none, sweetheart," she replied.

Jan knew none of this would tabulate into a satisfying answer for me.

Down in the ring, Shawn and 'Taker had one of the best matches of all time. Pure emotion, amazing storytelling, and two of the greatest ever to do it, giving everything they had. It was beautiful, memorable, with Shawn retiring in defeat, but on top.

As the show closed, Jan and I stood up to leave. A production assistant leaned into my ear: "Shawn and Undertaker said they're going to be by the buses."

"By the buses? What does that mean?" Jan asked me as the assistant walked off.

"Means I won't be going to the hotel," I told her.

WWE threw a lavish afterparty every year after the *WrestleMania* show finished. I wasn't in the party mood, and I didn't want to answer the same question a million times: "*Why didn't you call the match, J.R.?*"

She smiled. "Shawn and Undertaker sent for you?"

I nodded, my mood somewhat lifted: They had thought of me again on their biggest night. "You don't mind if I skip the afterparty?" I asked.

"Of course not," she replied. "Do you good to talk to the Boys."

Across from the hotel was a giant parking lot, and in that parking lot were several tour buses that the top talents used. Undertaker had positioned them in a horseshoe, effectively creating a private courtyard. Security made sure no curious onlookers got close.

When I got there, Shawn and Undertaker were already sitting on small seats in the "courtyard." I could see boxes of beer, three bottles of Jack Daniel's, and the makings of a campfire, ready to go.

Both men smiled huge smiles when they saw me. With a handshake and a hug, my spirit was immediately lifted.

Gone were wrestling costumes, the characters, and the need to perform. It was just three rednecks sitting in a parking lot, with a campfire crackling and a river of alcohol flowing.

Undertaker looked like a redneck king, sitting satisfied, chomping on a cigar, while Shawn downed his first beer in a long, long time.

The Heartbreak Kid had cut back considerably on his partying lifestyle since his "bad boy" days in the 1990s, but he wanted to enjoy a few drinks in private on the night of his retirement.

We all raised a toast to the classic match both men had just wrestled and to the careers we'd put together. Shawn was done, I knew my end was near, and 'Taker's full-time days were drawing to a close too.

We told stories, and laughed, and cried. We played country music on high and kept the flames of the fire higher. Our drinking became a competition, and the beers were suddenly followed by whiskey chasers—right from the bottle.

Each story led to another, as we'd all known the same people, worked in the same territories, and dealt with the same highs and lows over the years.

I suddenly realized I was having one of my best *WrestleMania* moments ever—in a parking lot, long after the final bell had sounded. I knew it was a gift: the warmth of the fire, the top-notch company.

"I love you guys," I said.

Both men nodded back in a manly way. I knew they loved me too.

I couldn't have been any more loyal to WWE. I knew I was a cranky bastard: moody, short-tempered, and gruff. But I was also passionate, and I gave everything to my job. I couldn't have worked any more hours, and, most important, I couldn't make myself younger or less facially paralyzed. But I could choose to be happier.

As I walked back to the hotel at five in the morning, I saw my future writ large. And I was ready to face *what* was coming, even with absolutely no control over *when* it came.

Soothe the Cranky

ABOUT A MONTH AFTER my private party with 'Taker and Shawn, the best way to describe my general demeanor was grouchy with others and down on myself. To soothe my crankiness, I knew I needed some clarity on my professional future. Since the closure of WCW, Total Nonstop Action Wrestling was trying to position itself as the alternative brand to WWE in the marketplace—and it was spending some decent money, backed by billionaire energy mogul Bob Carter.

In the classic circular nature of the wrestling business, TNA was originally set up by Jerry and Jeff Jarrett, after Vince had bought WCW and fired Jeff live on the air because Jeff had blindsided me in negotiations. But now TNA was about eight years old, Jerry Jarrett was gone, and Jeff was out of power. The Jarrett men had sold their shares to the Carter family, and Bob made his daughter, Dixie, head honcho.

TNA was looking to talk to me, and the offer was open to come meet the Carter family anytime. Given the vibe at WWE, I figured I had nothing to lose.

Of all people, it was former WWE writer Vince Russo who was urging me to talk to TNA.

"Bro," he said in his thick New York accent, "you gotta talk to these people, J.R. You'd do amazing here."

This was the same Vince Russo who'd mentioned me five years earlier in his book *Forgiven*:

> A large part of Vince McMahon's success can be attributed to surrounding himself with dedicated, hard-working people and then

putting them in key positions. But then what happened with J.R.? How in God's name did he get to be the head of talent relations—perhaps the most important position in the company?

He went on to say:

As Vince's television role grew, he brought in a Hollywood writer by the name of Ed Ferrara to help me. Over the past few years, Ed and I have had our differences. But I can never take this away from the guy—he was extremely talented. He easily could have been a stand-up comic. Not only does he look like a hedgehog, but the guy is just flat-out hysterical. Ed and I traveled everywhere with Vince, Shane, and Stephanie, and during every trip he would entertain the troops.

Even though Ed did many voices and characters, his staple was J.R. Yes it was cruel, but Ed's imitation of J.R. during his Bell's palsy era was beyond words. I'm going to go to hell for saying this, but as a good writer, I need to properly set the scene. When J.R. was stricken a second time with the disease—every time he spoke, his tongue would pop out of his mouth and roll about like a lost slug looking for a cool rock to crawl under. Ed had this down to a science. Now—get over it—we weren't being deliberately cruel, we were just spending way too much time on the road. Yeah, we may all one day meet again at Satan's gate, but at the time it was freaking hysterical!

That's how Ed Ferrara playing WCW's Oklahoma came about. We did it as a rib on J.R., and because we knew Vince would be dying on the inside, saying, "I can't believe those guys are doing that." Of course, the goodie-goodies at WCW made us kill the character because it may have insulted someone with Bell's palsy watching.

But, you know what? With Vince, it was always that part of him that stood out the most. It was really my privilege at times to get that glimpse of the real Vince. At work, he was somebody else—he had to be. But when you could break down that guard, when you were able to get those special one-on-one times with him, it was almost like being with your best friend.

I miss those times.

Russo, in fairness to him, apologized for how he spoke about me, and I accepted it completely. I was doing my best to try and live my life without negativity. Also, by now my contract extension had run out.

So I agreed to talk with TNA.

The Carters sent their private jet to pick me up in Norman. It was about a half-hour trip to North Texas, where a car waited to bring me to the ranch. It was Easter weekend, and when I arrived, Bob, his wife, Janice, their son, Todd, and the TNA president, Dixie, all welcomed me into their family home.

Bob and I fell easily into conversation. He was polite, charming, and straight to the point. "So, what is it going to take, Jim?" Bob asked me.

"For what?" I replied.

"To get you to TNA," he said.

In preparation for the meeting, I had been watching their programming and looking over their talent roster. TNA had a shot at being a great company, but there were some obvious problems.

"If I'm going to sign, I have to have control over the talent roster," I said.

Bob nodded—not affirming my statement, just letting me know he was listening.

"I need to buy some groceries. I need to get payroll under control," I said.

"Groceries?" he wondered.

"I need to cut a lot of the talent and bring in some newer, younger, fresher faces."

I could see Bob was getting a little more apprehensive. Not because he didn't trust what I was saying, but because of the effect the news of me controlling the players might have on his daughter, Dixie.

"My daughter is very loyal to the people who work there," Bob said.

I replied, "And no finer trait can you find in a person, Bob. But loyalty can put you out of business if it's blind."

"How do you mean?" he asked, already knowing the answer. Bob Carter hadn't made his billions without knowing exactly what I was saying.

"Look," I said, "you're Jerry Jones and I'm Bill Parcells is the way I'd see it. If I don't do good, you fire me. No bad feelings, nothing personal."

Janice called for us to come in for lunch. Bob put his hand on my shoulder as we entered the house. I knew we had a good understanding, and I began to think I might have a future with TNA.

"I'm so very glad you came to see us," Bob said.

"Me too."

After we'd had a little something to eat, Dixie brought me out on her four-wheeler around their massive ranch. "What would you change first, J.R.?" she asked me as we sped around the dusty trails.

"There's a lot of guys getting paid a lot of money but not contributing to the health of the company," I said. "I would fix that first. Bring the budget under control."

"You think we need to make that big a change?" she asked.

"Put it this way," I replied. "You're using talent who have already burned out. It's a natural part of the wrestling business that a body wears down or a worker's mentality becomes frayed."

I could tell by her sudden silence that she wasn't expecting—or wasn't comfortable with—me asking to clean house. Maybe Dixie thought it was a judgment on her hiring instincts, but it genuinely wasn't. Every new booker or higher-up wants to come into a new company and build things their way.

"What do you think are the challenges?" Dixie asked.

"I believe you're being sold a bill of goods," I said. "If you're really interested in signing me, just know that I'd come in and use my expertise to try and turn TNA around, financially and creatively. You have decent TV, but if you can't find your way to make drastic changes, you're going to be in trouble."

I could see in Dixie's face that she was struggling to bring change. She didn't want to let people go to whom she was paying big money, and I was interested in going to work there only if I was given the freedom to give the place a facelift.

"Sounds like a lot of changes, J.R.," she said.

"I'm not going to lie to you," I said. "A lot of changes are needed."

I could see there and then that Dixie couldn't pull the trigger emotionally on what I felt I needed to do. She didn't even ask whom I would clean out—just the mere thought of it was enough to stall our conversation.

"Let's head back," she said.

Product knowledge—especially in a niche business such as pro wrestling—is vital to survival. The Carters are wonderful people, but I felt they were being taken advantage of by some street-savvy talents who were essentially there on a money grab.

"There's bad weather coming our way," Dixie said as she drove us back toward the ranch.

"WE'LL FLY YOU HOME," Bob said as we parked outside. "Let me give you a traveler." He handed me a cup with their logo on it. "Something to see you home."

I thanked him and, to be polite, drank a sip before I left; it was a good stiff drink for the short flight home. As I left Texas, I wished I could have helped them, but I could see that giving up that much power, for Dixie, was a bridge too far.

TNA tried several times after that to hire me, but I wasn't interested in just taking their money if I couldn't meaningfully help them.

I figured I'd wait and see what WWE's next move was.

EIGHTEEN

A NEW OUTLOOK

Sit in the Closet

SOMETIMES VINCE DOESN'T NECESSARILY KNOW what he wants to do with a talent—he just knows he doesn't want anyone else to have them. And that's exactly what was happening when WWE offered me a new contract in the middle of 2010.

I wasn't trying to hide the fact that I had other offers and meetings—and suddenly, there they were on the phone.

Now, I could understand Vince's stance, but he had to know that people weren't going to just go sit in a closet until the next time WWE wanted to do business with them.

People *needed* to work, and people *wanted* to work.

Retirement has always been one of my biggest fears. I was brought up to work, and the mere thought of going home and doing nothing was mentally crippling to me. Some guys who've made a few bucks are happy to hit the beach or join a golf club. Me, I wanted to be in and around wrestling—and wrestling fans.

Jan and I were lucky in that we now had a few dollars, so I could have gone home, grown some nice flowers, gotten myself a Snuggie and a favorite daytime TV show if I'd wanted to. But the truth was, I wanted the validation, the rush, the feeling of forward motion.

I DECIDED TO ASK for more favorable terms and better money. I wanted to start fresh. Most important, I was going to try not to take things *so* personally that it affected my health.

The major concession I made was my on-air time. I could tell that the company had no plans whatsoever to use me in a full-time capacity at the announce table. The new agreement called for me to work more with the talent relations department—with John Laurinaitis still in charge—helping to book the house shows and doing the payroll. They also asked me to get involved in the developmental system.

As far as TV, they wanted me to be at the PPVs and to help the announcers, giving them any direction I could to help the story in the ring move a little smoother.

The trade-off I sought was fewer hours, more money, and more freedom outside WWE. I could go on speaking tours and do any book deals I wanted, I could write sports columns and announce any other sport—other than wrestling—that I wanted to.

It was a good clean contract that I was happy with. I signed the deal knowing that there would be more shit for me to eat, but I was going to try to do it without choking myself.

SO I WENT BACK TO WORK.

As we passed into 2011, I was paired with a big Oklahoma prospect named Jack Swagger.

It's Not Going to Get to Me

IT WAS LIKE MY FIRST DAY BACK AT SCHOOL—or my first day back at *old* school, to be precise. WWE wanted me to come back on a themed version of *Raw*, where we take the audience back in time by featuring names from the past.

"Maybe you shouldn't overthink things, sweetheart," Jan said to me. "Just let all the negativity go."

She could see I was packing my bag, ready to go back to work. Her words struck me, though. Most times in life it's not the words you hear that make a difference, it's when you hear them.

"I'm gonna put my head down," I said to my wife. "I don't care what they want me to do, I'll just do it. No more tension, no more stress."

"Promise?" she asked.

I nodded, and I meant it. I knew it wasn't going to happen overnight, but I was determined to change the way I processed things. "I'm going back there to do whatever it is they need me to do," I said.

"And you know they're going to mess with you," Jan replied.

"That's true," I said.

"And we're not going to allow that to get to us anymore. It's just a job, honey," she said.

I repeated back to myself: "It's just a job."

I knew I had been messed with, and I knew that probably wasn't going to stop, but I also knew that *I* wasn't the easiest to deal with either. I didn't stand before my wife a victim, I stood there a realist. I was taking WWE money to go back to do whatever it was they wanted me to do. I loved the company, loved the fans, and wanted to fight for whatever opportunities would become available.

This was going to be a new start, a new way of thinking. I was ready to hear anything that would make the journey easier.

"I love you," Jan said as she kissed my cheek.

"I love you too."

I packed up my cowboy hat, wheeled my case from my house, and headed to *Old School Raw* at the Giant Center in Hershey, Pennsylvania. I knew the vibe would be like a school reunion, full of stories, card games, smokes, and a few alcoholic drinks after the work was done.

All my anxiety faded away as I spotted all the other old-timers. I saw The Million Dollar Man, Ted DiBiase, whom I was asked to murder earlier in my career. (Check out my first book, *Slobberknocker*, for details.) After I caught up with Teddy, I bumped into my dear friend Dusty Rhodes. In spending just two short minutes with The American Dream, I was reminded for the millionth time in my career why he was the legend he was—Big Dust oozed charisma 24/7, whether the cameras were on or not.

"Hacksaw" Jim Duggan joined us, and we told stories about the old days, when Hacksaw and The Dream were major draws.

I visited with Arn Anderson, one of the greatest, most underrated wrestlers and mic workers of all time. Behind the scenes, he was also one of the best storytellers.

It wasn't hard to remember, in that moment, why I loved this place so much. WWE, for me, was like that secret backroom to which only the cool guys had access. I knew I was lucky—I had somehow stumbled right into my boyhood dream and found a place for myself.

I heard the familiar laugh of "Rowdy" Roddy Piper behind me, and I turned to see his smile as wide as his face. Hot Rod wasn't just a bombastic trash-talker with a wary eye for management in his TV persona—that's who he was in real life too. I think he appreciated just how many times I'd been fired, like it was a badge of honor for both of us.

Piper and I originally became friends during the *WrestleMania XII* build, where I took dozens of telephone calls and sitdowns to reassure Hot Rod that his discretionary pay would be to his liking.

And it was.

Roddy had grown up on the streets on Winnipeg and turned pro at age fifteen; he never graduated high school but had a Ph.D. in the game of life. His trust issues seemingly never went away, though.

"I hear you're not management anymore, J.R.," he said as he slapped me on the back.

"You'll have to torment someone else about your payoff tonight, Roddy," I replied.

Hot Rod howled with laughter. He seemed to like me even more now that I wasn't the Office anymore.

"You remind me of Bruce Dern's character opposite John Wayne in *The Cowboys*," I said to him. "You're the perfect villain to play opposite any hero."

Piper smiled. "The key is, I didn't give a shit about being cool, J.R. I just wanted everyone and their mothers to hate my guts."

And boy, did they.

Roddy and I shook hands and split to get ready for our respective assignments. Hot Rod's was a return to the classic *Piper's Pit* segment, and mine was to try to help a fellow Oklahoma native, Jack Swagger, get some traction on the roster.

Jack—or Jake Hager, as he was known away from the cameras—was a two-time All-American from the University of Oklahoma who had set a record of thirty pins in a single season. He was a dual-sport athlete who sat in my house after graduation, wondering what to do with his particular skill set.

I told him I could put in a word with my old colleague John Laurinaitis in WWE talent relations. John hired Jake immediately and turned him into Jack Swagger for the WWE audience.

My first act in aiding Swagger was to sit in on his match at *Old School Raw*. I waited behind the curtain until I heard the legendary voice of Howard Finkel announcing from the ring. "Ladies and gentlemen," he began, "at this time, would you please welcome your special guest commentator for the following match. He is WWE Hall of Famer good ol' J.R., Jim Ross."

Fink's voice was like a tonic. He was WWE's first employee, the best to ever ring-announce. Like me, he had been the brunt of many a joke behind the scenes, but he had WWE running through his veins.

I walked through the curtain into the arena, but what I didn't know as I walked to the ring was that Michael Cole, *Raw*'s lead announcer, was heeling up his hatred for me for the viewing audience at home.

"Did you do this?" Cole asked my former long-term partner, Jerry Lawler, on the air. "You do know this is my show now, right?"

I hadn't gotten the memo that I was walking out to not only commentate, but also to participate in a live, on-the-air, ad-libbed war of words with the guy who'd replaced me. I guess someone found Vince Russo's idea from back in 1999 and decided the J.R./Michael Cole war of words at the commentary booth must have been what made "the Attitude Era" work.

"Why would you bring this guy back?" Cole asked, as I high-fived the fans.

The King and I hugged as Cole ran his mouth behind me.

"Who invited you here? You're not going to even shake my hand, say hi to me?" Cole yapped as I put on my headset.

I decided that coolness was the order of the day. I had promised my wife that I wasn't going to let the same old stuff get to me like it had in the past. Vince could tell Cole to say whatever he wanted to me; I wasn't going to sell it.

"Hey, Michael, how you doing?" I replied, when I was good and ready.

In the ring, Jack Swagger was about to take on the amazing Daniel Bryan (a true overachiever who went on to become one of the best ever).

"Well, you've got the boring United States Champion in Daniel Bryan, might as well bring J.R. out to call his match," Cole said.

Despite what Cole was saying, I wanted the people at home to know just how special Daniel was—and I wanted the people in the back to know how dumb they were for running down their own talent on TV.

"Daniel Bryan is anything but boring," I said. "He's overachieved, overcome his lack of great size to become a great submission competitor. Anyone with any intelligence would recognize that."

"J.R., he's like you: He has no personality," Cole replied.

Vince was feeding Michael lines, and Michael was just doing his job. The camera guy knelt in front of us, hoping to catch some drama.

I just continued to call the match and do my job.

"You do realize I'm the voice of the WWE, guys," Cole said with the camera pointed at us. "You do understand that, right?"

"As I said, ladies and gentlemen, this is a one-fall match," I said, blanking

Cole and Vince altogether. I proceeded to tell the viewers about Jack Swagger and his great pedigree.

"Why don't you tell J.R. why you dislike Daniel Bryan?" King said to Cole. "It's a personal thing, right?"

"It *is* a personal thing," Michael replied. "The guy's a nerd, a goof, he's never had a date in his life. He attacked me and said that I was a poor man's J.R. I never wanted to be a J.R. Ever."

I no-sold the drama beside me and continued to call the match. But I knew Vince wouldn't stop feeding Michael lines.

"You guys calling this match is a cure for insomnia," Cole said. "And to think you guys did XFL games together. No wonder that league went out of business."

Now, for those counting at home, this was the weird dimension through which WWE travels from time to time. You had the CEO of WWE—the former owner of the XFL—tell one of his announcers to say his other announcers were so bad that they were the reason the XFL was dead.

"C'mon, J.R., we haven't heard it yet: We haven't heard 'slobberknocker,' 'stomping a mudhole,' we haven't heard 'government mule,' we haven't heard Stone Cold . . ."

I continued: "Daniel Bryan getting a head of steam . . ."

The King and I clicked into gear as the match picked up. It felt good to be on The King's frequency again.

"If you could hear paint dry, that's what this commentary sounds like," Cole said. The truck cut to him as he slumped in his seat, bored and bewildered.

"Please end this match, please," Cole said on cue. "Doesn't Oklahoma have a game tonight you have to be at?"

I've never heard a more Vince sentence come from another human's mouth. That was the crux of all this, I realized: I had gone home to Oklahoma when Vince felt I should have stayed by his side.

"How's the BBQ sauce working out for you, J.R.?" Cole asked.

"Very good," I said, acknowledging him for the first time. "Jrsbarbq.com."

The King laughed at my turning Vince's barbs into a free plug for my BBQ sauce. And, besides, I was proud that I'd continued using my time offscreen to further build my entrepreneurial ventures like my restaurants,

BBQ sauce, and beef jerky; it took me back to my beginnings in local retail in Oklahoma.

"I'm going to get a white cowboy hat for next week," Cole replied, his desperation rising. "I'm going to buy season tickets to Syracuse football games. I'm going to open a restaurant in Syracuse and bring out my own BBQ sauce."

In the ring, Daniel Bryan knocked Swagger cold.

"Boomer Sooner!" The King shouted. "Boomer Sooner!"

"That was a slobberknocker of a right foot to the face of Swagger," I said.

The ref counted three to end the match.

"Thanks for joining us," Cole said. "It's nice to have you back, J.R. Thanks for joining us. It was a lot of fun, you provided some great insight, it was wonderful having you back. See you in about ten years."

I turned to The King and shook his hand. "Great seeing you, King."

"J.R., loved having you out here."

"Great being back on *Raw*," I replied.

"Don't get used to it," Cole said, butting back in.

The cameras came back to us at the announce table. I stood up and bitch-slapped Michael Cole a couple of times with my hat before I left.

He wasn't happy. "Go home. Real professional. Go home to wherever you came from. Oklahoma or wherever."

I already did, Vince.

NINETEEN

PLEASE MAKE IT STOP

He's Been Carrying You

THE YEAR 2011 WAS UNUSUAL, even for me. Early that year, I came back to *Raw* in St. Louis to be a part of the ongoing Michael Cole/Jerry Lawler story that was unfolding.

Vince wanted an "attraction match" between Cole and Lawler to take place at that year's *WrestleMania*, with me sprinkled into the mix. I was totally fine and happy to do whatever was needed, because at least this scripted animosity would be going somewhere this time.

Despite having been a legend in the business for about forty years—and a WWE employee for almost fifteen—it was one milestone Jerry Lawler hadn't yet achieved: his own *WrestleMania* match. This year it was finally happening, and the company had decided to put Lawler, Cole, myself, and Jack Swagger into one mixing bowl and see if we couldn't make something of it.

Cole and I were obviously superior athletes, and I had been working on my 450-degree splash off the top rope during my time off. I was also happy to help Jerry realize a longtime goal *and* help a new talent, Jack Swagger, get some more spotlight.

WrestleMania XXVII was fast approaching, and it was time to pull the trigger on setting up the Cole vs. Lawler storyline—a match for the ages—on *Raw* in St. Louis. I warmed up backstage by standing completely still beside the curtain. I think I might have also flexed by accident too when I adjusted my hat. I was feeling so much like a wrestler that I even asked somebody passing if they, "Ever lift, bro?"

"J.R., get ready," Vince said, as my cue drew closer.

I thought, *I am ready, bro. Can't you see these guns from over there?*

That's not true: I looked like a big melted candle, but I was wearing a sweatsuit.

It went like this: Michael Cole—as a heel—had insulted Jerry's family and publicly called him out on the air. "You are pathetic, a loser, and at *WrestleMania* I'm going to put you in your place," Cole said, as he stood in the ring looking down at Jerry, who was at the announce table at ringside.

And that, ladies and gentlemen, was my cue. The Oklahoma fight song played, and I walked through that curtain once more. The people in the arena were loud and kind. I felt like John Wayne as I marched down to my duel with Cole. I had to fight every single fiber of my being to not backflip into the splits at the bottom of the ramp.

Cole stood in the ring with one hand on his hip, like a true badass.

I marched up the steps and reached the peak of my athletic prowess by successfully climbing through the ropes. The people were happy to see good ol' J.R., but Michael wasn't.

"I was wondering when this moment was going to come," he said. "I was wondering when you were going to do your best John Wayne impression and come riding in on your white horse, with the black hat on your head. I was wondering when you were going to show up to steal the spotlight. Must be a slow day in the BBQ business."

Man, I wanted to hit him right then and there with a dropkick, but instead I talked. "Don't you think this has gone far enough?" I asked. Cole turned his back on me, perfect for a German Suplex. But instead I reminded the audience about the nasty things Cole had said and done to try and embarrass The King. "Michael," I said, "come to your senses. This has gone far enough."

Michael pirouetted around with surprising grace to face me again. "J.R.," he said, "I got an idea: Why don't you go away? It's over, you're done. This is my show now, I'm the voice of WWE."

Man, little did he know that he was *that close* to getting a Hurricanrana from good ol' J.R. Now, there's two things you don't want if you're in our business, folks: that's a left hand from Harley Race or a Hurricanrana from Jim Ross. Both are devastating.

Cole was still running his mouth: "Michael Cole is the voice of WWE. Not. Jim. Ross."

"You know," I said, "I've been meaning to talk to you about that, about being the voice of WWE."

Michael folded his arms like a petulant child as I explained to him, "For many, many years I had the privilege and the honor of sitting right over there at ringside beside Jerry Lawler here on *Monday Night Raw*."

The crowd rose up and got louder as I told Cole that the only voices of *Raw* belonged to the fans around the world. I went for the cheap pop and BY GAWD did I get it. "You know," I said, "Lawler has been protecting you for a long time. He's been carrying you, Cole. He's been like a mother kangaroo carrying you around in his pouch and protecting you. You know, Michael, you're not a lovable, cuddly animal like a baby kangaroo . . . no, you're a different kind of animal. You are a . . . rat bastard."

Boom. Worse than a J.R. Hurricanrana. Job done. Cole was killed by words.

I moved to leave the ring.

"So, that's how it's going to be," Michael said, not actually dead from my sick burn. "This is how I always envisioned it: Michael Cole in his ring being a bigger man while J.R. walked into the sunset . . . his tail between his legs."

Well now, that's fighting talk.

I stopped and turned back around. Now it was time to see if I could get this crowd excited about two pasty announcers squaring off in a fistfight.

I slowly peeled off my hat as the crowd noise grew. Next, I tore off my suit in one go like a stripper. That's not true, but I did take off my suit jacket, and four ladies in the front row passed out. Not sure if that was because of happiness or horror. My tie was next, and I even loosened a top button to see if I couldn't whip up a further female frenzy.

Michael took off his suit jacket, and together we were officially the least fit, least trained, and least sixpacked dudes ever to square off in a WWE ring.

I showed that wretched Cole my Hall of Fame ring and warned him that I was going to punch him with it, right in his face. And to my surprise, the crowd began to chant, "J.R.! J.R.! J.R.!"

Then came the kicker—Jack Swagger jumped the barrier and attacked The King from behind before Cole and I could have our match of the year.

With The King down, Swagger turned his attention on me, and I knew another ass-whupping was coming my way. All my bravado left the arena as I was stalked in the ring by the "All-American All-American," Jack Swagger.

Cole shouted for my fellow Oklahoman to kick my ass, and I pleaded with him not to. Let me tell you, I didn't need to *act* scared.

Swagger kicked me in my toned gut, and I fell to the canvas like several pounds of soft cheese dropped from a height. Jack grabbed me in an ankle lock—which, outside the more theatrical world of WWE, is a legit hold—and he got so excited that he legitimately tore up my ankle and knee.

I was tapping and yelling like crazy, but the big ol' hoss that was stretching me was too in the moment to notice that I was almost sixty and not really that bendable.

The King got back up and tried to save me, but Swagger took him down too. Jerry and I, longtime friends and partners, got our asses kicked together, like any great team should.

But it wasn't over yet. Michael put the ankle lock on me too, and I can't impress upon you just how much it sucks to have your leg rewrenched after it's just been traumatized. But that's how it goes sometimes: Mistakes are made when the adrenaline is flowing.

The final image Vince wanted was Cole standing tall and running his mouth, so by God, that's what he got. "How does that feel, J.R.?" Cole shouted. "That'll teach you to come out here and disrespect me. You'll think twice again . . . both of you guys. This is my time. My time. Nobody else's."

The crowd booed accordingly, and Cole's expert heeling was punctuated when he grabbed Swagger's wrist, and both men stood over The King and I with their hands raised in victory.

Jerry knew what was coming for him: *WrestleMania* was fast approaching, and The King had revenge on his mind.

The Conga Line of Awfulness

I THOUGHT THE MICHAEL COLE/J.R. ANGLE was a dud, but it produced the greatest praise I ever received from Vince. "Goddamnit, J.R., you *finally* let me have it. You let me have all of you, J.R. I'm so proud of you," he said to me backstage.

I was floored.

The boss was elated, overjoyed, effusive in his praise of me—I'd never seen him react like that toward anything I'd done before. After eighteen years of calling my heart out and helping put together the greatest roster Vince had ever seen, he was finally proud of me. I'm not going to lie: It felt good to hear him say it. I'd come back through that curtain after triumphs and heartbreaks, I'd sat across his desk almost every day with news of another great signing or another tricky situation handled, but never in my WWE career had Vince lit up so brightly about my work.

I was both happy and confused—just what was *it* exactly that had made Vince finally so proud of me?

Probably not what you'd think.

First, I never imagined that my feud with Cole would become one of my "*WrestleMania* moments."

I'll start by saying I had great respect for Michael—I genuinely enjoyed being around him. When he first came into the company, I tried to help him as best I could, and when Bell's palsy struck, Michael stood in for me and did a great job. I enjoyed producing him—he was intelligent, and he had that thirst for knowledge that all great broadcasters need.

The problem for Michael was that he was being judged against the guy who preceded him. It happened to WCW announcer Tony Schiavone when the legendary Gordon Solie retired and Tony sat in Gordon's place. Schiavone ended up one of the great announcers of all time, but the first few years were shaky simply because the fans weren't hearing Gordon's voice—the voice they had grown up with.

Michael Cole suffered the same kind of unfortunate baptism when I was moved aside. The fans' focus was on who he *wasn't*, rather than who he *was*. Michael doesn't sound like me; he doesn't have my style or delivery. Now, in some ways that's exactly why he was on the air—Vince wanted something completely different. But the fans had gotten used to my voice, and for a lot of them I was the soundtrack of their favorite wrestling memories.

I think I also made it harder when I didn't retire or move on to another company. I was sitting backstage, ready to work, and the fans knew it—and, unfortunately, they took that frustration out on Michael sometimes.

Well, the company finally decided to lean into the fans' animosity toward Cole and made him a heel announcer drumming up even more hate.

And so came the angle with The King, Cole, Jack Swagger, and me.

Michael disliked this whole angle as much as I did. He didn't need the spotlight to be on him, and I'm sure he knew that once the audience turned on him, it would be hard to gain back his credibility when he needed to sell someone else's storyline in the future.

But from a selfish point of view, I was glad the match was on the card, as it meant I could be at ringside calling the action. I was also thrilled that my friend Jerry Lawler finally got his *WrestleMania* moment—even though I knew he would have much preferred a noncomedic bout.

I looked at Cole vs. King as a small little piece of business that helped get a few people to where the company wanted them in a mercifully short amount of time. I promised my wife that I wouldn't let things get to me, and I intended to keep that promise.

But boy oh boy, this one tested me.

The King and Swagger were pros, trained and adept at taking the audience on that journey between the ropes. Cole and I weren't, but we did what we were asked. We were all just following the play calls. All the talent, tenure, and goodwill in the world didn't mean anything when Vince stamped his approval on something—you were either doing it or you were moving on out.

And *WrestleMania* was *WrestleMania*, and no one wanted to miss that show. It didn't matter if it was your first time or your twentieth time, the"Grandest Stage of All" had an intoxicating allure that was hard to resist. If you were in the wrestling business, you wanted to be at *WrestleMania.*

And because Cole and King were on early in the show, I got to commentate on four *WrestleMania* matches after their match was over. It was a win/win for me, and if I had to do a little storyline with which I wasn't comfortable to get there, I was more than fine with that. Everyone knew that most stories culminate at *WrestleMania*, so Cole, Jerry, Swagger, and I would soon part company and move on to whatever else WWE had in store for us.

When *WrestleMania* came, I was back in my element, back on the headset, and back feeling like I could still do the job at a high standard. The Georgia Dome was full, and I knew, sitting there, that I would never be able to shake this business from my blood. I wanted to do nothing else with my professional life but to be at ringside.

But the moment of effusive praise didn't happen at *WrestleMania.* After the show finished, Vince said, "I want you back on *Raw* tomorrow night."

"Tomorrow?" I asked, kinda surprised that I was back on TV so soon.

"Good ol' J.R. is back," the boss said, before disappearing for the next item on his list of things to do.

THE NEXT NIGHT I SHOWED UP, sat at the announce table like I was instructed to do, and welcomed everyone tuning in. "Coming off the heels of an electrifying, memorable *WrestleMania XXVII*, we welcome you live to Atlanta. This is *Monday Night Raw*," I said.

Beside me, Jerry said, "How about it? Good ol' J.R. and The King back where we belong."

"I appreciate it, King. Back in Atlanta. The *WrestleMania* week just keeps on rolling. Tonight's going to awesome."

Turned out that was a lie. That night wasn't awesome, at least not for me. Cole showed up after the first segment in his orange spandex wrestling gear from the night before and squirted a bottle of J.R.'s BBQ sauce all over me.

Problem was, it got in my eye, and I was sent to the doctor to wash it out. If you ever want to feel like your eye just went to hell, dose it with J.R.'s BBQ sauce and blink a couple of times.

I tell you, it was no fun walking back through that curtain most nights and being laughed at. I might have been wrong, but it sure felt like bullying to me. When you grow up the fat kid, who wore Husky jeans for chubby kids, you become real good at absorbing shame and ridicule, but even I was reaching my limit.

I had worked so hard to become a public figure because I wanted to scrub away that very feeling of being laughed at rather than admired. And now I found myself ten years old again. I didn't know what was more painful: having an eye full of BBQ sauce or knowing that this angle with Cole, Jerry, Swagger, and me was going to continue as long as Vince wanted it to.

But I had made a promise to my wife, so I was just rolling with it rather than letting it get to me.

The following week, Jerry won a match that allowed him to pick the stipulation for a return match with Cole. The King picked a tag match, where he and I would "wrestle" Cole and Swagger.

Did you ever have that nightmare where you are being chased by a rotten corpse but you can't move any faster because you're stuck? Well, for me, that rotten corpse was this angle, and no matter how hard I tried, I couldn't outrun it.

Vince, of course, was having a great old time.

On another episode of *Raw*, to "get heat on Cole," they made me kiss Cole's foot live on the air. The segment lost us a couple of hundred thousand viewers, so not only did I think it was the shits, but the viewers at home did too.

So, naturally, Vince kept it going.

Another week on TV, he inflicted a "match" between Cole and me on the poor folks at home. It was a classic encounter during which Michael made fun of my weight, and I punched him so hard I split his lip and busted up my own hand, breaking my knuckle.

I was sure that would end the nightmare.

Nope.

No, we were going to take this feud off regular TV and bring it all the way to a Pay-Per-View, where I had to work with a splint on my hand because I'd broken one of my fingers on Cole's face, and Michael was bruised up from taking my shitty, nontrained punches.

I'm not sure where, but at some point in this conga line of awfulness I gave myself a legitimate hernia and needed surgery. In the storyline I was fired again and off TV anyway, so being laid up a week or two wasn't going to stall any plans the company had for me.

I did, however, tune in to see the *Capitol Punishment* Pay-Per-View, during which they ran an antibullying advertisement—literally the segment before WWE had a Barack Obama impersonator call me "a fat bastard" live on the air.

Yeah. They had the "President" insult me too.

But I managed to keep my promise to my wife, and Vince was about to be more proud of me than ever before in this storyline, remember?

Let's find out how!

Booked Me Simple

TWO MONTHS AFTER I WAS REMOVED FROM TV and had my hernia operation, I was brought back to TV. Vince wanted to freshen up the broadcast team, and I was installed back at the announce desk with Jerry Lawler *and* Michael Cole.

In the storyline, Triple H, who was now Vince's real-life son-in-law, was the new "COO of WWE," and his first order of business was to bring myself and CM Punk back to *Raw*.

Punk, a rebellious anti-authority figure, had been out after his contract ended, and he was legitimately talking about walking away. Vince felt that bringing us both back was a good way of resetting the creative slump and creating some buzz around the product.

The company pulled out all the stops to keep our appearance on the show a surprise—even going so far as to put us up in separate hotels from the rest of the talent and hiding us backstage until our segments were ready to go.

Funny business, wrestling: One day you're out because you're seen as old, and next you're back in because you're seen as new. Of course, by now I'd been in and out more than the activity in a well-booked brothel.

Triple H's voice echoed out from the microphone: "There's one name the WWE fans worldwide wanted back here on *Raw*. I have taken it upon myself this week to contact that man and re-sign him. So I would like it if, right now, you'd help me welcome him back to *Raw*."

My music hit, and out I came to another amazing ovation from the fans. They were happy to see me, and I was ecstatic to see them again. I knew that every time I was asked to walk that ramp might be my last, and I cherished every step.

"Cole, look at this ovation for good ol' J.R.," The King said from ringside.

Cole had his head in his hands. I was instructed, as part of our ongoing story, to shake Cole's hand and then go to work as normal. I put out my hand at the announce table, but Cole wouldn't shake it.

I knew then that something was up. Again.

Cole stood on the desk with the microphone and said to Triple H, "I refuse to sit down and work with this fat hayseed."

"Hayseed"? I wonder if that was directly from Vince.

Cole continued: "I refuse to work with this two-face—I mean, one-face . . ."

Yep, definitely Vince: Word was he liked to mock my Bell's palsy in writers' meetings.

Michael wasn't done yet. "What's the matter, J.R., you need the money since your restaurants went belly-up? What did you do, eat all the profits? Your ego couldn't let you sit home. The only thing bigger than your ego is your gut."

Jeez, a fella wouldn't want to be self-conscious about his weight or failed eateries around this place.

We gained a million people in the ratings for my return, so I was happy with that, but I still didn't like people making fun of my weight or poking fun at me in general. Throw in the digs about my Bell's palsy, and I was hanging on to the last sliver of the promise I'd made to Jan. My take was simple: I had signed the contract to come back. I had known what I was potentially coming back to. I had honestly hoped that Vince and the writing team would get bored of tormenting me on TV, but we were years into it, and it only seemed to be getting worse.

Michael was upset at having to deliver the childish, hurtful, and frankly embarrassing verbiage that was being written for him. What I quickly found out, though, was that not reacting to the provocation was worse than reacting to it.

It was week after week, month after month.

They even put me back in the ring to wrestle. John Cena, the company's biggest star since Austin and The Rock, was going to be my partner this time, and we were facing off against Alberto Del Rio and Michael Cole.

Now, Del Rio is a handsome native Mexican, whose family is practically royalty in the wrestling world down there, so of course WWE booked Alberto to play the bad guy in our match there. They had no idea that the guy was a star and beloved, so they constructed the match around the crowd hating him.

Cena knew better. He also knew how to do what the agents working backstage couldn't figure out: how to get me through a simple match in a way that made sense. John booked me in easy, basic spots, and he kept all the literal heavy lifting for himself. Cena could sense I was nervous—I said as much in our interview before the match. I was closing in on sixty years old, a grandparent, and I didn't want to be "wrestling."

When we got in the ring, I got a good reaction from the crowd, but Cena, the company's number one hero, was booed because WWE insisted on putting him in there against Del Rio.

"Mexico! Mexico!" the crowd chanted.

I mercifully got the win by putting Cole into an ankle lock.

When I got back through the curtain, John was very complimentary. I had signed Cena in the early 2000s and was proud as hell of what he had become. He was always a gentleman, with a rare passion for WWE.

Another week passed and Cole called me out again, and I could almost hear the collective groan across the world. I just wanted it all to stop and get back to announcing, but that wasn't in the WWE's plans. Instead they thought it would be a good idea to have Photoshopped pictures of fat people with my head on them as Cole ran me down again on the microphone. He issued a challenge to good ol' J.R. and put my job on the line. If I lost, I would BE FIRED.

You know, something original.

I presumed it couldn't get any more humiliating, so I didn't really care about getting into the ring again. I got the sense that Vince and the writing staff knew that wasn't really embarrassing me as much anymore, so my challenge wasn't a match at all.

This time it was three "battles" in the ring and they were all live on *Raw.* First was a rap battle, second was a dance battle, and third was a live weigh-in to see who was lighter.

At this stage I had gone past the point of giving a shit.

If this was really what got them their kicks, then I was going to do it and not let them see even a flicker of annoyance on my face.

Of course, when the time came I was so disinterested and uninvested in the whole thing that I forgot my "rap" battle lines, "danced" like a fool, and let WWE remind me once more that I was fat by weighing me live on the air.

And I lost my job. I was off the air again because Michael Cole had "won."

When I walked through the curtain, Vince was waiting. I'd never seen his face so lit up and happy. This was it, this was what I had done that made my boss the happiest he'd ever been with my performance.

"Goddamnit, J.R., you *finally* let me have it. You let me have all of you, J.R. I'm so proud of you," Vince said. He was clapping, euphoric, happier than I'd ever seen him toward me. All the calls I'd made, all the Superstars I helped get over, all the personal sacrifices, all the signings, the budgets balanced, the payroll never being a cent wrong, all the professional hurdles—and the thing that made Vince McMahon the most proud of me was him getting me to literally shake on live TV.

I'll never forget seeing the look of joy on his face—and feeling the look of confusion grow on mine.

Vince often said he wasn't in the wrestling business, but no other moment in all our decades together encapsulated that for me like this one. He knew my energy to fight against the awful creative impulses in the company was gone, and my white flag led me to just do whatever shit they wrote—and it made the boss glow.

I was finally what he wanted.

TWENTY

ANOTHER TURN IN THE ROAD

Very Few Things

I WAS MAKING PEACE with the fact my full-time on-air run in WWE had passed. I wasn't happy about it, I didn't feel it was right, but I was sure they would bring me in for special occasions, nostalgia nights, and have me on the bench in a "break in case of emergency"-type situation.

And as it turns out, in 2012, I was used for all of those scenarios.

Earlier in the year they brought me back to call a match at *WrestleMania XXVIII*, and it was my honor to lend my voice to Triple H vs. Undertaker, with Shawn Michaels as the referee. Cole and I shook hands on the air, to effectively end one of the most meaningless feuds in WWE history.

The match itself was billed as "The End of an Era," but everyone involved kept going in the business long after the match was over. The magical "never say never" is more prevalent in the wrestling business than just about any other field of sports or entertainment—very few "last time ever" or "retirement" matches actually stick. (Seven years later, all the men involved would be wrestling each other again in Saudi Arabia, of all places.)

But this was a helluva bout, with Hunter and Undertaker telling a classic story that built deliberately to an amazing finish. Both men were masters when it came to doing less to gain more, and with Shawn, all three knew exactly what to do to get the reaction they wanted. It felt big time because it was big time, and I was prouder than hell to be there at ringside, calling the action.

I was most proud, though, that the talent had requested me. Each time a legend went to Vince and asked for me personally, it made my heart swell.

But it was after that match that my next adventure in the wrestling business would take shape. Triple H, who was now also running the talent relations department under the title vice president of talent and live events, took me aside afterward and talked about his vision for WWE's developmental strategy.

Triple H—or Paul Levesque, as his parents named him—was taking over more responsibilities backstage as his full-time in-ring career wound down.

"I want to create something that will rival the best training systems in the world, J.R.," he said. "I'd love to get you more involved in that side of things."

Florida Championship Wrestling was where WWE had put most of their developmental eggs since moving away from its relationship with Ohio Valley Wrestling in Kentucky that we had when I left talent relations. Steve Keirn—one half of the amazing The Fabulous Ones, and Skinner in WWE—owned FCW, and had done an amazing job with very limited resources. But WWE wanted to control their own destiny in terms of new talent, so Triple H moved on from FCW and began creating WWE's own developmental brand, NXT.

The Game knew my passion for developing younger talent. When I was heading talent relations, it was a huge part of my work, and I always kept my hand in it because of my love for coaching. Even after leaving the post, I enjoyed being part of the system that showed our younger, newer talents how to bump properly and the basics of ring safety; I explained wrestling psychology and instilled in them a general business etiquette.

"I want you to go to Florida a few days a week and give your expertise to the next generation that's coming up," Hunter said. "I'm going to bring all the new talent under one umbrella, under one roof, if I can. So I'd love for you to go down there and help Dusty and the guys."

I was sunscreened and sitting on the plane in my shorts before Hunter could finish his pitch. The appeal to me was threefold: I loved coaching, I loved that developmental was a completely different atmosphere than WWE's main rosters, and I loved Dusty Rhodes, who was helping to guide the developmental league.

Dusty and I went all the way back to Jim Crockett Promotions (as told in my first book, *Slobberknocker*), in the late 1980s, and working with him was always enlightening, especially when he was "genius-ing," as he called it. We had a friendly rivalry during Texas vs. Oklahoma college games, but we loved each other dearly. People talk all the time about someone lighting up a room or someone being larger than life, but Dusty's ability to do both made him millions, as he sold out venues all over the world as a Superstar wrestler in his own right. The fact that he was now a beloved coach and trainer was a testament to the sheer range of his abilities.

The NXT name had gone through a few iterations in WWE, starting out as an initiative to pair up main-roster talent with rookies for a series of physical challenges on WWE television.

Funnily enough, that didn't get far.

But Hunter wanted to revamp the NXT brand with TV tapings in a new state-of-the-art training facility in Florida. Triple H knew what anyone in talent development knew: that the most important resource in the entertainment business is new faces. And with all the other wrestling companies largely out of business, it was time WWE took the development of its own talent seriously.

And what talent it had in training.

Roman Reigns, Seth Rollins, "Dean Ambrose" (as Jon Moxley was called in his WWE tenure), Paige, Sasha Banks, Bayley, Big E, Xavier Woods, Bray Wyatt, Luke Harper, Erick Rowan, Neville (as PAC was called in his WWE run)—the list of potential breakout Superstars who were wrestling, or being signed, to NXT at that time went on and on.

I knew walking in the door that I'd be happy.

"If I could do this for the rest of my career, I'd be happy," I told Jan on my first night.

"You think you will?" she asked.

"I don't see a path back to *Raw*," I said. "And I'm okay with that."

I was at peace and in a role that I knew could bring me happiness. But then my old partner Jerry Lawler had to up and die.

(Almost.)

Away from the Mothership

MAN, I LOVED FLORIDA. The weather, the work, the freedom, the people—it was the perfect blend for me. "My fat looks better tanned than white," Arn Anderson used to say, and living in Florida I was convinced he was right. Good ol' J.R. was strutting around the Sunshine State like a new man.

I was producing new announcing talent, going on the air myself, mentoring younger in-ring talents, but mostly I was decompressing from the tense atmosphere of WWE's main roster.

However, a little time and distance away convinced me even more that I wasn't blameless for my treatment backstage. I should have listened more, figured out better ways of saying what I felt needed to be said. I was sharp and angry more than I wanted to be, and it was a defensive thing. I'd just found myself in a toxic space—some of it self-created, some not.

But Florida gave me the time and perspective to see that I didn't want to be immersed in that atmosphere anymore. We all knew that what was going on in NXT was special; the trainees' passion and drive and optimism reignited my love for the sport itself. I even had a routine going: same hotel, same restaurants, becoming a regular to the waitstaff and owners.

I loved being first in and last out every night because my zeal for the business was sparking again. And I wasn't the only one—the general excitement and anticipation was infectious.

We moved TV production down to Full Sail University and unhooked NXT from WWE TV tapings completely. We were repackaged, realigned, and ready to tape our own pilot, aimed at the online audience.

I treasured my new voyage because I liked knowing that I didn't know:

Was this going to work? Were these new kids going to make it? Would the audience embrace a smaller, less story-driven product?

None of us knew for sure, but we all hoped the audience would feel as passionately as we did.

We taped the first four shows of NXT back-to-back, in Full Sail's state-of-the-art five-hundred-seat studio, giving it that old-school vibe that most wrestling shows had back in the day.

The production was similar to WWE, by design. It was modeled around a mini-WWE taping so the talent and crew got to experience what it would be like if they broke through and were called up to the main roster. Production was the same, and we mirrored the WWE infrastructure as much as possible, so I felt at home as the lights went down to start our countdown.

"You can't grow positivity unless you plant it first" was my mantra in the production meetings. Not only were the wrestlers new, but the crew was filled with students and first-timers too, and I wanted to make sure they knew how to engage the wrestlers right out of the gate.

I was adamant that we build these talented kids up. "They're already working through a lot of insecurities out there, so let's give them support and positivity," I said. "The worst thing that can happen to a performer is that they lose hope."

I could see my words landing; I truly felt like I had a lot left to give to this business. Maybe NXT would be not just a place for rookies to grow but a place where lifers like me could reinvent themselves too. For the first time in a long time, it felt like Jan and I were on a smooth road—no surprises, no more illnesses, and everyone was happy and healthy.

But then my old friend Jerry Lawler collapsed live on *Raw*.

"Honey," Jan shouted, "come quick."

Her voice let me know something was really wrong. I was in the kitchen on a call while *Raw* was playing in the lounge. I hurried back. Jan was crying while looking at the screen.

"What happened?" I asked her.

"Something is wrong with Jerry," she replied. "Looks bad."

"King?" I asked.

She nodded as Michael Cole appeared on our screen. My hand was shaking as I turned up the volume.

"Well, ladies and gentlemen," he said. His face was solemn. "I'm sure you've noticed Jerry hasn't been active in the last couple of matches. Earlier on tonight Jerry passed out at ringside. Jerry collapsed and was helped to the back . . . stretchered to the back. We understand now that Jerry is receiving medical attention in the back. They're preforming CPR as we speak. Again, this is not part of tonight's entertainment. Again, Jerry Lawler collapsed at ringside tonight and they're performing CPR in the locker-room area."

Michael looked shaken; his face was pale, his voice was trembling a little. I immediately began calling and texting people backstage. No one knew what the latest was. Jerry had gone straight to the hospital, and all they knew was that it was serious.

Luckily for The King, the WWE doctor was right beside him at ringside when he collapsed. His immediate attention saved Jerry's life.

He was dead. Then brought back. And then reports said he had died again, only to come back a second time.

I went back and rewatched it. Jerry was doing his job—I could hear his voice on commentary. But then he began to make snoring sounds. It was hard to watch, but Michael Cole handled the situation like a pro. His pre-WWE experience as a news correspondent kicked in, and he walked our audience through a truly difficult situation.

Back home, Jan and I cried for Jerry, as we weren't sure if he'd make it and couldn't get any answers. I think my fear of heart attacks kicked in too, because both my parents had died of a heart attack at age sixty-four. I also knew from my long friendship with The King that he never went to the doctor; if something was wrong, he didn't want to know.

By the end of *Raw*, Michael seemed a little more hopeful. The King wasn't dead, but he had dodged a massive bullet. If not for the doctor being right there, who knows what would have happened?

Once I made contact and knew Jerry was okay, I knew the call was coming.

"Vince would like you to fill in for King while he recovers," Kevin Dunn said to me over the phone.

"Anything you need," I replied.

Jerry was weakened but very much planning on a full recovery. I knew what the assignment was; I knew that it was only going to be a month or so.

"I look forward to it," I said to Kevin as I hung up.

But there was something about packing my bag to go back this time that felt different from all the others. It's like any relationship—there're only so many times you can break up without a bit of numbness setting in. And that's what was happening to me. I was thrilled to go back on commentary, but WWE wasn't my whole life anymore. Maybe at the age of sixty I had finally figured out how to do my job without it becoming my obsession. Maybe I could go back and just enjoy it in the moment, instead of plowing through old grievances and worrying about ones that hadn't happened yet.

Hell, during my little return, Vince even put on a "J.R. Appreciation Night" for me when *Raw* filmed in Oklahoma, to help boost local ticket sales.

I'm not going to lie: I was humbled and honored. When Vince took the mic and spoke, it really meant something to me.

He said, "Tonight is good ol' J.R. Appreciation Night, and I can tell you, no one appreciates J.R. more than I do. J.R. was born and reared here in Oklahoma . . . in the tradition of Oklahoma and Americana values of hard work and dedication. James Brown, the late James Brown, used to state that he was the hardest working man in show business—but he never met J.R. When it comes to dedication, most of you know J.R. as good ol' J.R. from behind the announce position. He certainly did that better than anyone else in the history of our business, including Gordie Solie. J.R., in terms of his work ethic, this is a true story: During a PPV, a three-hour PPV, J.R. passed a kidney stone; he would not leave his post—he passed a kidney stone and kept on commentating. As far as being on the other side . . . Many of you don't know J.R.'s executive skills. As far as dedication is concerned, there's probably no one any more dedicated in the history of our business than J.R. is to WWE. Whether it was talent recruitment, development, and management or whether it was television production and presentation; whether it was the untold hours and hours he would sit at his desk in the office, or at home, twenty-four hours a day, trying to conjure up matches that would be enticing for you to wanna see. J.R. would do anything for the business. And a testament to that would be something that in this ring here, this arena, some time ago, when J.R. joined a certain special club that we won't mention. Again, J.R. would do anything for the business. When you think of J.R., you have to think of legacy and what he continues to leave. When you think of the fact his product now is in at least thirty different languages and in at least one hundred and thirty different countries all over the world, J.R. is a household name worldwide. You'd have to wonder, however, how some of J.R.'s terms translate. How would 'Slobberknocker' translate in Chinese? Or 'stomp a mudhole and walk it dry,' maybe in German? How about some of the other J.R. terms he said so many times, like 'business is about to pick up'? It always picked up when he was right there, or behind the scenes contributing to WWE. There're many people who could say many, many wonderful things and accolades about Jim Ross. I would just like to state that Jim Ross is an American icon, and my friend. Thanks, Jim."

Vince then called me to the ring. I expected the worst, but he simply shook my hand, and it felt like a closure of sorts. He gave me a plaque, and I got to stand in front of my people and say hello without anything bad happening.

Even though I knew The King wouldn't be back for a few weeks, this was my swan song. I tried to let go of the WWE decisions that I could not change; I knew that road led nowhere.

Instead, I tried to focus on the good.

When I got home, Jan had the plaque hung in my office because she knew how proud I was of it—and I knew how proud she was of me.

TWENTY-ONE

RESET, RETIRE, OR REINVENT

The Principal's Office

ON SEPTEMBER 10, 2013, Vince's assistant called me and said the boss wanted to meet me in his office. I knew there and then what was going to happen.

"What do you think he wants?" Jan asked me.

"He's going to fire me," I said.

"No," she replied. "He wouldn't, would he?"

I chuckled; she'd seen Vince fire me plenty of times before.

My new troubles had started a few weeks prior, when WWE asked me to host a live symposium to promote the new and lucrative 2K video game in Los Angeles. My panel was a mix of legends and current stars: Paul Heyman, Mick Foley, Daniel Bryan, Rey Mysterio, Steve Austin, Ric Flair, and Dolph Ziggler.

The brief was largely unknown, because we had no production meeting and no walk-through. There wasn't even anyone in my ear giving me direction once we hit the air. I was simply handed a script at the last second and shown the stage when the time came.

I knew we had a mix of natural talkers from different eras who were more than capable of keeping the proceedings interesting and fast-paced. But it wasn't the other panelists I was worried about—it was me. Everyone seemed to have faith that good ol' J.R. could handle things without a net. The execs at the game publishing company had watched my work for years and presumed I needed little or no input. WWE obviously thought the same. But I knew the second the lights came up that I was rusty, that my time on the bench had hurt my timing and delivery.

But I didn't want to say anything because I felt I was on shaky professional ground already, and I didn't want WWE to think I couldn't handle anything I was given.

In the green room before the show, a few of the talents were enjoying the free cocktails on offer. Usually I wouldn't dream of drinking before a gig, but I took one cocktail and brought it onstage with me to calm my nerves. After all, the cool kids were being slightly rebellious, so I was too.

I take full responsibility for that.

We kicked off the symposium, and I tried to slip in some one-liners to lighten the mood; I railed against the script I was given. I genuinely felt the ad-libbing was entertaining the audience, and I knew our goal was to get eyeballs on the product. The fans in attendance seemed engaged and entertained, and my wrestling brothers were having a good time too.

I thought we were crushing it.

I had misread the situation completely.

As the show rolled on, I saw Ric down at the end of the dais and noticed that he was in no state to be part of the freewheeling panel discussion with WWE brass present.

A few months before, Ric had found his twenty-five-year-old son, Reid, dead of a heroin overdose in the hotel room next to his. Father and son spent a lot of time together, because Reid was training to be a professional wrestler, just like his old man. Obviously, nobody should find their son dead, but Ric's conviction that he could have prevented it amplified his grief.

We all knew Ric was drinking more than ever to try and cope, and I questioned why they had flown him out at all. The man needed grief counseling, not to "be around his friends" or to use the event as a "diversion to help keep his mind off it," as some suggested.

The Nature Boy took the 2K conversation to a more bar-room type atmosphere when he told behind-the-scenes stories about clean-cut John Cena's drinking and other potential headache-inducing stories WWE might not want aired in public—and I had a hard time keeping my hands on the wheel. It didn't help that I kept trying to add my own "edgy" one-liners to mask my insecurity.

After the show had ended, the sponsors were thrilled when they got word of record traffic on their servers. Well, I'd soon come to learn that there's good kinds of traffic and bad kinds of traffic.

Not that I knew that standing backstage, as we all mingled and said our goodbyes.

Three weeks later Vince asked his assistant to call me in.

And so I went to Stamford.

I entered Vince's office, like I had done a million times before, and I read the room before he even opened his mouth. "I know you're going to fire me, so could you get it over with so I can make my flight back home?" I said.

Vince was a little taken aback by my straightforwardness; I guess I was too. "I'm disappointed in you, J.R.," he said. I wanted to be defiant, but the truth was I was disappointed in myself too. "I was embarrassed by what I heard," Vince continued. "What were you thinking going up there drunk?"

"Drunk?" I said.

"Were you not?" he asked.

"Absolutely not. I had one drink that I didn't even finish," I told him. "All the other stuff, the off-the-cuff remarks, the unprofessional behavior, all of that is true. I fully take responsibility for my part in that. But me being drunk is not true at all."

I could tell Vince was torn; he knew I didn't bullshit, but he'd heard what he'd heard. "People told me I had a drunk guy handling my business, Jim."

Vince only called me "Jim" when he was serious.

"Vince," I said, "I'm not running from this. I'm happy to take an ass-whipping or whatever else is coming my way. But I wasn't drunk."

"I was counting on you," Vince said. "Is this what you are now, unreliable?"

Vince knew my first point in picking talent was their reliability, so his words stung, as I'm sure they were meant to. But the boss was right. This was out of character for me and I'd let him down. I also knew that I hadn't done my career any favors. Anyone who was in Vince's ear about moving me on now had the perfect cover story.

I had basically let myself get flanked by my own stupid behavior—and it broke my heart. My paranoia about being let go was turning into a self-fulfilling prophecy. I knew by Vince's face that he didn't want to fire me, but he'd assured his inner circle that he was going to "handle it"—and backed himself into a corner based on bad information. He couldn't do nothing, or he'd look weak.

"Well, J.R.," he said. "I need to do something here."

"I understand," I said. "The train went off the rails, and I was driving. I wish I could do it over, and I apologize."

Vince stood and shook my hand. "You're always in the principal's office, J.R.," he said with a laugh.

"Trust me, I'd prefer to be by my pool in Norman," I said.

We hugged and, again, it felt different than it had in the past. It wasn't a back-slapping, manly affair. It was genuine.

"You could have done this over the phone," I said in our embrace.

"I respect you too much not to do it face-to-face," he replied.

We separated; both of us had tears in our eyes. My bridge with Vince and WWE was charred but not burned down completely.

"So long, J.R.," he said.

I tipped my hat and left.

I think we both knew that this was it: the moment between us that would change everything. I had been admonished before, fired before, replaced before, but this was different.

This was that part in every failing relationship when both parties have no fight left in them and just want to go their own separate ways for a while. Whatever else happened between me, Vince, and WWE from here on out, the balance had shifted.

By the time I got to my cab, the official WWE tweets were out announcing my retirement. Vince had fired me—although he never said as much in the room—but he'd ultimately done me a PR favor. The chairman could have easily put out a statement echoing the rumors that I was drunk, and there wouldn't have been much I could do about it. But instead he put the word out that I had retired from WWE, which gave me some breathing room and also saved the company from having to say they'd fired me again.

It was a "best of a bad lot" type of scenario.

The many previous times I'd been fired from WWE, I felt scared and adrift. This time I felt free. I knew I had game left, and employment wasn't going to be hard to find. I had confidence in my abilities, and I just had to make sure I didn't take myself out of the game.

From the WWE offices in Stamford to LaGuardia Airport I thought about what I should do. Could I actually retire, or should I reinvent? Was I going to fish, play golf, or maybe burn through my million-plus air miles and see the world? Or was I going to tell them all to kiss my ass?

I knew I'd be back in WWE again; it was just a matter of when. I also knew one other thing for sure: I was finally excited to see what else the world had for me.

TWENTY-TWO

LIFE OUTSIDE THE WALLS

Working Through My Retirement

FOR THE FIRST TIME SINCE I WAS A BOY, I was without work—and totally happy about it. Working for WWE had already secured my financial future. I'd made a great living from being a commentator there—but the life-changing money didn't come until I became a company administrator with stock options. It was then that Vince helped make my future secure and, hopefully, the future of my grandkids too. So I walked out into the free market. I knew WWE would always be my home, and I'd probably find myself back there someday, but for now I was excited about new horizons.

I wasn't looking for *a* role outside of WWE—I was looking for several. I knew I wanted to continue the speaking tours I had undertaken, and I wanted to write an autobiography—those I knew for sure—but I didn't have any set plans afterward. It was exhilarating—and a little scary—to be in my sixties and looking to start fresh.

"You should do a podcast," my old friend Steve Austin said over a call. "I can set you up with my guys."

"Okay," I replied, then immediately went to find out what the hell a podcast was. Turned out it was a medium right up my alley, as it reminded me of doing my old radio show when I worked for WCW.

"Do one show a week," Steve advised.

He was contracted for two, so he knew the level of commitment involved. I was proud of the Texas Rattlesnake for making his way into a new industry that, at the time, wasn't being exploited to its fullest by people in our business. A talented independent wrestler named Colt Cabana was the first I knew of with a wrestling podcast, but Austin was the first mainstream star to take the leap.

I was glad those guys had paved the way in podcasting, because it was exactly the kind of challenge I was looking for. I wasn't very good with new technology, but I loved learning new skills.

The company Steve introduced me to gave me a deal: a blank-sheet type of setup where the pay was linked to the number of listeners I attracted. I liked that, because it was akin to the pro-wrestling model of one's money being attached to the size of the house he drew.

I was energized, and I wanted to hustle for my money again. I liked that my success was in my own hands, and I could put in as much or as little effort as I wanted. It turned out the very first podcast I ever heard was my own first episode.

Not long after I signed the podcast deal, Mauro Ranallo—an extremely gifted commentator—left AXS TV to join WWE. Mauro's departure meant that AXS TV, the U.S. broadcaster for New Japan Pro-Wrestling, was looking for a new voice to fill his slot.

NJPW was a longtime, major brand in the wrestling world, and even though its primary market was Japan, it has cultivated an intense and loyal fan base in the United States too.

My manager, Barry Bloom, called to say that NJPW would like to know if I was interested in the gig. AXS TV was majority-owned by billionaire Mark Cuban, and his executive in charge was a great guy named Adam Swift. Turned out Adam had grown up in the wrestling hotbed of North Carolina, and he told me on our first call how my voice was the voice of his childhood. I learned that one of the very cool things about getting older is that some of the kids who'd grown up on my work were now men and women in positions of power in the broadcasting industry.

"We want you here, J.R.," Adam said. "Hiring you for AXS TV would be one of the most exciting things I could do here."

Boy, was it good for my fragile old ego to hear those words.

Adam and Barry negotiated a nice deal for me to fly out to Los Angeles a handful of days a month to record my commentary for the New Japan shows.

It was there I met Josh Barnett, a legit badass, former UFC Heavyweight Champion, and my new announce partner. Josh was amazing to work with, and we hit if off right away.

I knew immediately I had some catching up to do, though, because New

Japan is so different from WWE style-wise. I had spent a huge amount of my career in WWE emotionally invested in the people viewers saw on the screen. They were "my guys"—I'd signed them, I knew them, I understood what the audience needed to know about them. I was as invested in them as anyone watching at home. With NJPW, I was commentating about guys I didn't really know, and from a sound booth thousands of miles away, instead of being there live.

It was a whole new world for me to master.

Josh and I worked hard on our chemistry and timing, and after a few shows I began to feel a little more comfortable, even if I still struggled to get my Oklahoman tongue around a few of the wrestlers' names. But, thankfully, a small band of Internet trolls helped by calling me an asshole and wishing for me to be fired.

The situation was further complicated by the fact that New Japan, the promoter, already had an English-speaking team that called its matches on a pay-monthly subscription service. It was AXS TV—the broadcaster—who hired me, as they wanted to target the lapsed wrestling fan who might try a brand other than WWE if they heard a familiar voice.

In some fans' minds, this pitted us against the other announce team. Nothing could be further from the truth. I thought the other team was supremely talented, and there was no ill will or animosity between us. I even asked AXS TV to let Kevin Kelley—the voice of NJPW online—work with me on their station when Josh couldn't make a taping.

Kevin and I had worked together at WWE twenty years earlier, and I always found him to be talented and professional. I was happy for him that he was making a living outside of WWE.

"There's no clash here, J.R.," he told me. "We're working for a completely different set of fans."

I agreed with him. Some fans online were voicing their displeasure, but the business of it all was more simple—I understood that, and Kevin did too. He was announcing for the hardcore fan who was already on board, and I was announcing for the more casual fan who might be taking a look because my voice was familiar to them.

In my few years with AXS TV, I had no ego whatsoever when it came to who was "the voice" of NJPW.

Even when New Japan put on shows in Long Beach to catch the American market's eye, I offered to step aside and let Kevin take my spot. It seemed he and his broadcast partner, Don Callis, weren't told that Josh and I were calling the show, so they arrived with no work to do. I wanted to hand over the reins, but our paymasters wanted what they wanted and Josh and I were asked to call the action.

With more places to work, and more fans looking for an alternative to WWE, I knew the wrestling business was changing. It was in Long Beach that I met one of the men who would crystalize that change in the future. But neither he or I knew it at the time.

Tony Khan came along to see the New Japan show, and we were introduced by our mutual friend, SiriusXM NFL Radio host Alex Marvez. I came to learn that Tony's family was in the football business—both here and in the UK—and that Tony had an encyclopedic brain for professional wrestling. He was young, smart, and had a lot of money behind him. But mostly, I noticed just how much of a fan he was.

Through the course of our conversation, it struck me that he said more than once when talking about the wrestling business, "If I owned a company I would..." Not that I thought Tony was solidly planning to enter the wrestling business at that stage—but it seemed to me to be at least a germ of an idea in his mind.

We carried on our conversations after the New Japan show was over, and it was easy to tell how passionate and knowledgeable Tony was about many different promotions across many different eras in my world. These conversations with Tony and Alex would come back to save my wrestling career several years later when Tony would, in fact, enter the wrestling business with All Elite Wrestling on TNT.

My few years away from WWE were much needed, and they planted many seeds for future opportunities and adventures.

I was still hurting that I'd left WWE in the way I had, but the new experiences and offers were amazing, to say the least. I got to tour my spoken word show, write my book, make my podcast successful, and keep commentating on professional wrestling via New Japan and another venture in the UK with ITV.

And then came the call, and the offer to again go home.

"Vince wants to give you a two-year deal, J.R.," Kevin said. "What do you think?"

"What's his plan for me?" I asked.

"He wants you to call the main event of *WrestleMania* this year," Kevin said.

"I've heard that before," I replied. "And I'm working on projects I really like right now."

"Vince said you keep working wherever else you like. He just wants you back in the fold."

Vince never let anyone work outside of WWE. I was taken aback, so I needed clarity. "Vince told you I can keep my podcast, tours, and New Japan work?"

"Yes," Kevin said.

It was a win/win for me. I get to work a light schedule with WWE, keep doing what was making me happy, *and* I'd get to end my story there on a better note.

"Tell Vince he's got a deal," I said.

TWENTY-THREE

GOODBYE

The Unimaginable

THE SMOLDERING BRIDGE I'd left with WWE when Vince "retired" me was about to be reopened again. *WrestleMania 33* was the planned return date, and they wanted me to call Undertaker vs. Roman Reigns in the main event.

Jan was excited as hell that I was being asked to rejoin the team. She wanted me to walk away from WWE when the time came, on my own terms, instead of being forcibly retired.

The truth was, the thought of going back to my team added an excitement to our house because we both missed our friends in WWE. Jan never held any grudges, and I was trying to be more like her in that regard. My wife implored me to look at what we had, how lucky we were. "You should go back there in peace, sweetheart, and not in defiance," she said.

And she was right.

Vince and I had a relationship that many people couldn't figure out—me chief among them—but I loved him for all he did for me and my family. "Happy Christmas, Jim," he said in a text around the holidays. "One helluva run. Thanks for being there for me. Love U."

It meant the world to me. The older I got, the less drama I wanted and the more wrongs I wanted to make right.

I knew I had made the right decision when I saw my wife. She was already planning her dress for the Hall of Fame ceremony, and I was feeling freer too. I was no longer caught up in my need to be the best or my need to prove myself. I was excited to go back and just enjoy what an amazing privilege it was to make a living doing what I had always wanted to do.

Jan and I were feeling grateful, thankful, hopeful, and blessed.

And then came the call.

I was driving home along Interstate 44 toward my home in Norman. I had just finished recording my podcast out of a small radio station in Chickasha and I was looking forward to getting home. We were less than two weeks away from *WrestleMania*, and everything was clicking nicely into place. Suddenly my phone lit up with a number I didn't recognize. Normally I would let it go to voicemail, but for some reason, I answered this time.

"Is this J.R.?" the female voice at the other end of the line asked.

"Yes, ma'am, who is this?" I asked.

"My name is Katy Perry," she replied.

I thought it was a rib. *What the hell would Katy Perry be doing calling me?*

"Mr. Ross, I'm calling from the Norman PD," she said. "Your wife has been in an accident, and you should get to OU Medical Center as quickly as you can."

"Are you serious?"

"Yes, sir. I'm afraid I am."

The medical center was about half an hour north of where I was, so I hurried right there. I had no idea if I was arriving to find a broken finger or something much worse.

I got to the hospital, and Officer Perry had a parking space cordoned off for me close to the front door. It was then I had a feeling that this wasn't good.

I was led through the hospital with no idea what to expect.

They brought me to an examination room where Jan was lying. They had shaved half her hair off, and her head was cut open to let her brain swell outside the skull.

My world flipped upside down. She looked so small on the bed. I couldn't believe what I was seeing. I froze; my whole world instantly shattered.

Wires and tubes were everywhere, moving from machine to machine and back into her body. Doctors and nurses talked to me, but I couldn't hear anything. I knew from their eyes that Jan was in serious trouble. She was just so small, and the damage so great.

When I had left the house earlier, Jan said she was going to the gym. There was nothing unusual about that; she worked out at the same place no less than five days a week. She took her black Vespa and wore her WWE ballcap—there was no helmet law in Oklahoma. A few minutes from our house, she was run over by a 2000 Mercury Grand Marquis, driven by a seventeen-year-old who hit her from behind.

They took her down for surgery.

I sat alone and waited.

The longest wait of my life.

I panicked and prayed, I cried and I hoped. I have never wanted anything more in my life than for my Jan to wake up.

After what felt like an eternity, the top neurologist at the medical center spoke to me. I watched his eyes—not much hope there. "If she makes it," he said, "she would be a different person and you wouldn't recognize her, nor would she recognize you."

His words were to the point and very clear.

"She would not be able to communicate at all or manage her bodily functions," he said.

I knew Jan would never accept that fate.

They transferred her to her own room.

I talked to her.

I tried to make her laugh, saying how mad she'd be at me for letting strangers cut her hair.

I sobbed and I held her little hand.

I squeezed as gently as I could, time and again, hoping she would squeeze me back.

But she didn't.

She couldn't.

My wife was there in front of me, but she was already gone.

I hated the tubes in her, and I hated that her hair was shaved like it was—only because I knew Jan would hate it too. She took such pride in her appearance. Each second she wasn't trying to fix herself reminded me that our time together was gone.

I was alone.

And I loved her more than anything.

That's when I came to the agonizing realization that it would be up to me to take my wife off life support.

No warning, no goodbye, but twenty-five amazing years together.

All of us only get one true love, and mine was no more.

My kids were hundreds of miles away, and my wrestling family was crisscrossing the country. I didn't know whom to call or in whom to confide.

I looked at my phone, and it was filled with messages of love and support. The McMahon family, offering anything I needed. Mark Cuban told me he'd personally fly in the top neurologist in the country if I needed him to. The Rock called, Austin called, Triple H and Stephanie called. Knowing that people loved Jan so much meant the world to me. I was offered all the love, money, help, and support in the world. But as the hours rolled past, it became more and more apparent that there was nothing anyone could do.

Jan never regained consciousness.

Two days after the collision, I called some friends to find me a priest to read Jan the last rites. I was too heartbroken for a memorial service.

I regret that decision from time to time, but at that moment, I just wasn't capable of it. I didn't need any more heartbreak; I had all the grief I could handle.

There was no one at home except for our cat, Mickey, a silver Persian who was literally afraid of his shadow. My wife loved him so much that she gave him his own entrance music, Living Colour's "Cult of Personality," except Jan changed the words to "The Cat with Personality."

I found myself relieved to have Mickey in the house with me. I was struggling being there on my own.

I found myself turning on the TV when I left the house because I liked to fool myself into thinking she was at home when I got back. Those seconds of hope were worth the pain of remembering all over again that she was gone. I just needed to hear some voices when I got back from the store. I needed to think that God had made a mistake, and He'd put her back in the chair she loved, in front of the TV.

Days passed. My family was amazing. Her family too. But everyone goes home. I knew I didn't want to be alone. If I heard the right song at the wrong time, I'd crumble. I began to get annoyed at myself that I couldn't really control the crying. I hated feeling so raw. But my tears for Jan were different than any others I'd ever shed. I was completely broken, painfully alone.

And I learned that there's no science to grieving. We all have different hearts, and there's no manual. My sadness was challenging me to even stay upright. My face was unshaven, my watch stopped. I was slipping into a hole, and I knew I needed to throw myself a lifeline.

I didn't want to be a burden to my daughters and their lives, so I packed my bags for my other family—my wrestling family. I needed a reason to shave, a reason to put on my watch. I knew that if I stopped moving, I wouldn't be able to get going again.

My life was empty.

My home was empty.

My Angel wasn't coming back.

I needed to be around people who loved me.

TEN DAYS AFTER JAN DIED, I arrived in Orlando, at the site of *WrestleMania 33*, like a man with nowhere else to go. It was supposed to be me and my wife together, but instead I showed up alone because she was gone and I was afraid of myself alone at home.

I got word from home that Mickey the cat had died too. I had asked my landscaper, Stephen Link, to look out for Mickey, as the cat was more down than normal around the house. Stephen told me that when he couldn't find Mickey he searched high and low and then found him under our bed, on Jan's side.

I wasn't looking forward to coming home at all.

I signed my WWE contract with no agents or managers needed. It was more than I would have paid myself; Vince saw to that. He wanted to look after me, and even though I didn't need the money, I sure as hell treasured the opportunity to stay busy.

When the chips were down, Vince McMahon looked after me. He knew me well enough to know that I was better off around something I loved. As I signed the agreement, I remembered a drive the chairman and I took once. "Jim," he said. (Again, he always calls me "Jim" when he's being serious.) "You and I are the same."

I laughed. To take a cursory look, Vince and I are anything but "the same."

"How do you make that one out?" I asked.

"We're just two rednecks," he said.

"I find it very interesting, Mr. Chairman," I replied, "that you told me this information with no witnesses."

Vince laughed. I did too.

Just seconds after crying for my wife, and minutes after not knowing how I was going to get through what I was going to get through. Vince knew I wasn't in my hour of need in terms of money. But I was in my hour of need in terms of hope.

WHEN I GOT TO CAMPING WORLD STADIUM, everyone made it their business to come and tell me how much Jan had meant to them. Turned out my beautiful wife had been sending the wrestlers' wives gifts for their kids' birthdays and other big occasions.

My old friend and road brother Jerry Lawler reminded me how my wife had gotten his girlfriend, Lauryn, into Louis Vuitton by saying she needed "a big girl's bag." King wasn't happy. His reaction to the price of purses still brings me joy.

And the wives and girlfriends made sure to find me. Jan really did have a massive impact on them all. I was glad I'd come, but I was feeling a little overwhelmed, so I knocked on the door of Undertaker's tour bus. He embraced me and invited me in to seek refuge. He hugged me, comforted me; made sure no one bothered me. I knew I could sit with 'Taker and talk all day, or I could say nothing if I didn't want to. He was the quiet company I needed.

We prepped in silence, dressed in silence, and left each other to take the walk we each needed to take on our own.

When the time came I waited by that curtain, that portal between two worlds, and I thought of my Angel.

As I stood there I promised her—the woman who stood by me, steered me, endured me, helped me, loved me, listened to me, journeyed with me, cried with me, lived with me, and died before me—that I wouldn't give up.

As I broke through that curtain one last time in Orlando, the stadium packed, the air warm, I could think only of her. My Angel. The one who made me so much better.

She had wanted to be here with me so badly; but she couldn't. And I had no idea how I was going to make it from the top of the ramp down to the announce table below—but she helped me. As the crowd chanted my name, and my lips quivered, Jan's memory urged me to put one foot in front of the other. She gave me the strength I never had on my own. I couldn't have loved her more, and still I felt she deserved even more.

Wrestling soothed me, comforted me, opened its arms to me once more when I needed to be embraced. The fights, the hardships, the struggle, the payoffs, the careers made, and the highs and the lows—wrestling was always there to help me forget. Ever since I was a boy playing with action figures on my bed, and now as a man brought low, wrestling loved me back when I needed it most.

I had business to attend to and a woman to make proud. I was going to call my heart out for her. For one more night I was going to be the man she knew I could be, using the talent she knew I had.

I pointed every single word I spoke toward the sky. I was broken, and even among tens of thousands of people I was lost. But I at least knew I was lost within a giant circle of *my* people. And when the waves of pain grew too big, I looked around and listened.

My life meant something. I had done something good with my time. I had met someone truly special. I loved. I fell. I stood. And I walked on again. Even without my Angel, my feet carried me forward down that ramp.

The people cheered. Their kindness toward me almost reduced me to tears. I hugged my old "nemesis," Michael Cole, as I sat down at ringside.

"Absolutely incredible," Michael said for the people at home. "I know it's been a rough couple of weeks for you, J.R., but I want you to do what you do best, as the greatest of all time—and that's call the main event at *WrestleMania*."

"I'm very excited to be here," I said, with every drop of passion I could muster at that time. "Let's raise some hell and have some fun."

As the music hit for the main event, under the Orlando night sky, I almost drowned in memories. I just wanted Jan to know that I'd be okay until we met again. My heart was smashed, but my love for her would sustain me for as long as I needed it to. Because ever since I met my wife, all I ever wanted to do was impress her.

I knew I would spend the rest of my life with my heart broken, but also knowing that I was truly blessed, and that I was truly loved back.

I could want nothing more from a life lived.

EPILOGUE

Looking Ahead

MY FINAL CONTRACT WITH WWE ran out in April 2018, just before *WrestleMania 34*. It was the fitting end to a twenty-five-year relationship, which started with a baptism of fire at *WrestleMania IX* and went on to encompass more than I ever dreamed possible.

Back then, all I wanted was the opportunity to call matches. I was lucky to do much more than that in my two and a half decades with Vince.

Despite our ups and downs, I still love WWE—and the McMahon family. This may sound strange, given the way I was sometimes treated over the years. To be honest, I don't always understand it myself. But some jobs are more like family than business: You can fall out and make up, but the baseline pretty much stays the same.

I had far more great times in WWE than bad times. I met countless wonderful people there. I forged lifelong friendships, made great TV, and earned enough money to look after the people I love—forever.

Most important, I got to be the thing I dreamed of being when I was a kid. How many people can say that? As my granny used to tell me, "Jimmy, someone is going to be what you want to be, so why not that someone be you?"

I was the voice of WWE during the Monday night cable wars—a war we won, thankfully. I got to recruit and develop the greatest roster in WWE history. As the head of talent relations, I watched Mick Foley and Steve Austin soar when others had doubted them. I signed a handsome young Dwayne Johnson over a meal he couldn't even afford to pay for at the time. I brought in the best talent that WCW had to offer—not just the nWo or Jericho and the Radicalz, but Booker T and Rey Mysterio as well.

I had the privilege of watching new talent like John Cena and Batista—who, along with The Rock, are now bona fide Hollywood stars—come up through the ranks in Ohio Valley Wrestling, alongside future Hall of Famers Randy Orton and Brock Lesnar. It was thrilling for me to see WWE take up the mantle of building the stars of tomorrow with our own developmental system, NXT. And I'm incredibly proud that my talent relations team helped change the perception of what a WWE Champion could be, making room for smaller guys, lighter guys, guys from different backgrounds and with different strengths. When I first brought Chris Jericho and Eddie Guerrero around, there was major skepticism. But both became champions and fan favorites.

Why? Because true talent trumps size every single day of the week.

These successes opened the door—and not just in WWE—for smaller but hugely talented names like Daniel Bryan, A.J. Styles, CM Punk, Seth Rollins, Kofi Kingston, and so many others who are defining the next generation of wrestling.

And it wasn't only on the male side: During my time at WWE, the perception of what a women's division could offer was rapidly changing too.

We went from pudding matches and "puppies" to legitimate, top-billed female stars breaking through. I watched the likes of Trish, Lita, Jackie, Ivory, Molly Holly, Jazz, Victoria, Gail Kim, and Mickie James toss the old wisdom out the window, changing the system from the inside out. These pioneers then passed the baton to up-and-comers like Sasha Banks, Asuka, Bayley, and Charlotte Flair to blow the doors off what a Diva could be. One of the last people I had a hand in hiring was Becky Lynch, who is now a true headliner, drawing cheers as loud as any of the Boys.

And there was no shortage of opportunities outside the ring, either. Thanks to WWE, I got to sell my own branded products, run restaurants, launch live events, build a podcast with the Podfather, Conrad Thompson—and, yes, even write a few books.

But as grateful as I am to WWE, it's important to separate my love of the sport from my love of the company. As this book comes out, I find himself, for the first time in many years, the weekly voice of a wrestling company once again. It was a simple, pleasant meeting with a young man named Tony

Khan, at a New Japan event in California, that would save my life when I most needed it.

After Jan died, I worried that if I sat alone at home, I'd go crazy. Tony and his father, the auto-parts billionaire Shahid Khan, were planning the launch of a starry new venture, All Elite Wrestling—and they wanted me on board. Their contract offer was more than I had ever made before—but, more important, it was a chance to once again feel vital and worthwhile in a business that can be cruel and cold.

I may be a sixty-seven-year-old widower with Bell's palsy, but goddamn if I don't still love the chase. And it's like old home week in the new locker room. AEW's first big signing, Chris Jericho, is that guy for whom I went to bat with Vince twenty years ago. Another of our top stars is that kid from Oklahoma, Jake Hager, whom I brought to WWE and worked into a storyline at *WrestleMania* as Jack Swagger. The roster also includes some folks who were coming through NXT when I was there, guys like Jon Moxley and Pac. Backstage is littered with old friends and colleagues: people like Dean Malenko, one of the disaffected WCW stars we brought in twenty years ago, and my old friend Arn Anderson.

I jump out of bed on filming days and happily battle airport delays and flight cancellations because I am so grateful to be back on a team that wants me. The job is fun again—and I'm no longer treated as less-than because of my Oklahoma drawl, my facial paralysis, or my age or build.

I am confident in who I am and what I bring to the table. I'm not ready for the scrap heap just yet. I'm starting fresh, cutting through the few noisy trolls and loving the many passionate fans. There's nothing like a new player in town to make things exciting again.

Even if it is hard to imagine doing this without Jan, I'm choosing to be happy. I'm choosing to be positive. I'm choosing to bet on myself again, because that's the man she fell in love with in the first place.